Jim Wyngaarden

with regards from

John Swets

Evaluation of Diagnostic Systems
Methods from Signal Detection Theory

This is a volume in

ACADEMIC PRESS
SERIES IN COGNITION AND PERCEPTION

A Series of Monographs and Treatises

A complete list of titles in this series appears at the end of this volume.

Evaluation of Diagnostic Systems

Methods from Signal Detection Theory

John A. Swets
Ronald M. Pickett

Bolt Beranek and Newman Inc.
Cambridge, Massachusetts

1982

ACADEMIC PRESS

A Subsidiary of Harcourt Brace Jovanovich, Publishers
New York   London
Paris   San Diego   San Francisco   São Paulo   Sydney   Tokyo   Toronto

ACADEMIC PRESS, INC.
111 Fifth Avenue, New York, New York 10003

United Kingdom Edition published by
ACADEMIC PRESS, INC. (LONDON) LTD.
24/28 Oval Road, London NW1 7DX

Library of Congress Cataloging in Publication Data

Swets, John Arthur, Date
    Evaluation of diagnostic systems.

    (Cognition and perception series)
    Bibliography: p.
    Includes index.
    1. Signal detection (Psychology)   2. Imaging systems.
3. Imaging systems in medicine.   I. Pickett, Ronald M.
II. Title.   III. Series.
BF441.S85   001.53'8   82-3885
ISBN 0-12-679080-9   AACR2

PRINTED IN THE UNITED STATES OF AMERICA

82 83 84 85   9 8 7 6 5 4 3 2 1

Contents

Preface

The contents of this book attempt to address the many issues that arise in evaluating the performance of a diagnostic system, across the wide range of settings in which such systems are used. These settings include clinical medicine, industrial quality control, environmental monitoring and investigation, machine and metals inspection, military monitoring, information retrieval, and crime investigation. The general problem of diagnostic systems is to discriminate among possible states of the object under study, and to decide which one actually exists. We treat here extensively one of the more complex means of doing so—the interpretation of visual images by human observers. In the process we include as well the somewhat simpler systems in which the data of the system are numerical or textual, or in which the interpreter is a machine.

Diagnosis in any of its forms can be viewed as a problem of signal detection and classification, and modern signal detection theory supplies the best methods available for evaluating diagnostic systems. These methods provide a reliable and valid index of diagnostic accuracy and thereby satisfy the first objective of evaluation. They do so by isolating a system's intrinsic discrimination capacity, or accuracy, from the factors that affect the translation of discriminations into decisions and that confound other indices of accuracy. The concomitant ability of these methods to measure decision factors independently helps to satisfy a second evaluation objective: an overall assessment of the efficacy, or usefulness, of a system in terms of costs and benefits. To the extent that the relevant costs and benefits can be estimated, the usefulness of a system can be assessed relative to its optimal operation. In this book we describe the two kinds of indices and detail the experimental and quantitative methods required to derive them.

This book is written for the scientist or engineer in any technical specialty who desires to evaluate the performance of one or more diagnostic systems. It should be useful as well to the applied, quantitative, or experimental psychologist who is engaged in the study of the human processes of discrimination and decision making in either perceptual or cognitive tasks.

For the general audience we acknowledge that a wide variety of systems exist, involving primarily hardware, software, or people, or two or all three of these elements. Necessarily, therefore, some of the discussion is restricted to issues that must be addressed in arriving at the specifics of a particular study. Because the intended audience is so broad, however, this book is framed as a how-to-do-it manual to the extent that this is possible. Its recommendations are highly specific, for example, with respect to perceptual testing and the statistics of study design and data analysis. For the psychologist, this book brings together recent developments and contains new material relative to experimental method and quantitative analysis. We expect that the practical or engineering advice dispensed here will not distract these readers (who claim the methods of this book to be in their province) from recognizing that these methods will undergo continued development. Indeed, we hope that this structured compilation of methods will be an effective stimulus to further advances.

In Part I we describe quantitative methods for measuring the accuracy of a system and the statistical techniques for drawing inferences from performance tests. Part II covers study design and includes a detailed description of the form and conduct of an image-interpretation test. In Part III we examine the case study of a medical imaging system that serves as an example of both simple and complex applications. The Appendixes provide study protocols, a computer program for processing test results, and an extensive list of references that will assist the reader in applying those evaluative methods to diagnostic systems in any setting.

This book grew out of a project sponsored by the National Cancer Institute (NCI) of the National Institutes of Health (NIH) at the firm of Bolt Beranek and Newman Inc. (BBN) during 1976–1979. The intent of the project was to develop a general methodology for evaluation that NCI could use as a standard for its research on medical imaging. To further that aim, two studies were conducted at BBN to evaluate competitive imaging systems: one comparing computed tomography and radionuclide scanning for detection of brain lesions and another comparing xerographic and film mammography for the diagnosis of breast cancer. These case studies reveal the great variety of methodological issues that require explicit treatment in almost any diagnostic setting, expose the many difficulties that attend their adequate treatment in a practical application, and indicate the extensions and adaptations of general methods that must be developed for such applications.

Advisory Panel

S. James Adelstein *Harvard Medical School*
Harold L. Kundel *University of Pennsylvania School of Medicine*
Lee B. Lusted *University of Chicago*
Barbara J. McNeil *Harvard Medical School*
Charles E. Metz *University of Chicago*
J. E. Keith Smith *University of Michigan*

Consultants

William D. Kaplan *Harvard Medical School*
George M. Kleinman *Massachusetts General Hospital*
Norman L. Sadowsky *Tufts University School of Medicine*
James A. Schnur *Harvard Medical School*

Staff of Bolt Beranek and Newman Inc.

Barbara N. Freeman
David J. Getty
Joel B. Swets
Terry Timberlake-Kinter
Mildred C. Webster
Susan F. Whitehead

Representatives of the National Cancer Institute

R. Quentin Blackwell
William Pomerance
Judith M. S. Prewitt
Bernice T. Radovich

Acknowledgments

The staff at BBN was supplemented for NCI's project by a six-member advisory panel that spanned the contributing disciplines of radiology, physics, nuclear medicine, psychophysics, and quantitative methods. Local consultants were a neuroradiologist who met regularly with the staff, and specialists in radionuclide scanning, mammography, and pathology. Four NCI and NIH staff also collaborated in the project. The names of these contributors to the effort appear on the facing page.

The two imaging evaluations conducted at BBN were based on images and related clinical data collected in two collaborative studies sponsored by NCI. Principal investigators and institutions participating in the collaborative study of computed tomography and radionuclide scans were Hillier L. Baker, Jr., Mayo Clinic; David O. Davis, George Washington University Medical Center; Sadek K. Hilal, Columbia University; Paul F. J. New, Massachusetts General Hospital; and D. Gordon Potts, Cornell University Medical Center. Data coordination for this collaborative study were supplied by C. Ralph Buncher, University of Cincinnati Medical Center. The collaborative mammography study involved three institutions, but we used only materials collected at the University of Texas Medical Center. The principal investigator there was Gerald D. Dodd, who was assisted by David D. Paulus and Dennis Johnston. We appreciate the cooperation of all individuals mentioned in facilitating our central analysis of the clinical materials they collected.

Twenty-four radiologists served as image interpreters in the performance tests conducted at BBN and advised the staff on evaluation methodology from that perspective. They are L. Reed Altemus, Richard A. Baker, Andrew W. Duncan, Daniel Kido, Joseph Lin, and Thomas P. Naidich (computed tomography); Harold L. Chandler, John P. Clements, Thomas C. Hill, Leon Malmud, Frank Deaver Thomas, and Donald E. Tow (nuclear medicine); Peter Barrett, Arnold L. Berenberg, Carl D'Orsi, Ferris Hall, Marc Homer, Lester Kalisher, Sidney A. Kaufman, Ronald J. Messer, Jack E. Meyer, Dorothea R. Peck, William E. Poplack, and Peter K. Spiegel (mammography). Their very helpful advice, as well as their perseverance through several days of image interpretation, is much appreciated.

This project was a remarkable team effort, with many individuals contributing well beyond the special expertise they brought to it and making substantial contributions too numerous to mention. We single out Charles E. Metz, who, during a 3-month sabbatical leave spent at BBN, contributed greatly to Chapters 3 and 4 and carefully reviewed most of the remainder. The roles of two others were critical: Judith M. S. Prewitt, of the Division of Computer Research and Technology, NIH, conceived the project, encouraged NCI's interest in it, and did much to guide its development; and William Pomerance, chief of the Diagnosis Branch of NCI, made the project happen. Until his death near the end of the effort, he provided the strong personal and administrative support that is essential to a task of such complexity and did so in the perceptive and friendly way that was his hallmark. To reflect the high regard in which he was held by all involved, we dedicate this book to the memory of Bill Pomerance.

Introduction

THE GENERAL SETTING

Diagnostic techniques of obvious personal and societal importance are used to determine the presence and form of abnormal cells in body fluids, cracks in airplane wings, incipient storms, enemy weapons, oil deposits, relevant documents in a library, malfunctions in a power plant, criminal activity, defects in assembly-line products, and so on.

The "techniques" are usually realized in a "system," which may include a *data-collection device* and a *display* of data, and usually includes an *observer* and a *decision maker*. The data-collection devices are often sensing devices—"active" as when some kind of energy (e.g., X ray) is sent at or into the object under study and then collected again as transformed by the object, or "passive" as when the device picks up some kind of emission (e.g., sounds) generated by the object under study. The display of data may be in the form of an image of the object (e.g., a cross section of a brain shown on a video screen), in some abstract pictorial form (e.g., a tracing of a magnetic pattern), in numerical form (e.g., describing meteorological conditions), or in verbal form (e.g., key words associated with a document in a file). The observing and decision-making functions are often combined and may be carried out by a person or programmed machine. We use in this book a variety of terms to refer to these latter two functions—observer, decision maker, data interpreter, image reader, and diagnostician—depending partly on the kind of system under discussion.

In general, the systems attempt to *detect* "signals" in a background of interference or "noise"; they may attempt to *localize* the signals; and they may attempt to *classify* (*identify* or *recognize*) the signals. The results of these processes are often followed directly in a predetermined way by a general decision, which we shall speak of as a "diagnosis." The diagnosis is a statement about which of the possible states of the object under study actually exists. A choice of action may follow directly upon the diagnosis, or additional information may be taken into account.

THE GENERAL PROBLEM

In all cases the data on which the diagnosis is based are insufficient to permit certainty or complete accuracy over repeated applications of the system. Indeed, the error rates of useful systems may be quite high. These diagnostic techniques are used because obtaining fuller data is more invasive, costly, or time-consuming than is desired, or actually destructive of the object being studied.

But, for the most part, we do not have very precise ideas about the accuracy of these techniques nor of the systems that implement them, and therefore we cannot have very precise ideas about the efficacy, or the usefulness, of the systems in an overall cost–benefit sense. Most of the current measures of system accuracy are demonstrably inadequate, and no acceptable index has reached the status of a standard. Also, experimental methods for formal testing have received scant attention. As a consequence, one usually does not have good data for

1. electing to use a given technique or given system,
2. choosing between competitive techniques or systems,
3. isolating the major cause of error in a technique or system, or
4. deciding to attempt to develop new techniques or systems.

Indeed, the very concept of formal evaluation of diagnostic systems is not widely recognized: Often, inventors come up with a system, and practitioners gain evidence of its worth through slowly accumulated experience with it. In view of the many critical applications of diagnostic systems and the large financial outlays for those systems, this state of affairs is tremendously risky and expensive.

THE PROPOSED SOLUTION

In this book we attempt to spell out an acceptable method of measuring accuracy that could serve as a standard, and, indeed, the method described is rapidly gaining currency. Its essence is an analytical procedure called the "relative (or receiver) operating characteristic" (ROC). The ROC is based in statistical decision theory (e.g., Wald, 1950) and was developed in the context of electronic signal detection (Peterson, Birdsall, and Fox, 1954). It has been applied extensively to human perception and decision making (Green and Swets, 1966/1974; Swets, 1973) and to diagnostic systems in clinical medicine (Swets, 1979), and in a preliminary way to industrial quality control (Drury and Fox, 1975), military monitoring (Swets, 1977), information retrieval (Swets, 1969), crime investigation (National Academy of Sciences, 1979), and weather forecasting (Mason, 1980).

The three main accomplishments of the ROC are unique to it. Together they give the methods and performance indices that are based on it a degree of reliability, validity, and generality not provided by any others. Each of the following topics is carefully developed in Chapter 1.

1. The ROC analysis supplies a pure index of accuracy, that is, of the inherent capability of the system to discriminate one object state from another. That is to say, the index of accuracy is independent of whatever criterion is adopted in the system for making a particular decision or of whatever bias exists in the system toward one particular decision or another. These two aspects of performance—discrimination capacity and decision tendencies—are confounded in other indices of accuracy.

2. The ROC supplies estimates of the probabilities of decision outcomes of the various kinds (e.g., of true-positive and true-negative decisions, and of false-positive and false-negative decisions) for any and all of the decision criteria (biases) the system might use. That is, the decision-outcome probabilities stand in a trading relationship with one another, and the different possible balances among them—any of which may be attained by shifting the decision criterion—are revealed.

3. The ROC analysis supplies an index of the decision criterion, which reflects together the subjective probabilities and utilities that usually determine this criterion. This index also makes it possible to use a more precise knowledge of prior probabilities of possible object states, along

with carefully calculated judgments about the values and costs of correct and incorrect decisions, to determine which decision criterion is optimal for a given system in a given setting. Then an assessment of system efficacy may be made for the system operating at its best (Metz, 1978; Swets and Swets, 1979).

FOUR TYPES OF EVALUATION

We suggest that the ROC provides a desirable index of *accuracy* and the appropriate basis for an index of *efficacy*. Let us pause briefly to compare these two types of evaluation and two others often used, namely, *fidelity* and *consistency*.

Fidelity

The fidelity of an imaging system may be assessed by means of carefully constructed test patterns and by perceptual observations and physical measurements that indicate how faithfully the system represents the contrived signals. The measurements reveal various properties of the system, as related, for example, to the noise or artifacts it introduces, and may provide a basis for calculating the so-called transfer characteristics of a system. The use of simulated rather than real test cases often realizes substantial savings in the time and cost of an evaluation study.

Consistency

Measurements of the consistency of one decision maker making repeated, independent, standardized judgments (about signal presence, location, or class), or of the consistency of different decision makers working independently, are used to provide another level of evaluation. Consistency can be expressed in terms of the percentage of trials on which the judgments agree or in the form of a correlation index. Either way, the measure of consistency is very useful in determining the extent to which the inaccuracy of a system is due to decision-making error, and consistency is often measured for just that purpose. Consistency can also serve as an indication of the upper bound of accuracy. When real test cases are used, consistency improves on fidelity in that the practical relevance of the information shown to be transmitted by the system is less questionable. However, since the truth of the judgments is not considered, all that is being measured is the *potential* diagnostic value of the information transmitted. That is why consistency serves only as an upper bound on accuracy.

Accuracy

In evaluating accuracy, standardized reports about test cases are scored for correctness relative to the diagnostic truths associated with those cases. The "truth" may be contrived, as with artificial test cases, or approximated for real cases on the basis of external evidence (evidence entirely separate from information obtained via the systems under study). Various measures of the degree of diagnostic accuracy can then be computed to assess and compare diagnostic systems. When real test cases are used, the main advantage of accuracy measures over consistency measures is that they reflect the *actual* diagnostic value of the information being transmitted. Moreover, they provide a basis for estimating the *potential* practical value of that information. The main difficulty in securing accuracy measurements is that reliable and valid truth is often expensive to obtain. Constraints on study resources serve in varying degrees to degrade truth data and the validity of the study results.

Efficacy

In assessing efficacy, standardized reports are necessarily obtained on real test cases and scored against the truth as determined independently. Here, however, one attempts to determine the various benefits, risks, and costs of diagnosis and to compute various cost–benefit indices for the diagnostic system. The great advantage of efficacy over accuracy assessment is that it provides a measure that reflects the *actual* practical value of the information that systems transmit. The great difficulty attending attempts to go beyond accuracy to efficacy is that of placing values on variables that are difficult to assess in monetary terms. And the complexity of a reasonably full assessment of efficacy often makes for a very expensive study.

Comparison of the Types

The four types of evaluation can be ordered in terms of whether or not, and how definitely, they are able to assess diagnostic systems on two fundamental dimensions: (*a*) diagnostic value, that is, how much the diagnostic system helps in determining the actual state of the object under study, and (*b*) practical value, that is, how much benefit the system provides relative to its risks and financial costs. Table 1 provides a summary view of this ordering of approaches.

We appreciate, then, that the bottom line of an evaluation of a diagnostic system is a statement of the efficacy of that system, that is, an assessment of its actual impact in terms both of benefit and costs. Such an analysis is obviously very difficult to accomplish with assurance and completeness. Various approaches to it are discussed in Chapter 5, which is devoted to the topic. Whether the analysis of efficacy to be attempted in a particular study is ambitious or restricted, one can attempt to assess reasonably adequately the actual diagnostic value of a system in terms of accuracy. For this purpose, estimates are made of the probabilities of the various possible decision outcomes. These probabilities are then combined as discussed in Chapter 1.

GENERAL ISSUES IN TEST DESIGN

The needs for an unbiased index of system accuracy and for some assessment of system efficacy are general to performance tests in all diagnostic applications. In support of fulfilling these needs, certain issues of test design must be considered in every application. Thus, for example, one must always attend to the character and quality of both the test cases of system data and the data interpreters that are used in a performance test.

The sample of test cases—whether they are in the form of images,

Table 1

TYPES OF EVALUATION AND SCORING DIMENSIONS

	Diagnostic value	Practical value
Fidelity	Measures of questionable relevance	No measure
Consistency	Measures only potential value	No measure
Accuracy	Measures actual value	Measures only potential value
Efficacy	Measures actual value	Measures actual value

graphs, numbers, wave forms, or words—must be representative of the population to which the system is directed. Each case must be accurately typed as to signal or noise and perhaps as to location and category of signal. And they must be collected and presented in a manner that is fair to each system under test. If the system's data interpreter or decision maker is a machine, the related issues of design may be quite straight-forward, although again fairness to competitive systems may be a concern, especially if they operate on different forms of data or typically make decisions in different formats. If humans are the data interpreters and decision makers, one must be concerned about their training and skill levels.

For any application, a test procedure must be carefully designed—with regard to data presentation, format of interpretation or decision, general background information available for the interpreter, particular information given about individual test cases, and test environment—and, if humans are involved, with regard to timing of trials and sessions, orientation, feedback, and the role of the test administrator. Some specifics of test procedure are determined by the goals of the study, and, in general, the goals must be developed in detail in advance.

The goals of the test in any application are spelled out in terms of the kinds of conclusions desired to be drawn. These conclusions depend upon the statistical inferences that can be based on the test results, which, in turn, depend on the size and logic of the test. Size is measured primarily in terms of the number of test cases and the number of interpreters or decision makers, and logic is represented in such terms as independent versus matched test cases and independent versus matched interpreters.

SOME APPLICATION VIGNETTES

To illustrate the generality of the issues just described, we briefly sketch the test parameters for five applications of diagnostic systems. In these sketches the several design choices to be made are usually merely implied to ease the exposition, but it can be seen that they are there to be made and that they condition the range and value of the study.

Forecasting the Weather

A meteorologist (Mason, 1980) desired to compare the accuracy of two mathematical techniques for predicting frost, one based on a multiple linear regression and the other on an empirical Bayes's method. He chose measures of 10 meteorological variables (taken at 6 p.m.) to enter into the prediction and a method for deciding on occurrence or nonoccurrence of frost on the following morning. These measures and events were accumulated for each day of a given month in midwinter, over an appropriate number of years and locations. The proportions of true-positive and false-positive decisions were calculated for each of several values (decision criteria) of the continuous output of each system, and overall indices of accuracy were derived from these data. The relative efficacies of the two techniques were to be calculated for different users of the forecast, who vary with respect to the cost of taking the appropriate precaution against frost (which they take for positive forecasts, whether or not they are correct) and with respect to the loss incurred if unpredicted frost occurs. Indeed, one predictive method was found superior in accuracy at low false-positive probabilities, whereas the other was superior at high false-positive probabilities; so different users would use one method or the other, depending on the ratio of the costs involved in their operations.

Retrieving Relevant Documents

An information scientist (Swets, 1969) desired to evaluate the state of the art of information-retrieval systems and to determine how new computer-based systems compare with traditional library operations. He obtained experimental results from two developers of prominent computer-based systems and from an extensive study of human effectiveness in comparable settings. Some 50 different retrieval methods were represented—based on titles, key words, abstracts, or full text; thesauruses or statistical word-association devices; hierarchical subject arrangements or syntactical relations of subject identifiers; fully automatic or user-controlled search; automatic or manual indexing; short or long queries; and so forth. Files of items of varying sizes had been used in six different subject fields of science and engineering, and 50–200 queries had been addressed to each. The queries in some cases were drawn directly from documents in the test files, in other cases, were not. Panels of subject-matter specialists judged the relevance of each retrieved document to the question that elicited it. Estimates were made by various means of the number of relevant documents corresponding to each query, including exhaustive review. An ROC analysis showed the three systems (two computer-based and one manual) to perform about equally well and leave considerable room for improvement. Assuming a file of 3000 items and queries to each of which 10 items are relevant, on average, retrieving 4 of the 10 would also bring 30 irrelevant items, while retrieving 9 of the 10 would bring 300 irrelevant items.

Monitoring Manufactured Items

Two industrial engineers at a glass-manufacturing company (Drury and Addison, 1973) wished to examine the performance of a team of "100% inspectors" before and after provision was made for immediate feedback of the results of their inspection. The change was effected by moving a team of "special examiners," who made a sample inspection later, closer to the 100% inspection and making known their results to the 100% inspectors more quickly and directly than before. Results were available for 12 weeks prior to the change and 11 weeks after the change for all types of defects considered together. The change was found to reduce the defects missed by one-half. A subsidiary finding concerned the manner in which inspectors varied their criteria for calling a defect as the quality of the items varied at input to inspection. They were found to adjust their decision criteria so as to keep the outgoing batch quality (percentage defective) constant.

Detecting Deception

Two psychologists (Szucko and Kleinmuntz, 1981) sought to determine the absolute and relative accuracies of human interpreters and a statistical formula in discriminating between truthful and untruthful subjects by means of the polygraph records obtained in lie detection tests. Thirty undergraduate volunteers were randomly assigned to theft and no-theft conditions, and the 15 in the first condition were encouraged to steal a $5 bill. Four examiners trained by a polygraph firm, who were not told of the experiment, administered polygraph tests in the usual format. The resulting records were submitted to six experienced interpreters, who knew only that half of them represented individuals who had stolen something and who judged each individual as truthful or untruthful on an 8-point rating scale. The same records were digitized and subjected to a statistical prediction formula that used the optimal linear combination of the physiological indices or cues in the records. The formula outperformed all of the humans by a wide margin. Four of the six humans performed better than chance would have it, but the difference was small. The human interpreters' accuracies were not related to amount of experience, and their decision criteria, as indicated by their tendencies to classify a truthful subject as untruthful, varied widely. For example, the interpreter with the most experience detected more of the untruthful subjects than the other interpreters (82%), but called almost as many of the truthful subjects untruthful (76%). The authors suggest that the next study should better reflect field conditions—with real rather than volunteer suspects and with the interpreters given access to more information on each case than just the polygraph records.

Finding Flaws in Metals

In each of the four applications just sketched, the investigators traced out an empirical ROC curve (showing the probability of a true-positive decision as a function of the probability of a false-positive decision) as the decision criterion varied. In each case that information was of practical importance: Users of meteorological forecasts, library users, factory managers, and crime investigators want to see that function so that they can choose the operating point on it that is best for their own particular purposes. Our final sketch here comes from the field of nondestructive evaluation in industry and illustrates the main difficulty that presents itself when the ROC function is not obtained. This difficulty is not just an inability to select an appropriate operating point, but a basic inability to determine the accuracy of a diagnostic system.

Metallurgists in the United States Air Force (see Gulley, 1974, and a review by Berger, 1976) wished to determine the accuracy of a magnetic particle technique for detecting flaws in the metal structures of aircraft. They collected a set of 24 test cases consisting of real parts that were rather confidently judged to contain flaws and carried these test cases to 11 industrial laboratories across the country that had an appropriate inspection system in use. The comparative results were reported only in terms of the percentage of flaws found—an estimate of the probability of a true-positive decision for each system in normal operation. The eleven laboratories showed percentages ranging from near 20% to near 90%, with nine laboratories scoring between 30% and 60%. The difficulty in knowing only the true-positive percentage or probability is that it will surely increase if the false-positive probability is allowed to increase, and will surely decrease if the false-positive probability is made to decrease. Thus, we have no idea how the several systems performed, absolutely or relative to each other. Any of the systems with a percentage less than 90% could have produced that percentage with a more lenient criterion for a positive decision. That criterion could have been attained by instructing a human observer to make positive decisions on the basis of weaker evidence than before. Alternatively, the same result might have been achieved by turning a knob on the apparatus to increase its signal (and noise) amplification.

ORGANIZATION OF THIS BOOK

This book is divided into three parts: The first deals with quantitative methods in evaluation; the second, with experimental methods; and the third presents an evaluation case study.

In Part I the quantitative methods first described are those that provide an index of a system's accuracy and an independent index of a system's decision criterion. Chapter 1 presents the fundamental ideas behind these indices as well as the specifics of their measurement. Chapter 2 describes certain extensions of those ideas and indices to treat more complex diagnostic problems and to aid in summarizing and interpreting test results. Statistical issues in the design of tests and in drawing inferences from them are spelled out in Chapters 3 and 4. Chapter 5 presents a general review of ways to measure the efficacy of a diagnostic system, with content drawn from the medical context.

Part II begins with Chapter 6, which offers a general discussion of study design, with an emphasis on experimental aspects. In Chapter 7, we describe quite specific matters in the design and conduct of an image-interpretation test. Chapters 8 and 9 then take up the selection of samples of test cases, and Chapter 10 considers some issues in the selection of human diagnosticians for test purposes.

With the exception of the chapter on efficacy assessment, the quantitative methods in Part I are discussed in rather general terms, though examples throughout are drawn from the medical context. Part II, on the other hand, exemplifies our conviction that a particular setting must be examined in detail if the general experimental methods are to be adapted to practical use; therefore, all of the chapters in this part focus on one diagnostic setting, specifically, the interpretation of medical images by human diagnosticians. Again, we believe the interpretation (or "reading") of visual images by humans to be among the more complex kinds of diagnostic system, and therefore the methods discussed in Part II should cover tests of other kinds of systems. And much of what we have to say about lesions or other medical abnormalities will apply to the states to be diagnosed in other contexts, whether defects or malfunctions, desired resources or threats. Part II is written so that it may be read before Part I, but reading both parts will facilitate understanding of Part III.

Part III presents one of two case studies of medical imaging systems that were undertaken to refine and illustrate the general methods. It compares Xeromammography with two forms of film mammography in the diagnosis of breast cancer. This study has not been published separately because the images and other clinical data we were able to obtain were not adequate to a fair and representative test of the three alternative systems; however, those materials were adequate to a methodological study that is suitable for our present purposes. The other study we conducted compared computed tomography (CT) and radionuclide (RN) brain scanning in the diagnosis of brain lesions, and was published in *Science* (Swets *et al.*, 1979). Certain results of this CT/RN study are reproduced here for convenience (and it is used along with the mammography study to illustrate points throughout the book), but the full journal article should be consulted for an exemplar of a study and report based on the methods of this book.

Five appendixes are included. Appendix A outlines the sequence of steps that should be taken in a full and complex evaluation, according to the precepts set forth in the text, and therefore includes the steps pertinent to less complex evaluations. It can serve as a guide and checklist for study design, conduct, and interpretation. Appendix B demonstrates a means of determining how well a sample of test cases represents the population of cases to which one desires to generalize test results. Appendix C contains an example of a questionnaire an investigator may wish to give test observers after their participation. Appendix D gives a listing of a computer program that gives a maximum-likelihood fit of an ROC curve to test results, and calculates various performance indices along with their variances. Appendix E gives references to applications and other discussions of ROC-based methods in the four fields of application in which a substantial number of papers have been published: medicine, military monitoring, industrial monitoring, and information retrieval.

PART I

Quantitative Methods

Chapter 1 shows how discrimination and decision aspects of diagnostic performance can be measured independently of each other in detection problems and in simple localization and classification problems. It describes recommended indices for both aspects of performance and criticizes some commonly used, but inadequate, indices of diagnostic accuracy. Chapter 2 extends the ROC analysis, though in a less powerful manner, to problems that involve detection along with complex localization and classification. It also suggests how one may go beyond the recommended performance indices to certain quantitative descriptions that may be related more directly to the practical setting. Chapter 3 is devoted to the statistical and logical design of a performance test. In it we develop from first principles the elements of sampling variance whose quantities are helpful in determining how many test cases and observers and observations are required to yield a desired reliability of an accuracy index. And we examine, for comparisons of systems, how case and observer matching will affect the reliability of any obtained difference.

Chapter 4 develops the related computational formulas for making statistical inferences from obtained data. In Chapter 5 we discuss quantitative approaches to assessment of system efficacy, proceeding from the
model of a full cost–benefit analysis to various more practical alternatives.

CHAPTER 1

Fundamentals of Accuracy Analysis

In assessing the quality of diagnostic judgments, it is desirable to separate two aspects of performance: (*a*) the capacity to discriminate among the alternative states of the object under study and (*b*) the effects of decision factors that contribute to the selection of one diagnostic alternative over another. Often, one is interested primarily in the discrimination aspect (which is also termed here "accuracy"), and then one wants to separate out the decision aspect so that it does not confound or contaminate the measurements of intrinsic accuracy. Thus, in evaluating the potential of a new imaging system, the investigator may not be particularly interested in the influence of the decision factors on the individual test readers once steps have been taken that permit ignoring them. Of course, the objective in another setting, such as in training, may serve to put the decision aspect at the center of interest at one time or another. Moreover, in attempting to assess the efficacy (as opposed to just the accuracy) of a diagnostic system, one would like to use estimates of the probabilities of the various possible diagnostic outcomes that reflect decision factors in the manner most appropriate to the particular diagnostic context at hand.

The purpose of this chapter is to lay out in detail the techniques available to measure the two aspects of performance independently. We assume here that just two alternative states are under consideration. This emphasis on discrimination between two alternatives reflects the fact that the most satisfactory techniques for separating the two aspects of performance apply fully only to the two-alternative situation, and the fact that many diagnostic problems can be treated as a sequence of two-alternative decisions. We consider extensions of the analysis to multiple alternatives in Chapter 2.

As already indicated, the relative operating characteristic (ROC) is our principal means of analysis. Applications of the ROC to human discrimination and decision making have been described in textbook form by Green and Swets (1966/1974). McNicol (1972) has written an extensive primer on that subject, and Egan's (1975) book provides a tutorial introduction to the ROC concept as well as a theoretical treatment of various forms of ROC curves. An article by Swets (1973) summarizes the history of the ROC and reviews applications in psychology; a chapter by Swets and Green (1978) describes several applications of ROC analysis outside of psychology; and an article by Swets (1979) reviews medical applications to date along with theoretical issues of particular interest in the medical context.

We proceed now to a further discussion of the two aspects of performance and of the factors that affect these two aspects. This discussion is tutorial; it is intended to lend an intuitive appreciation to someone who has not previously considered the matter formally or in detail. The discussion leads to an explication of the separate measurement of the two aspects of performance by means of the ROC graph. The principal outcome is the recommendation of certain indices of diagnostic performance for the two-alternative situation. After a description of simple graphical techniques for determining these indices, we make reference to objective statistical techniques for determining them and describe a computer program that provides objective estimates of the indices and their variances.

1.1   TWO ASPECTS OF PERFORMANCE

Diagnosticians want to make more correct than incorrect judgments, but not necessarily as many more as possible. They are concerned with the total value of their performance, and so desire to minimize errors

1.1.4   The Capacity for Discrimination

The other aspect of diagnostic performance besides the decision criterion or response bias is the capacity for discrimination that it reflects. What is the capacity of a particular diagnostic system to discriminate, say, abnormality from normality? That capacity will depend on the *quality of the information* that the system acquires and represents, and on the perceptual and cognitive competence of the reader.

1.2   ANALYSIS OF PERFORMANCE VIA THE ROC CURVE

Formally, all two-alternative decision tasks can be represented by the intersection of the two possible states of the object under study (or "stimuli") and two possible "responses." That is, performance can always be completely summarized in terms of a 2×2 matrix. Table 2 shows such a matrix, with the stimulus alternatives as the columns and the response alternatives as the rows of the matrix. We could have listed specific alternatives (e.g., "appendicitis" and "transient abdominal pain" as columns, and "operate now" and "wait" as rows), but have chosen to represent the more general situation of "normality" and "abnormality." We have earlier identified the cells of the matrix as true- and false-positive and true and false-negative responses—denoted *TP*, *FP*, *TN*, and *FN*—but here we must use a slightly more complex notation.

Table 2

2×2 MATRIX OF STIMULI AND RESPONSES*

Response	Stimulus	
	a	*n*
A	M_{Aa} true-positive $P(A|a)$	M_{An} false-positive $P(A|n)$
N	M_{Na} false-negative $P(N|a)$	M_{Nn} true-negative $P(N|n)$
	$M_{Aa} + M_{Na}$	$M_{An} + M_{Nn}$

* Symbols are described in the text.

Our symbolic convention for this discussion is to label the stimuli by lowercase letters (n, a) and the responses by capital letters (N, A). Then the occurrence of a stimulus a and a response A, for example, leads to an entry in the upper left-hand cell. The total number of entries in that cell is designated M_{Aa}. Similarly, the raw frequencies of the other stimulus–response conjunctions are designated M_{An}, M_{Na}, and M_{Nn}. The total number of times stimulus a is presented is $M_{Aa} + M_{Na}$, and the total number of times stimulus n is presented is $M_{An} + M_{Nn}$.

We can now associate the cells of the matrix with certain conditional probabilities of interest—probabilities of a certain response given the occurrence of a certain stimulus. We designate these conditional probabilities by a term such as $P(N|a)$, which is the probability of the response "Normal" being made given that the stimulus is "abnormal." Thus, a conditional probability refers to a correct response when a capital letter is followed by the same lowercase letter, and to an incorrect response when the two letters are different.

We designate "conditional," as opposed to "joint," probabilities. Thus, $P(N|a)$ is not the probability of N and a occurring together, but the probability of the occurrence of N given the occurrence of a. This conditional probability is estimated by dividing the number of N responses made when a is present by the number of times a is present. In our notation, $P(N|a)$ equals $M_{Na}/(M_{Aa} + M_{Na})$. The other four conditional probabilities are similarly obtained. To exercise the terminology given earlier: $P(A|a)$ is the conditional probability of a *true-positive* or *hit*; $P(N|n)$, of a *true-negative* or *correct rejection*; $P(A|n)$, of a *false-positive* or *false alarm*; and $P(N|a)$, of a *false-negative* or *miss*. [Because we think they are easier to read, we shall frequently use in later sections the symbols $P(TP)$, $P(TN)$, $P(FP)$, and $P(FN)$ to denote these probabilities, but the reader should keep in mind that we have reference to conditional, not joint, probabilities.]

If the decision between A and N is made repetitively, and if the decisions are independent of one another, then this matrix specifies the task and the decision behavior completely. It is important to note that the quantities in the matrix are not independent of one another. In fact, each column adds to 1:

$$P(A|a) + P(N|a) = 1.0,$$
$$P(A|n) + P(N|n) = 1.0.$$

These two equations indicate that a particular case, whether normal or abnormal, must be labeled one way or another by the diagnostician. (We consider a third response—"Equivocal"—in Section 2.2.) So there are only two independent probabilities in two-alternative decision tasks—not four, as the entries of the matrix might imply.

Because the matrix contains just two independent probabilities, we can represent discrimination-and-decision performance by only two probabilities. The ROC analysis is based on the true-positive probability, $P(A|a)$, and the false-positive probability, $P(A|n)$. Specifically, the ROC curve shows the (trading) relationship between the two probabilities as the decision criterion varies. Note that the first probability is the complement of the false-negative probability, by the first equation above, so we could think of the ROC as representing the relation between the two kinds of errors—false-negatives and false-positives. These errors, in the imaging context, are promoted by "underreading" and "overreading," respectively.

The ROC graph, specifically, is a plot of $P(A|a)$ versus $P(A|n)$—true-positives versus false-positives, or hits versus false alarms. Figure 1 shows such a graph with a single point located on a smooth curve. The point represents one possible decision criterion; the curve represents the locus of possible points for a particular discrimination capacity. (We show the complements of our two main probabilities on the upper and right-hand axes to emphasize that the ROC graph represents all four.)

As indicated, we have represented a particular performance as a single point in the ROC space. Presumably, however, one could alter the decision criterion that produced that point (essentially at will) and, hence, alter the hit and false-alarm probabilities. If the curve of Figure 1 represents a given discrimination capacity, then changes in the decision criterion would move the probabilities along such a curve. That is, if one adopted a very stringent (conservative) criterion, very low false-alarm and hit probabilities would result—a point near the lower left-hand corner. Conversely, if one adopted a very lenient (aggressive) criterion, then very high false-alarm and hit probabilities would result—a point near the upper right-hand corner. These criteria represent the extremes. The ROC curve represents all potential decision criteria, and hence all potential discrimination performances for a diagnostic system of fixed accuracy.

We can note here that "stringent decision criterion" is essentially equivalent to "bias against a positive response" and that "lenient decision criterion" is tantamount to "bias toward a positive response." "Bias," in short, is not a pejorative term in the present context; a decision maker's performance, perforce, lies somewhere along a bias contour, and may indeed be at the "optimal" location. Note also, in a preliminary way, that the location or level of the decision criterion can

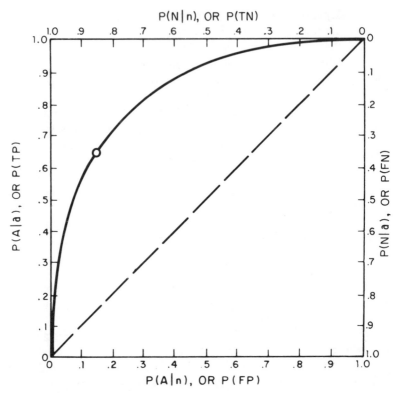

Figure 1. The ROC graph, with one point representing a single performance at a single decision criterion. The curve shows the locus of performances possible with a variable decision criterion for a fixed discrimination capacity.

be rather simply indexed. One possibility is the probability of a false alarm yielded by the criterion. Another possibility is the slope of the curve at the point corresponding to the given criterion. Because the ROC is monotonically decreasing, progressively more lenient criteria yield points at progressively lesser slopes.

The *major diagonal,* indicated as a dashed line in Figure 1, is the locus of points for which the hit and false-alarm probabilities are equal. This diagonal represents situations in which the diagnostic information is so poor that abnormal and normal cannot be discriminated at a better than chance level. In this situation, one could ignore the information and make the two responses at random; one would still achieve a point somewhere along the dotted line. The *solid curve* of Figure 1 represents a quality of information that enables some discrimination between the two stimulus alternatives, and hence the hit probability exceeds the false-alarm probability for every point along the curve. (Note that points or curves below the diagonal can occur only as chance variations of data from true discrimination that is at a level on or above the diagonal, unless the decision system is perverse.)

Figure 2 shows a set of three hypothetical ROC curves that represent different degrees of discrimination capacity. This fact can easily be appreciated if we take a single false-alarm probability, say, 0.1, and note that the hit probabilities for these three curves are 0.3, 0.6, and 0.8, respectively. The same ordering of curves holds no matter what false-alarm probability we take. Another way of viewing the relative performances represented by these curves is to observe that they encompass beneath them different amounts of area in the ROC space and that more

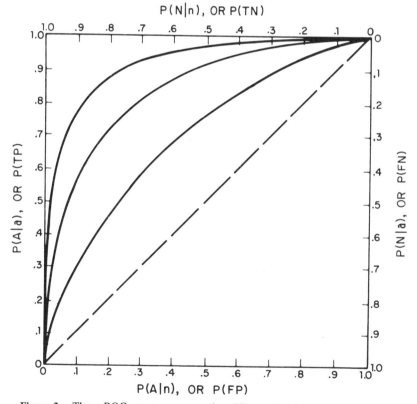

Figure 2.   Three ROC curves, representing different discrimination capacities.

area is better. Still another possible comparison is based on the different distances by which the curves deviate from the major diagonal—in the direction of the northwest corner of the graph, which represents perfect discrimination. We shall shortly specify, more precisely, certain indices of discrimination capacity.

These comments complete our introductory treatment of the ROC analysis. Its contribution is a means of separating two independent aspects of discrimination performance. The importance of that contribution is twofold.

1. Performance may be good or poor with respect to the location of the decision criterion, and it may be good or poor with respect to the ability to discriminate between the alternatives. Any recommendation to change the performance of a human being, a human and a machine working together, or a fully automatic system must distinguish these two aspects of performance.

2. The evaluation of discrimination capacity, or accuracy, by itself is fundamental, because the decision criterion is relatively labile.

1.3   OFTEN USED, BUT INADEQUATE, INDICES OF ACCURACY

There are several alternative indices of accuracy not based on the ROC curve that are used frequently in the literature on clinical evaluation and elsewhere. We warn against them here because they do not separate discrimination accuracy from the decision criterion; they are therefore specific to a given decision criterion, which may or may not be appropriate, and when that criterion varies in an unmeasured way they incorporate spurious variation. We specifically describe here five of these indices:

1. the conditional probability of a true-positive response;
2. the conditional probability of a true-positive response (sometimes called "sensitivity") paired with the conditional probability of a true-negative response ("specificity");
3. the probability of a true-positive or true-negative response (i.e., the total probability of a correct response);
4. the a posteriori probability of a true-positive response; and
5. the ratio of the a posteriori probability of a true-positive response to the a posteriori probability of a true-negative response, a quantity

variously called the "incidence ratio," "relative risk," or "odds ratio."

1.3.1   Conditional Probability of a True-Positive Response

The difficulty with using as an index of accuracy only the conditional probability of a true-positive response is obvious from the foregoing discussion: It can vary from 0 to 1.0 as a result of variation in the decision criterion alone. A fixed capacity to discriminate, in other words, can yield the full range of this particular index of accuracy.

Of course, this index is ordinarily used along with the assumption that the decision criterion is relatively stable. But how stable is the criterion, and how do we know how stable it is if it goes unmeasured? Even if one is willing to assume that the decision criterion is so stable as to yield values of $P(FP)$ within the range from 0.05 to 0.15, the index $P(TP)$ can still vary considerably. For the three curves of Figure 2 for that amount of variation in the decision criterion, $P(TP)$ will vary from 0.20 to 0.38 for the lower curve, from 0.43 to 0.67 for the middle curve, and from 0.66 to 0.84 for the top curve. That amount of variation in $P(TP)$ is in addition to the inherent statistical variability of the quantity and is introduced by criterion variation alone. That much variation is enough to obscure true differences in $P(TP)$ that are practically significant or to produce apparent differences that do not truly exist.

Furthermore, the use of $P(TP)$ as an index in comparing two systems requires the assumption that the decision criterion is the same for the two systems, which strikes us as an extreme assumption. How likely is it that the same decision criterion is used, for example, in CT of the head as in RN brain scanning? If not demonstrably likely, then what do we know if told that CT has $P(TP) = 0.90$ while RN has $P(TP) = 0.80$? We believe, indeed, that it would be a reasonably simple matter to ask RN interpreters to adopt a more lenient decision criterion and thereby to reach a higher $P(TP)$, including one of 0.90.

1.3.2   Sensitivity and Specificity

An improvement over using the conditional probability of a true-positive response alone is to report another conditional probability that stands in a trading relationship to it and with which it is paired. Thus, one may report a given value of $P(TP)$ and the coincident value of $P(FP)$.

It is common in medical literature to report $P(TP)$ along with the associated complement of $P(FP)$, namely, $P(TN)$. The first quantity is termed "sensitivity" and the second, "specificity."

The difficulty with using a single such pair of values as an index is that we do not know specifically how they trade off against each other as the decision criterion is varied. They may represent a point on a curve where considerable sensitivity can be gained with little loss in specificity, or they may not. Furthermore, the comparison of two systems is ambiguous. Is system A with sensitivity of 0.90 and specificity of 0.30 more or less accurate than system B with values of 0.70 and 0.50? Such a question is answered only by having the full curve for each system.

1.3.3 Probability of a True-Positive or Negative Response

Another common index is the overall probability of a correct response, that is, the probability of a true response of either kind. This index of accuracy may be viewed as an attempt to capture sensitivity and specificity in a single-parameter index, and thus to provide an unambiguous comparison of systems. Note that this particular index of accuracy is often defined as "accuracy," co-opting what we use here as a more general term.

Note also that in this index each conditional probability is multiplied by the appropriate a priori probability. In our terminology, the overall probability of a correct response is

$$P(C) = P(A|a)P(a) + P(N|n)P(n).$$

This probability, then, is the sum of two "joint" probabilities; $P(A|a)P(a)$ equals the joint probability $P(A \cdot a)$, and, similarly, $P(N|n)P(n)$ equals the joint probability $P(N \cdot n)$.

As noted earlier, employing a coincident value of a second variable along with $P(A|a)$ is a good idea; and, to be sure, we might have defined the ROC in terms of $P(N|n)$ rather than in terms of its complement, $P(A|n)$. However, simply adding two independent quantities from the 2×2 matrix obscures their covariation; the simple addition fails to use one of the quantities to calibrate the other.

This fact is seen easily in Figure 3. For the particular ROC curve shown, which is labeled by the hit probability $P(A|a)$, and for equal a priori probabilities of a and n, the variation of $P(C)$ due to criterion variation alone is as shown. Thus, criterion variation of a magnitude that yields $P(A|n)$ or $P(FP)$ ranging from 0.00 to 0.25 will induce variation in $P(C)$ ranging by as much as 40% (in this instance, from 0.50 to 0.70).

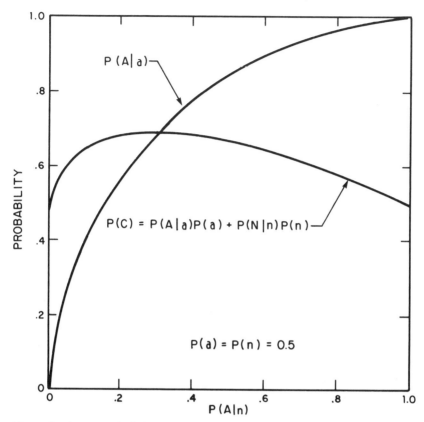

Figure 3.   A portrayal of the variation in the true-positive probability, $P(A|a)$, and in the overall measure of percentage correct, $P(C)$, that is due to variation in the decision criterion alone. (After Egan and Clarke, 1966.)

1.3.4   Inverse (A Posteriori) Probability of a True-Positive Response

An index that we would all like to use is the inverse probability of a true-positive response, $P(a|A)$. Practically, what we want to know is the probability that an abnormality exists when the system says it does. Unfortunately, however, that probability is also highly dependent on the particular decision criterion employed. If the decision criterion is very lenient, $P(a|A)$ can be as low as the a priori probability of abnormality. If the criterion is very strict, $P(a|A)$ can be as high as 1.0.

One might try to overcome this problem by using $P(a|A)$ as one element of a kind of ROC. The response analysis characteristic (RAC) has been defined elsewhere (Swets and Birdsall, 1967) as $P(a|A)$ plotted against $P(a|N)$. But the RAC does not aid us in our present purpose. This is because the RAC takes forms not easily described or indexed, the range of the RAC depends on the a priori probability of abnormality, and the curve associated with a given a priori probability crosses all curves with higher a priori probabilities.

The general effect is indicated in Figure 4. The left panel shows a particular ROC and indicates points at five decision criteria, 1, . . ., 5. The middle panel shows the corresponding RAC for $P(a) = 0.50$ with the same decision criteria indicated. The right panel shows the corresponding RAC for $P(a) = 0.20$ with those decision criteria indicated. In addition to seeing the three unwieldy properties of the RAC just listed, we can see that, as mentioned earlier, $P(a|A)$ varies from the a priori probability at one extreme to 1.0 at the other as the decision criterion varies from lenient to strict.

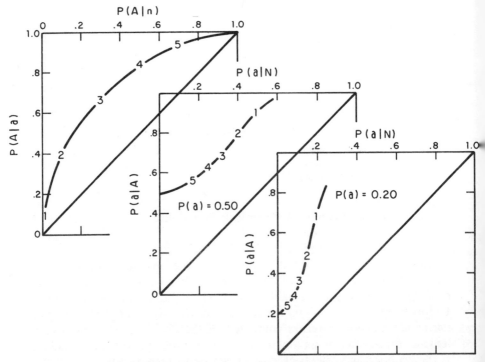

Figure 4. An ROC with data points, 1, . . . , 5, at five decision criteria (left panel); the so-called RAC for those data points for $P(a) = 0.50$ (middle panel); the corresponding RAC for $P(a) = 0.20$ (right panel).

1.3.5   The Odds Ratio

Another index of accuracy based on a posteriori probabilities is simply the ratio of the two probabilities mentioned, $P(a|A)/P(a|N)$, for any given decision criterion. This ratio is known as the "incidence ratio" or as "relative risk." A closely related ratio is the odds ratio, or the log-odds ratio described by Goodman (1970).

The difficulty with the incidence ratio, relative risk, and the odds ratio (as with a pair of values of sensitivity and specificity) is that they are based on a single 2×2 data matrix, or, equivalently, on a single decision criterion or a single point in the ROC space. That dependence on a single ROC point would be acceptable if empirical ROCs always took the same form, but they do not. A major recommendation of this book is that the full ROC be traced out for each evaluation, and an index derived that depends on the full ROC. If assumptions are made about the form of the ROC, and indexes are based on single points, one can easily conclude that system A is superior to system B when, in fact, the reverse is true (Goodenough, Metz, and Lusted, 1973; Metz and Goodenough, 1973).

1.4   RECOMMENDED INDICES OF ACCURACY

Several alternative ways to index the accuracy reflected in an ROC have been devised and used (Green and Swets, 1966/1974; Simpson and Fitter, 1973; Swets, 1979). In this section we describe one of them that we recommend for general use and another that might be used on occasion. The primary performance index is defined as the proportion of area of the ROC graph that lies beneath an ROC of a particular theoretical form, one that is based on normal (Gaussian) probability distributions. This index is termed A_z. An alternative index is defined as the perpendicular distance of such an ROC (plotted in a manner described shortly) from the center of the ROC space, and is called d_a. The latter index gives quantities in the range of the various indices used first with the ROC (those in the d' family) and may be a convenience on those grounds; it is also useful in certain theoretical comparisons.

In addition to those two indices of accuracy, we describe a simple numerical way of conveying quite precisely the position of entire ROC curves without showing them graphically. A two-parameter fit of the ROC, again based on normal distributions, is termed $D(\Delta m, s)$, and serves this purpose. Those two parameters could serve to measure accuracy, but we prefer to think of them as a description or summary of ROC data.

Both of the accuracy indices described and the data summary are based on a highly robust, empirical result, which is now substantiated in dozens of diverse applications; namely, that the empirical ROC is very similar in form to a theoretical ROC derived from normal probability distributions. In practice, in other words, the ROC curve is adequately described by a straight line when plotted on a binormal graph (see, e.g., Dorfman, Beaver, and Saslow, 1973; Green and Swets, 1966/1974). By a "binormal" graph is meant a graph whose coordinates are "probability" scales or, more specifically, coordinates on which the normal-deviate value of the probability is scaled linearly, as in Figure 5. That figure shows the ROC quantities $P(A|a)$ or $P(TP)$ and $P(A|n)$ or $P(FP)$ on probability scales. Those probabilities are spaced as shown when

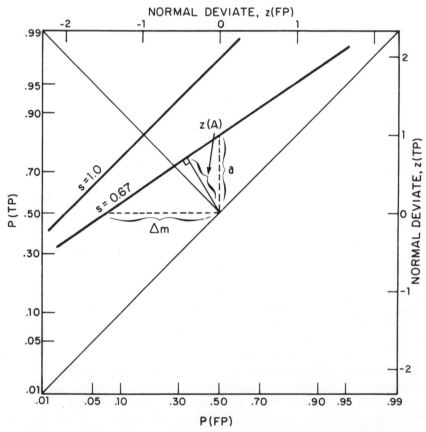

Figure 5.   Binormal ROCs of two slopes (s), with various parameters indicated; see text.

their respective normal-deviate values, denoted z, are scaled linearly: $z(TP)$ on the right ordinate and $z(FP)$ on the upper abscissa. On such a graph, the slopes of empirical ROCs will vary, but the ROC curve is generally a straight line. Figure 5 shows ROCs with slopes (s) of 1.0 and 0.67.

We point out that for slopes other than unity on a binormal graph, the ROC on the linear probability scales considered earlier will not be symmetrical about the minor diagonal as are the curves of Figure 2. For slopes less than unity on a binormal graph, which is the most frequent case, the curvilinear ROC on linear probability scales will rise more steeply from the lower left corner and at some point bow over and approach the upper right-hand corner almost linearly.

The straight-line ROC is called a "binormal ROC" because of its theoretical basis in normal or Gaussian probability distributions. It is relatively easy to fit by eye and is easily fitted by statistical techniques that give maximum-likelihood estimates of its slope and intercept. The two terms of the data summary mentioned are an intercept Δm and the slope s of the straight line, as described shortly.

1.4.1   Area under the Binormal ROC, A_z

Our recommended index of accuracy A_z is the proportion of the total area of the ROC graph that lies beneath the binormal ROC. (Strictly speaking, it is the proportion of area under the binormal ROC when the ROC is plotted on the linear probability scales of Figures 1 and 2.) A_z thus ranges from a lower limit of 0.50 for an ROC lying along the major diagonal, defining performance at a chance level, to an upper limit of 1.0 for an ROC following the left-hand and top axes of the graph, defining perfect performance.

We point out that this index of area under the binormal ROC, A_z, is practically superior to an area index described earlier, called $P(A)$ by Green and Swets (1966/1974), because A_z is less affected by the location or spread of the points that define the ROC. $P(A)$ is obtained by connecting empirical ROC points on linear probability scales (as in Figure 2) by straight lines and then computing the subtended area by the trapezoidal rule. $P(A)$ has a theoretical advantage in being free of any assumptions about the form of probability distributions that might underlie the ROC, but it underestimates the area beneath a complete ROC when the empirical points are not well spread across the ROC space.

The range of the area index—from 0.50 to 1.0—is consistent with the fact that it is equal to the probability of a correct response in a two-alternative, forced-choice test (Green and Swets, 1966/1974). Such a test presents on each trial one sample of each of the two alternatives under consideration—for example, one sample of "signal-plus-noise" and one sample of "noise alone" in a detection problem. The observer knows this to be the case and must say which is which or, more simply, which sample is of the designated alternative, for example, "signal-plus-noise." Equivalently, the observer ranks the two samples according to which is more likely to be from the designated alternative. Bamber (1975) has pointed out that the area index is closely related to the Mann-Whitney U statistic, familiar as a nonparametric statistic.

1.4.2 A Function of the Perpendicular Distance to the ROC, d_a

Figure 5 shows a quantity $z(A)$ as the perpendicular distance in normal-deviate units from the origin of the ROC space $[z(TP) = z(FP) = 0]$ to the binormal ROC. That quantity $z(A)$ is, in fact, the normal-deviate value that corresponds to the area measure A_z when A_z is expressed as a probability. Multiplying $z(A)$ by the square root of 2 yields the index denoted d_a. The index d_a is like the indices d' (which applies only when the straight-line ROC has a slope of unity) and d'_e (which is d' measured at the minor diagonal), but has an advantage in statistical nicety (Brookes, 1968; Simpson and Fitter, 1973). Like d', d'_e, and Δm, the value of d_a ranges from 0 to a practical upper limit of 4 or 5. All of the indices just mentioned (d', d'_e, Δm, and d_a), by the way, are equal when the linear ROC has unit slope.

1.4.3 A Two-Parameter Measure, $D(\Delta m,s)$

The binormal ROC is not fully described by A_z or d_a, because given values of those indices can result from linear ROCs of different slopes and intercepts. The binormal ROC is fully described by the two parameters of slope and intercept. Figure 5 shows the intercept indexed as the normal-deviate value at the intercept of the ROC with the x axis, that is, the axis corresponding to $z(TP) = 0$. This value (with sign reversed) is denoted Δm. The ROC slope s is the ratio of the quantity denoted in the figure as a (i.e., the normal-deviate value of the intercept of the ROC with the y axis) to the value of Δm: $s = a/\Delta m$. The two parameters are combined in the term symbolized as $D(\Delta m,s)$. If, for example, $\Delta m =$

1.0 and $s = 1.0$, we would write $D(\Delta m,s) = (1.0,1.0)$. (Those two values characterize the illustrative curve shown earlier in Figure 1.) The quantity Δm ranges effectively from 0 to 4 or 5; almost all empirical slopes lie between 0.5 and 1.5.

The term $D(\Delta m, s)$ conveniently represents the entire curve, allowing a report reader to reconstruct the entire curve from just those two numbers and hence to examine coordinate values at any point throughout the range of the curve even when the curve is not reported. The calculation of $D(\Delta m,s)$ also points up comparisons of ROC curves that may differ significantly in slope. For those comparisons, the single-parameter measures that describe an entire curve without regard to slope (such as A_z and d_a) are inappropriate. A single-parameter measure that may be used in such instances is the value of $P(TP)$ at some particular value of $P(FP)$, as discussed later in Section 1.6.

1.4.4   Graphical Determination of Indices

One can plot ROC points on a binormal graph, fit a straight line to them by eye, and easily obtain from the graph and a few calculations all of the quantities just mentioned.

Beginning with the normal-deviate values of the x and y intercepts, namely, Δm and a as read directly from the upper and right-hand coordinates of Figure 5, one calculates $s = a/\Delta m$ to obtain $D(\Delta m,s)$.

The quantity $z(A)$ is equal to $s(\Delta m)/(1 + s^2)^{1/2}$. Taking $z(A)$ to a table of the cumulative standardized normal distribution gives A_z as the area under the normal distribution up to the normal-deviate value equal to $z(A)$. The quantity d_a is equal to $2^{1/2} z(A)$.

1.4.5   Statistical Estimates of Indices

Alternatively to the graphical determinates of indices (and usually preferably) one can use an existing computer program to obtain (1) an objective fit to empirical ROC points with a chi-square index of the goodness-of-fit and also (2) maximum-likelihood estimates of A_z, d_a, Δm, and s. This program is a slight revision by the original authors of one described in the literature (Dorfman and Alf, 1969). Dr. Dorfman has kindly made a listing of this computer program available to us, and we have reproduced it in Appendix D along with his *User's Guide* to the program.

1.5 A COMPUTATIONAL EXAMPLE

We describe now the construction of an ROC curve from what are termed "rating-scale" data and then calculate the various indices of accuracy described above.

Consider again the diagnostic problem in which the two possible states of the patient are "normal" and "abnormal." A point on the ROC graph may be obtained from the conditional probabilities of the corresponding decision alternatives ("Normal" and "Abnormal"), which are obtained while the diagnostician attempts to maintain a particular decision criterion for this binary response. A second point can then be obtained from a second group of trials during which the diagnostician adopts a different criterion—more or less stringent—and again makes a binary response, and so on, until enough points are obtained (say, four or five) to define adequately an entire ROC curve.

The preferred alternative to this procedure—preferred for reasons of reliability of estimates and economy of time—is to ask the diagnostician to give a *confidence rating* that each case is *abnormal,* or, in other words, to respond on a *rating scale,* which has, say, five or six categories that represent graded levels of confidence. The diagnostician is asked in effect to maintain several decision criteria simultaneously, and he or she yields at once the desired number of points on the ROC graph.

Consider the hypothetical data of Table 3, which represent numbers of rating responses made in each of five categories of a rating scale both for cases truly abnormal and for cases truly normal. In each cell the raw frequencies of responses are given at the left. The cumulative response proportions given in parentheses at the right of each cell (moving downward) are the estimates of conditional true-positive (*TP*) probabilities (left column) and conditional false-positive (*FP*) probabilities (right col-

Table 3

ILLUSTRATIVE RATING-SCALE DATA

	Stimulus	
Response	Abnormal	Normal
Very likely abnormal, 1	350 (0.70)	25 (0.05)
Probably abnormal, 2	50 (0.80)	50 (0.15)
Possibly abnormal, 3	40 (0.88)	75 (0.30)
Probably normal, 4	35 (0.95)	150 (0.60)
Very likely normal, 5	25 (1.00)	200 (1.00)

umn). The *TP* and *FP* probability estimates are simply obtained by successively considering each rating-category boundary as if it were a binary-decision criterion.

Thus, considering only ratings of 1 as Abnormal, and considering ratings of 2 to 5 as Normal, we obtain an estimate of $P(A|n)$ or of the *FP* probability of 0.05, and an estimate of $P(A|a)$ or of the *TP* probability of 0.70. This ROC point of (0.05, 0.70) is the equivalent of one generated by a binary-decision criterion that is relatively stringent. Move on now to regard ratings of both 1 and 2 as indicating Abnormal, and ratings of 3 to 5 as indicating Normal—a somewhat more lenient criterion. Then $P(FP)$ equals 0.15 and $P(TP)$ equals 0.80, and so on, through the fifth rating category, yielding the points (0.30, 0.88), (0.60, 0.95), and (1.0, 1.0). We see, incidentally, because the last category always yields $P(FP) = P(TP) = 1.0$, that rating judgments yield a number of ROC points 1 less than the number of judgment categories.

The four ROC points calculated in Table 3 are plotted as circles in Figure 6. The coordinates of the ROC graph in this figure are linearly scaled in terms of the normal deviate, hence we would expect on normal assumptions an ROC curve approximating a straight line. (This graph paper is printed by the Codex Book Company, Inc., of Norwood, Massachusetts, and bears their No. 41,453.)

The graphical determination of the recommended accuracy indexes, and of the data summary, begins with fitting by eye a straight line to the data points of Figure 6. The value of Δm associated with such a line is equal to the normal-deviate, or z value at the x intercept with the sign reversed; here Δm equals 2.50. Again, the slope s equals $a/\Delta m$; here $s = 1.50/2.50 = 0.60$. The term $D(\Delta m, s)$ equals (2.50, 0.60).

Applying the computer program of Appendix D to the hypothetical results given in Table 3 and Figure 6 yields estimates of $a = 1.484$ and $s = 0.592$. Thus, $D(\Delta m, s)$ equals (2.51, 0.59). These values are essentially those we obtained graphically; they indicate that our hypothetical ROC points were susceptible to being fitted well by eye. Another comparison of this sort is supplied by Dorfman and Alf (1969), who reported maximum-likelihood estimates for four observers whose data were earlier fitted by eye (Green and Swets, 1966/1974, pp. 104, 105). For two of those observers, the estimates by the two procedures are very similar as above, whereas for the other two observers the estimates differ by 5–10%.

The quantity $z(A)$ obtained graphically is $s(\Delta m)/(1 + s^2)^{1/2}$ or 0.60 (2.50)/$(1 + 0.36)^{1/2} = 1.286$. The latter quantity is the normal-deviate value corresponding to a cumulative probability of 0.901, our measure A_z. The computer program yields $A_z = 0.899$.

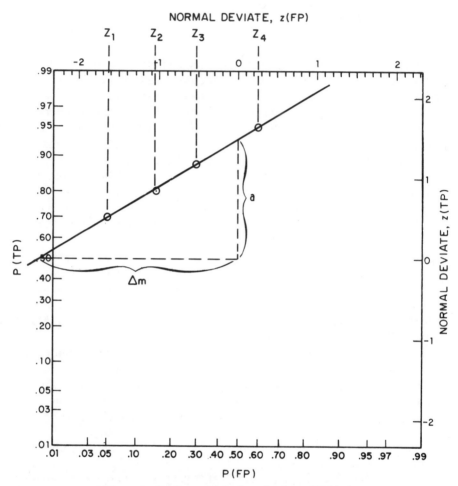

Figure 6. ROC curve based on the data of Table 3.

Obtained graphically, the index d_a equals $2^{1/2} z(A)$, which equals 1.414 × 1.286 = 1.818. The computer program gives a maximum-likelihood estimate of $d_a = 1.806$.

The computer program yields a value of $\chi^2 = 0.135$ for the goodness-of-fit of these hypothetical data to the straight line fitted. The number of degrees of freedom associated with the χ^2 test is $n - 2$, where n is equal to the number of data points; so with our four points we have two degrees of freedom (d.f.). $\chi^2 = 0.135$ for 2 d.f. has an associated probability of >0.90, quite consistent with the ability to fit these four points well by eye and with the close agreement of indices as derived graphically and statistically.

In our opinion, graphical estimates of the accuracy parameters made from ROC curves fitted by eye are adequate for many purposes: for example, to determine the approximate level of accuracy of a system or to make a preliminary comparison of two systems. However, analysis via computer is essential to a definitive comparison of systems, especially when a difference between them might be asserted. In that event, one should have an objective fit of the curve and the greater precision of the computed estimates. Most important then are the estimates of sampling variance yielded by the computer, for the purposes of determining confidence intervals on the accuracy parameters and the statistical significance of observed differences in those parameters (see Chapter 4).

1.6 A SUITABLE ACCURACY INDEX BASED ON ONE ROC POINT

So far we have treated accuracy indices that are based on an entire ROC curve and that provide general assessments of system performance without regard to the decision criteria or ROC operating points that may characterize the specific settings in which the system may be employed (Sections 1.4 and 1.5). Also, we have warned against accuracy indices based on one point in the ROC space when the remainder of that system's curve is undetermined (Section 1.3).

However, an investigator may decide to use an accuracy index based on one ROC point when the full ROC curve *is* determined, because the use of such an index is (*a*) desirable or (*b*) necessary. Here we first identify a suitable index of that sort and then compare and contrast the conditions under which it is appropriate with conditions under which the general measures like A_z and d_a are appropriate.

In our opinion, the most direct and easily interpretable single-parameter index based on one operating point of a fully determined ROC is the value of $P(TP)$ corresponding to some carefully selected reference value of $P(FP)$. One may choose to work instead with $P(FP)$ at a reference $P(TP)$ or with the complements of those probabilities, but what we have to say here applies to all of these possibilities and we refer further in this volume only to $P(TP)$ at a reference $P(FP)$.

We emphasize the more general measures in this book because we believe that a given diagnostic system will likely be used with widely varying decision criteria or operating points. The variation may be deliberate—ranging, for example, from the necessarily strict criterion in a screening setting to a relatively lenient criterion in a referral setting. An evaluation from a general vantage point, as might be taken by a government agency, for example, can treat the entire range of possible settings with a general index. On the other hand, the variation in operating points used with the system may be inadvertent. Optimal operating points are often difficult to determine precisely, depending as they may on value judgments about morbidity and mortality and on adequate prevalence data; and the process of translating a calculated optimum into consistent practice, though conceivable, is not altogether direct and simple. Thus, even for a given type of diagnostic setting, the operating points used will probably vary across locations, across diagnosticians at one location, and within individual diagnosticians over time. Again, a general index seems best. Whether the variation in operating points is deliberate or inadvertent, at present it will probably not be well known. In most diagnostic settings of interest, the data bases, data rates, and data analyses are not up to the tasks of ascertaining the geographical and personal variation and of tracking the temporal variation. A corollary of this uncertainty is that one will rarely be able to establish that two systems being compared have essentially the same operating point, and therefore one will not meet a fundamental requirement of a comparison based on a single operating point. For example, the CT and RN brain scan modalities have very different structures and may well differ in the operating points typically used.

However, let us acknowledge the possibility that the focus of practical interest may at times be rather specific with regard to diagnostic setting and that an investigator may be reasonably confident about at least the approximate single operating point, or the limited range of points, that will be employed by the various systems under test. Then concentrating on that point or on a few alternative points in a narrow range will surely give a sharper analysis than is given by treating the entire curve. This investigator will want to know the confidence interval of an index derived only from a point—such as $P(TP)$ at the reference $P(FP)$—and the statistical significance of an observed difference in a pair of such indices. Statistical information about the general indices A_z and d_a will not satisfy the analytical requirements.

Quite apart from the desirability of sharper analyses when single operating points exist and are known is the fact that single-point indices may be demanded by the nature of the ROC data. Specifically, the use of the general indices is properly restricted to a comparison of binormal ROCs with slopes that are similar or not materially different. The issue here is quite clear when two ROCs cross within the ROC space as usually graphed, that is, within the space that includes probabilities between 0.01 and 0.9—and is especially clear when they cross in a region of the space that is likely to contain operating points of practical interest. Then one system is more accurate for operating points to the left of the crossing point, and the other is more accurate to the right of that point. The general indices will not reflect such a condition, and therefore one has to determine the operating point or points of particular interest and base an accuracy index on the point(s) determined.

What constitutes a "material" difference in slope when the ROC curves do not visibly cross is a difficult question, and we believe one that is best left for the investigator in each specific study. One reason for not attempting to state a general rule is that a given difference in slopes might matter for curves close together and not matter for curves far apart. Another reason is that a given difference may matter or not, independent of whether it is statistically significant. We made the judgment in our CT/RN study (Swets *et al.*, 1979) that a difference in slopes approaching 0.20 was not material, given a difference in A_z of 0.10.

We believe that ordinarily the ROCs one wants to compare will have slopes sufficiently similar to permit use of A_z or d_a. Nonetheless, basing an accuracy index on a single operating point may be necessary in some instances, and then, despite the attendant difficulties, one must select that point as best one can. Some considerations in selecting the point are raised in Section 1.7 in the context of a discussion of ways to index such a point.

1.7 INDICES OF THE DECISION CRITERION

There are, as in the case of accuracy, several alternative means of indexing the decision criterion, or the response bias, that is reflected in any point of an ROC curve. Ten or so of these indices were recently reviewed in the psychological literature (DuSoir, 1975). The two best indices, in our view, are (*a*) the value of $P(FP)$ at the point in question—or the normal-deviate value corresponding to that $P(FP)$, denoted Z_k ($k = 1$ to n for the n points of an ROC); and (*b*) the ROC slope at the point, denoted β. As we shall see, these two indices correspond to different concepts of the factors that determine the decision criterion. For this reason, the choice between them may depend on the investigator's opinion about which factors are properly and/or actually determining the placement of the decision criterion in the particular situation under investigation.

1.7.1   The Normal-Deviate Value of $P(FP)$, Z_k

Either Z_k or β can be used to represent any ROC point, of course, no matter how it is arrived at, but the use of Z_k is most consistent with the assumption that the decision criterion is set in order to achieve a given $P(FP)$. It is consistent with the Neyman-Pearson definition of the optimal criterion, familiar from traditional hypothesis testing in statistics. This is the criterion that maximizes $P(TP)$ while satisfying an upper limit on $P(FP)$; see Green and Swets (1966/1974). Ordinarily, in statistics the value of $P(FP)$ selected is 0.05 or 0.01.

Note that the Neyman-Pearson definition lets the maximum $P(TP)$ fall where it may. Thus, two observers may have the same criterion in the sense of Z_k, but very different values of $P(TP)$, and, thus, very different accuracies. They will therefore have a very different balance between $P(TP)$ and $P(FP)$, between hits and false alarms. If, however, accuracy is essentially constant over the observers compared, then Z_k is a reasonable index quite apart from any theoretical connotation.

1.7.2   The ROC Slope, β

Recall from Figures 1 and 2 that the ROC slope is decreasing throughout the ROC's extent so that its slope ranges from infinity to zero and uniquely identifies any ROC point. (This assertion holds strictly only for binormal ROCs with $s = 1.0$, but its failure for ROCs with $s \neq 1.0$ is limited to extremes of the ROC and need not concern us here.)

Underlying the use of β as the index of the decision criterion is the assumption that the criterion is set to achieve a desired balance between hits and false alarms. False alarms have no special status in having a certain limit as conceived in the Neyman-Pearson definition of optimum.

The definition of the optimal criterion most in accord with the use of β is the expected value (EV) definition. In this case, positive values are associated with the two correct decision outcomes (true-positives and true-negatives), and negative values or costs are associated with the two incorrect decision outcomes (false-positives and false-negatives). The criterion is set in order to maximize the total payoff. The total payoff will be maximized for a given accuracy at a particular balance between true-positives and false-positives, that is, at a particular value of β, no matter what accuracy is involved. Specifically, the EV or payoff will be a maximum when the expression $P(TP) - \beta P(FP)$ is maximized, where

$$\beta = [P(n)/P(a)] \cdot [(V_{TN} + C_{FP})/(V_{TP} + C_{FN})],$$

where $P(n)$ and $P(a)$ are the a priori probabilities of normal and abnormal

cases, and where the V's and C's are the values and costs of the four
possible outcomes (Green and Swets, 1966/1974). (Thus, it is possible
for two observers to have the same decision criterion, as indexed by β,
and quite different values of $P(FP)$ if their accuracies differ.)

To exercise the equation just given, note that an operating point on
an ROC having $\beta = 0.5$—and thus representing a relatively lenient decision criterion with a high $P(FP)$—would be indicated when the V's and
C's are equal, and $P(a)$ is twice $P(n)$, or when $P(a) = P(n)$ and the sum
of V's and C's associated with abnormal cases is twice the sum associated
with normal cases. Conversely, a stricter criterion with $\beta = 2.0$, say,
is appropriate when the two sums of V's and C's are equal, and $P(n)$
is twice $P(a)$, or when $P(n) = P(a)$ and the premium on identifying
correctly a normal case is twice that of an abnormal case.

1.7.3 Computation of the Two Indices, Z_k and β

Graphically, Z_k is obtained by drawing the perpendicular distance from
an ROC point to a point on the fitted ROC line, finding the x coordinate
at that point on the line to be $-Z_k$, and changing the sign. (Thus, Z_k is
derived from a point along the ROC in the same manner that Δm is.)
In Figure 6, we see that $Z_1 = 1.64$, $Z_2 = 1.05$, $Z_3 = 0.52$, and $Z_4 = -0.25$. Estimates of Z_k may also be obtained from the computer program
in Appendix D. That program's estimates for the points of Figure 6 are
1.625, 1.054, 0.525, and -0.255. Of course, ROC data more difficult to
fit by eye than our hypothetical data would yield larger deviations of
estimates made by the graphical and statistical techniques.

The value of β corresponds to the slope of a utility line tangent to the
ROC at the point yielded by a given decision criterion. Hence, one can
proceed to a set of empirical ROC points (plotted on linear probability
scales as in Figures 1 and 2), draw a smooth curve to fit the points, and
measure the slope of the line tangent to the curve at a point of interest.
The simplest technique is to lay a ruler along the tangent at the point,
draw the tangent line on the graph, measure the x and y distances to
the line from any point below the line, and take $y/x = \beta$. If one measures
off 10 cm horizontally to the right from the left-hand end of the line,
then the vertical distance in centimeters from that point to the line equals
β.

The available computer program does not calculate β, but a simple
calculation employing the maximum-likelihood estimates of that program
is

$$\beta = s \exp\{+\tfrac{1}{2}[(1 - s^2)Z_k^2 + 2s^2(\Delta m)Z_k - s^2(\Delta m)^2]\}$$

in our present notation; in the notation of the computer program as given in Appendix D, we have

$$\beta = B \exp\{+\tfrac{1}{2}[(1 - B^2)Z_k^2 + 2ABZ_k - A^2]\}.$$

1.7.4 Example: Data from the CT/RN Study

In our study of CT and RN brain scans, a five-category rating scale yielded the four points shown for each modality in Figure 7. The points for each modality are based on a pooling of the raw response frequencies of six observers (a procedure discussed in Section 2.3).

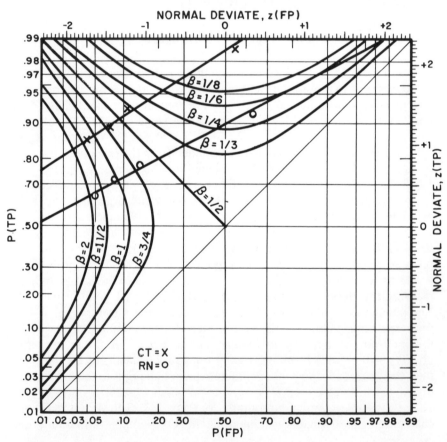

Figure 7. Curves of constant β for linear ROC curves of slope of one-half, and the ROC data of the CT/RN study.

Expressed in terms of $P(FP)$ or Z_k, the criteria are rather similar across the scale for the two modalities. Reading from left to right with CT values first and RN values second, $Z_k = (1.765, 1.680)$, $(1.50, 1.346)$, $(1.192, 1.013)$, and $(-0.115, -0.335)$.

The figure shows contours of constant β, sometimes called "iso-bias" contours, for linear ROCs having a slope of 0.50. The slope of 0.50 approximates the observed CT slope of 0.61 and the observed RN slope of 0.51. [The difficulty, by the way, with using such a set of theoretical contours to estimate empirical β's is that the contours depend on the slope of the *linear* ROC. For an ROC of unit slope, for example, $\beta = 1$ is at the negative or minor diagonal, where $\beta = \frac{1}{2}$ appears in this figure, and, indeed, all of the quantities in the figure move two curves to the right.]

The values of β are seen to diverge more than the values of Z_k for the two modalities. Approximately, listing CT values first and RN values second, $\beta = (1\frac{1}{2}, 1\frac{3}{4})$, $(\frac{3}{4}, 1)$, $(\frac{1}{3}, \frac{3}{4})$, and $(\ll\frac{1}{8}, \frac{1}{5})$. To make a single comparison, in terms of β, the (pooled) CT reader viewed the second rating category much as the (pooled) RN reader viewed the third rating category.

1.7.5 The Choice of a Decision Criterion

Ordinarily, the intent of a performance test is to obtain an index of accuracy independent of the observer's decision criteria. This intent is satisfied by the simple use of a rating scale and the ROC analysis. The rating scale serves to spread out four or so ROC points, and therefore to define adequately the ROC curve. As long as the curve is adequately defined, a valid index of accuracy can be obtained without regard to where exactly the points lie.

Thus, in an evaluation study, one need not be concerned with the observers' decision criteria as such. One need not take any special steps to assure that the observers all think of the rating categories in the same way—whether, for example, they choose to distribute numbers of responses across the categories according to a normal distribution, rectangular distribution, or U-shaped distribution. All of this is fortunate, because the laboratory setting may affect different observers differently and may affect all observers differently than does the practical setting. Observers in practice may adopt a Neyman-Pearson sort of limit on $P(FP)$, and, upon entering the laboratory, where immediate actions do not follow upon their decisions, may switch over to the criterion that maximizes the percentage of correct responses. This latter condition is

met, incidentally, when $\beta = P(n)/P(a)$, the ratio of the two prior probabilities (Green and Swets, 1966/1974). Therefore, unless special pains
are taken with the definition of laboratory criteria, one would not be
inclined to generalize from them to the practical setting.

Even if the intent of the study is to go beyond an index of accuracy
to obtain an assessment of the efficacy or overall usefulness of a diagnostic device, the investigator still need not be concerned about the test
observers' criteria. Any given criterion—for example, any value of β
selected by the investigator according to the prior probabilities and utilities thought to characterize the practical diagnostic setting—can be used
with an ROC representing the several test observers. From that criterion
and the observers' ROC, one can calculate that probabilities of the various decision outcomes and the payoff from using the system. If the
efficacy or usefulness of a given system is maximized at a given criterion,
the task will be to adjust the observer's criterion in the practical setting—
not in the laboratory—to match the optimal criterion. We do not take
a position here as to whether the Neyman-Pearson definition or the EV
definition is most suitable to a given practical setting. Efficacy may or
may not be synonomous with EV. Satisfying a limit on $P(FP)$ may be
critical.

1.8   SUMMARY

We have seen how the discrimination capacity of a diagnostic system
(i.e., its accuracy) may be separated from its decision tendencies in
problems involving discrimination between two states. The ROC curve
is a means of determining indices for each of these aspects of diagnostic
performance. Graphical estimates of the indices are simply obtained, and
an existing computer program provides maximum-likelihood estimates
of the indices and their sampling variances.

Two indices of accuracy were detailed: the perpendicular distance to
the linear ROC, denoted d_a; and one the authors prefer, the proportion
of area beneath the binormal ROC, denoted A_z. Two indices of the
decision criterion are the corresponding false-positive probability $P(FP)$
or its associated normal-deviate value Z_k and the corresponding slope
of the ROC, denoted β. The optimal value of the decision criterion may
be determined under several definitions of optimum, including one that
merely fixes $P(FP)$ and another that takes prior probabilities and utilities
explicitly into account. The optimal criterion can then be used in assessments of system efficacy.

An index of accuracy specific to one point on the curve will be desirable in certain instances, and a simple one is available. However, several common indices of accuracy are based on what amounts to one ROC point in an inadequate way. In particular, they do not choose the single point, let alone in an advised fashion, and so fail to use one of the point's coordinates to calibrate the other. Then unassessed variation in the decision criterion produces an unknown amount of variation in the accuracy index.

CHAPTER 2

Extensions of Accuracy Analysis

.

The first part of this chapter treats some issues involved in indexing diagnostic performance when more than two alternative states are considered—a consideration that arises when attempting to make a detailed analysis of localization and classification performance. A general ROC solution has not beeen achieved for the multiple-alternative situation, but we recommend an accuracy index based on an extension of the conventional ROC that we believe to be adequate for most purposes.

The second part of this chapter shows how certain manipulations of ROC quantities can yield quantitative interpretations of diagnostic accuracy (*a*) that may be more directly meaningful than are the ROC indices required for rigorous assessment, and (*b*) that help to reflect the practical import of an ROC index of any particular value. The third and concluding part of the chapter describes ways to index the performance of a typical diagnostician, or of a group of them, as an aid in summarizing data.

2.1 MULTIPLE ALTERNATIVES

In this section, we (*a*) acknowledge the lack of a general ROC analysis (for more than two alternatives), (*b*) suggest that a general ROC analysis might be unwieldy anyway, (c) discuss the percentage of correct responses as a possible measure, (d) dismiss two other approaches that have been considered, and (e) recommend for use what we term the "joint ROC."

2.1.1 Lack of a General ROC Analysis

Several attempts have been made over the past 25 years (a few published, but more unpublished) to develop a general ROC analysis for multiple stimulus and response alternatives. Although some progress has been made, these attempts have not been completely successful. Specifically, developments to date have not yielded a general and workable analysis of a diagnostic system's ability to identify the correct site of a signal (localization) or the correct type of a signal (classification) when several alternatives are considered at once.

The basic goal of these efforts has been twofold. Just as with the ROC analysis of two alternatives, we would like an analysis of multiple alternatives that (a) yields independent measures of stimulus identifiability and of decision criteria or response biases and (b) permits deriving the response probabilities that would result from any given identifiabilities of the stimuli for any selected decision or response strategy.

Achievement of the first goal would assure us of a relatively pure measure of stimulus identifiability, one unaffected by variation in decision factors. Achievement of the second goal would permit us to calculate the probabilities of the various diagnostic outcomes that optimally reflect the stimulus probabilities and the utilities in a given diagnostic context. The ability to make that calculation would be useful in those situations in which enough data on incidences and values and costs are available to attempt a rather full assessment of the efficacy of a diagnostic system.

A recent review by Metz, Starr, and Lusted (1977) indicates the complexities that must be faced and the uncertainties that must currently be entertained even when dealing with three alternatives.

"Generalized ROC curves" describing the relationships among the relative frequencies of the various types of decisions in almost any diagnostic decision-making experiment can be imagined and can, in theory, be determined experimentally. In some situations, however, the resulting relationships can be complex, difficult to measure to acceptable statistical accuracy without large numbers of trials, and difficult to interpret if an underlying theoretical structure is not available.

Consider, for example, analysis of the "detection and recognition" situation in which an observer must decide whether an image contains a lesion of type "a," a lesion of type "b," or no lesion at all. Let "a," "b," and "n" represent the three states and let "*A*," "*B*," and "*N*" represent the corresponding decision. Nine *types* of correct and incorrect decision are thus possible. Because of the fact that decision probabilities conditional on the same true state must add to unity, three constraint equations exist:

$$P(A|a) + P(B|a) + P(N|a) = 1;$$
$$P(A|b) + P(B|b) + P(N|b) = 1;$$

and

$$P(A|n) + P(B|n) + P(N|n) = 1.$$

Thus any combination of decision frequencies can be represented by a point in six-dimensional space, and observation of the relationships among six types of decision frequency can always serve as an empirical description of observer performance in this situation.

Since more than one confidence threshold [decision criterion] can be varied in this kind of experiment, however, the relationship among these decision frequencies is not necessarily represented by a *line* in the six-dimensional space. The number of degrees of freedom—and hence the theoretical and experimental complexity—actually necessary to describe human observer performance in a detection and recognition situation is not yet established. Luce's "choice theory" (Luce, 1963) suggests that specification of *two* conditional decision frequencies should serve to determine the other seven, while a general signal detection theoretical approach (Swets and Birdsall, 1956; Whalen, 1971, p. 140) designed to maximize average decision utility by adoption of a theoretically optimum decision strategy suggests that *five* conditional decision frequencies must be specified in order to determine the other four. The practical usefulness of the generalized ROC curve concept for analysis of decision performance in detection and recognition situations—and, indeed, in any situation requiring the use of multiple confidence thresholds—seems to depend upon our ability to discover theoretical points of view, similar to those described above for the detection-and-localization and multiple signal detection tasks, which can be used to illuminate fundamental relationships among the various decision frequencies. [From Metz, C. E., Starr, S. J., and Lusted, L. B. Quantitative evaluation of visual detection performance in medicine: ROC analysis and determination of diagnostic benefit. In *Medical Images,* G. A. Hayes (ed.), pp. 230, 231. Copyright © 1977. Reprinted by permission of John Wiley & Sons, Ltd.]

We shall return shortly to the so-called detection-and-localization task just mentioned and the method of data analysis associated with it, because that method provides a useful way of dealing with multiple alternatives; but first let us ask how valuable a general solution for the multiple-alternative situation would be.

2.1.2 Difficulties with Practical Application of a General ROC analysis

We have said that the general ROC solution for three alternatives— say, lesion of type a, lesion of type b, or no lesion—has eluded us. As it happens, when the three-alternative problem is worked out, we shall thereby have the solution for four and more alternatives as well. But at this point we must acknowledge that the generalized ROC we seek will not necessarily permit us to work neatly in all diagnostic settings.

Witness the response format we used to represent site and differential diagnosis in our study of CT compared to RN brain scans (Section 7.2.4). An attempt to let the two modalities show their full capabilities led us to make 40 boxes available for checking off the location of a lesion, and also to list 11 categories of type of lesion (not to mention a twelfth alternative labeled "none of the above"). The generalized ROC in that study might yield 40 (or more) indices of stimulus identifiability and 40 (or more) indices of response bias for localization, and upwards of 11 of each for classification, but then we would have to make sense out of that many numbers. We might find a way that makes sense within localization or within classification, but then we would have the problem of merging our results on localization and our results on classification into a set of final diagnoses.

Moreover, even if we analysts could handle that many numbers, we could hardly expect future image readers to adjust so large a number of response biases to near-optimal settings. Even computer-aided diagnostic systems (e.g., Leaper, 1975) would experience difficulty with that many quantities.

We might, to be sure, selectively collapse our response alternatives into a smaller set for purposes of analysis, but we might still have to accomplish the merging of localization and classification results if we wanted to get an overall assessment of accuracy or cost–benefit relationships. Moreover, the suggestion that a number of response categories be reduced to a smaller number raises again the possibility of using only two categories for each decision and using as many two-category decisions in sequence as might be required. Still, some merging of the multiple indices of accuracy is required for a general summary.

The next few paragraphs set forth some ideas about a very simple index of accuracy for localization and/or classification. This index does not possess the central advantages of an index derived from the ROC graph, but it does give a way of dealing with a large number of alternatives and with alternatives that are organized into more than one set.

2.1.3 The Percentage of Correct Responses $P(C)$

One index available for use with multiple alternatives is simply the percentage of correct responses. This index is surely not free of response bias, and such bias is a substantial drawback. We might, however, take some comfort in supposing that somewhat less bias exists in the selection among several sites or types of abnormality than in the yes–no decision about abnormality or in other two-alternative decisions with strong polarity, such as malignant versus benign.

A distinct advantage of this index—here denoted $P(C)$—is that it simplifies the merging of multiple sets of multiple alternatives. In short, correctness can be defined at several levels. To begin with, $P(C)$ can be determined for just the localization alternatives, for example, and at the same time, for just the classification alternatives—to give separate assessments of these two aspects of diagnosis. Alternatively, or in addition, a response may be considered correct only when correct in both respects. If the test reader goes beyond a detection response only when it is positive, the latter value of $P(C)$ is tantamount to an overall measure, which consists of the fraction of trials in which a lesion is correctly detected *and* correctly localized *and* correctly classified.

Note that this overall measure as it was just stated ignores nonlesion trials, whether or not the reader issued a positive detection response, a matter to which we return shortly. Note also that the procedure on which it is based approximates what has been termed a "forced-choice" procedure in the literature of psychophysics. Ordinarily, a forced-choice procedure carries the assurance to the observer that a signal is in fact present on every trial and calls only for a localization or classification choice. In the evaluation of clinical diagnostic systems, however, the question of detection is likely to be fundamental, so that a pure forced-choice procedure—in the sense that the signal is known to be present on every trial—would have to be conducted, if at all, as a separate experimental condition. Moreover, the clinical evaluator may not want to call for a localization or classification choice on every trial when nonlesion trials are included: Achieving rapport with the test readers may preclude asking them to go on to identify the site and type of lesion after they have responded (perhaps confidently) that no lesion is present.

We should realize, then, that the $P(C)$ we would obtain in the medical context is not exactly the same quantity usually obtained in forced-choice tests. Specifically, determining $P(C)$ in the manner just described permits it to fluctuate with the reader's detection criterion. Readers with liberal detection criteria will tend to choose among lesion sites and types with less information than that typically available to readers with conservative detection criteria. Thus, the evaluator may want to determine $P(C)$ as a function of the detection criterion. A comparison of values of $P(C)$ for two systems should be made only at a given false-positive detection probability. Section 2.1.5 amplifies this suggestion.

2.1.4   Other Approaches to Multiple Alternatives

We have considered other, more complex approaches to multiple alternatives and have implemented one in our study of CT/RN brain scans. One possible approach is to ask test readers to distribute 100 points over the several alternatives in order to convey rather finely the intensity of their belief in the possible truth of each alternative. In pilot studies we found this task a difficult one with attendant difficulties in interpreting the results. The somewhat simpler approach that we used more extensively with classification was to ask test readers to rank up to four choices and give a percentage figure to represent their confidence only in their first choice. An analysis of the data on confidence percentages should prove interesting, although probably will not contribute in any important way to an evaluation of the competing systems.

Still another way to assess performance in choosing among multiple alternatives, considered by others, is to calculate the amount (in bits) of information transmitted by the readers' responses. A possible advantage of this index over the $P(C)$ index is that it might be insensitive to the number of alternatives considered (Garner, 1962). Though that number is usually fixed for any particular comparison, situations can arise where fine classifications are appropriate for one modality and relatively coarse classifications are appropriate for a modality to be compared. The major drawback of the information index is that it reflects only the consistency with which stimuli are mapped onto responses; therefore, for more than two alternatives, it ignores the correctness (accuracy) of the reader's judgments (see, e.g., Coombs, Dawes, and Tversky, 1970, p. 335.)

2.1.5   Recommended Approach: The Joint ROC

The detection-and-localization task referred to in Section 2.1.1 is one in which the observer makes both a detection response (perhaps a rating of confidence) and a localization response (a forced choice among m alternatives). The so-called localization ROC (LROC) is a plot of the probability of a false-positive detection response on the abscissa, as usual, with the probability of both a true-positive detection response and correct localization response on the ordinate. The LROC leaves the lower left-hand corner of the ROC space in the usual manner and has an asymptote at a value less than 1 on the ordinate, depending on m. Illustrative LROC curves are shown in Figure 8.

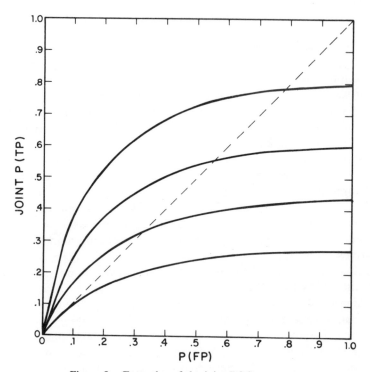

Figure 8. Examples of the joint ROC; see text.

Starr *et al.* (1975) show how the LROC can be predicted from the detection ROC as a function of the number of locations considered. The basic assumptions made are that the location alternatives are "orthogonal," or independent, and of equal detectability. They used experimental conditions thought to satisfy those assumptions—specifically, a field of radiographic mottle containing either no signal or a signal consisting of the image of a Plexiglas disk in exactly one quadrant of the field. The theory was amply confirmed by the experiment, which showed very good fits of empirical LROCs by predicted LROCs.

One conclusion of this work is that localization tests need not be conducted in situations to which the theory applies. The theory probably does not apply, however, when the location alternatives are complex and interrelated. Whether or not the alternatives we used in our study of CT and RN brain scans can be considered to be of equal detectability and orthogonal with respect to location is a matter for further study.

In our study of CT and RN brain scans, we have expanded the concept of the LROC to include classification as well as localization. The results were quite satisfactory, and we suggest this generalization, which we term the "joint ROC," for use with multiple alternatives. One can plot as the ordinate of the joint ROC the probability of a true-positive detection response *and* a correct classification response—or, for that matter, the probability of a true-positive detection response *and* a correct localization response *and* a correct classification response. In relation to issues raised earlier in Sections 2.1.2 and 2.1.3, the joint ROC thus permits a merging of localization and classification data and shows $P(C)$ as a function of the detection criterion.

Note that we have expanded the empirical concept of the LROC to the joint ROC, and have not necessarily expanded to the joint ROC the theoretical ideas that permit prediction of the LROC from the detection ROC. We are not immediately concerned with the validity of the assumptions of equal detectability and orthogonality of alternatives. Both assumptions may be seriously violated and still leave useful a comparison of two modalities if the assumptions fail in roughly the same way for the two modalities.

A question arises as to how to index the location of an empirical joint ROC. One could connect the data points by straight-line segments (probably with a horizontal line from the rightmost point to the right-hand side of the graph in Figure 8) and use the trapezoidal rule to calculate the area beneath the joint ROC. One could alternatively use the ordinate value of the rightmost point on the joint ROC, at $P(FP) = 1.0$; this probability is equal to $P(C)$ in a forced-choice test for the signal-present alternatives considered. Our preference, however, is to use the joint probability on the ordinate—termed "joint $P(TP)$"—at some value of $P(FP)$ deemed realistic in the diagnostic setting at hand. In our CT/RN study we chose $P(FP) = 0.10$.

Figure 9 shows CT and RN data for six readers combined in each modality. The combination of readers was effected by pooling their rating responses in each category as described in Section 2.3. Three points are present on each curve because the reader went on to a site and type response only after a detection rating in the first three categories. The figure shows four joint ROC curves for each modality and the simple detection curves for comparison. Shown are joint ROC curves for

1. localization,
2. classification when any of the four ranked classification responses was scored as correct,
3. classification when only the first classification choice was scored as correct, and
4. localization combined with first-choice classification.

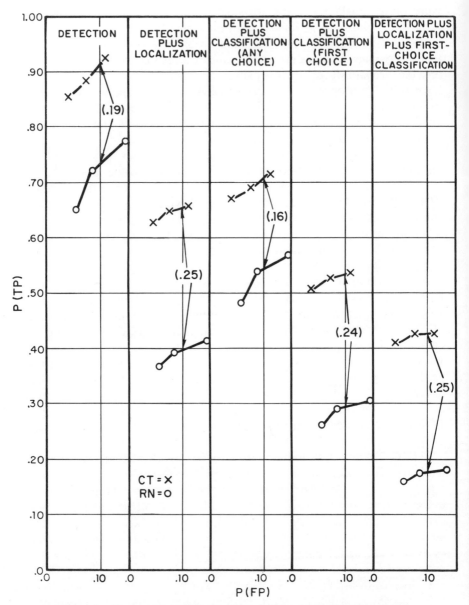

Figure 9. Various joint ROCs for CT and RN and their detection ROCs.

The differences between the curves listed in the figure are differences between the ordinate values at $P(FP) = 0.10$. These differences are fairly constant at about 0.20 across the five panels of the figure. Performance levels drop for both modalities and the ratio of CT performance to RN performance grows (from left to right) as the task becomes more complex.

2.2 OTHER INTERPRETATIONS OF ROC DATA

The quantities represented in the conventional ROC curve may be manipulated in various ways to give various views of performance accuracy. We illustrate here five interpretations of ROC data that go beyond the one-parameter accuracy indices such as A_z and d_a, as applied to a single or typical diagnostician. These additional analyses express results in ways more immediately related to the practical setting; thus, they add richness to an assessment of the quality of performance. Of course, the practical importance of an accuracy index of a given value—or of a reliable difference of a given size between the accuracies of two modalities—is determined ultimately by an analysis of efficacy, as outlined in Chapter 5. Still, we would like to be able to say in advance of a thorough efficacy analysis whether a reliable accuracy difference of a given size is likely to have practical consequences. The interpretations of ROC data discussed next may be helpful in that regard.

2.2.1 Admitting the "Equivocal" Response

As indicated in Section 1.5, we usually construct the conventional ROC curve by means of a graded series of five or so responses, but we have not yet treated the possibility (or necessity) of a graded response in the practical setting. Diagnosticians will frequently withhold a positive or negative response and report that the evidence available so far is equivocal. Making use of the Equivocal response permits diagnosticians to keep both probabilities of error, $P(FP)$ and $P(FN)$, within desired bounds. They may, for example, desire that neither error probability exceed 0.10 and may issue as many Equivocal responses as necessary to achieve that objective (Swets and Swets, 1979).

We can easily derive from an empirical ROC the probability of an Equivocal response that will result from any specified limits on the error probabilities, because of the constraint that the probabilities of responses to positive stimuli must add to 1.0, as must the probabilities of responses to negative stimuli. Thus,

$$P(FN) + P(\text{Equivocal}|\text{positive}) + P(TP) = 1.0,$$

and

$$P(FP) + P(\text{Equivocal}|\text{negative}) + P(TN) = 1.0.$$

We now illustrate these equations with data from our study of CT/RN brain scans. The two ROCs representing the performance of those modalities in our tests are shown in Figure 10. We see from the figure that for CT to maintain $P(FP) \leq 0.01$, its $P(TP)$ would be 0.75. Reading the right-hand and upper scales, we find that maintaining $P(FN) \leq 0.01$ yields $P(TN) = 0.40$. The equations then show that maintaining both error probabilities at 0.01 would give $P(\text{Equivocal}|\text{positive}) = 0.24$ and $P(\text{Equivocal}|\text{negative}) = 0.59$. These values are listed in Table 4, along with the corresponding values for RN. (The columns list stimuli and the rows list responses.) If the prior probabilities of positive and negative cases were equal, permitting a simple averaging of the probabilities of equivocal responses to the two kinds of cases, then CT would issue that response for 42% of the cases whereas RN would issue that response for 72% of the cases.

If we relax our limits on the errors and permit error probabilities of 0.09, we have the outcome given in Table 5. Here we see that CT attains correct probabilities of both kinds, *TP* and *TN,* of about 0.90, while sorting essentially all of the cases into Positive or Negative. RN here attains $P(TP) = 0.72$ and $P(TN) = 0.45$ while failing to sort 19% of the positives and 45% of the negatives. For equal prior probabilities of positive and negative cases RN would remain equivocal on about one-third of the cases presented.

Such analyses of response probabilities clearly lend additional meaning to results expressed in terms of A_z. The observed difference between

Table 4

THE PROPORTION OF "EQUIVOCAL" RESPONSES NECESSARY TO MAINTAIN BOTH ERROR PROBABILITIES AT ≤ 0.01

	CT		RN	
	positive	negative	positive	negative
Positive	0.75	0.01	0.52	0.01
Equivocal	0.24	0.59	0.47	0.97
Negative	0.01	0.40	0.01	0.02

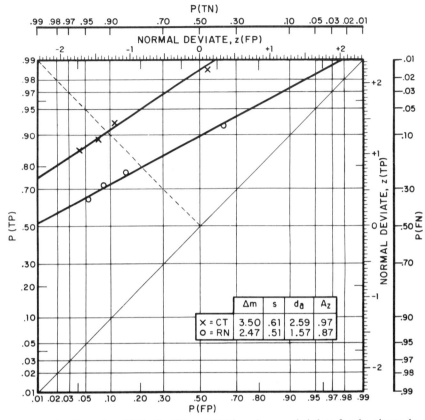

Figure 10. Detection ROCs for CT and RN based on pooled data for the six readers of each modality with various curve parameters.

Table 5

THE PROPORTION OF "EQUIVOCAL" RESPONSES NECESSARY TO MAINTAIN BOTH ERROR PROBABILITIES AT ≤ 0.09

	CT		RN	
	positive	negative	positive	negative
Positive	0.91	0.09	0.72	0.09
Equivocal	0.00	0.01	0.19	0.46
Negative	0.09	0.90	0.09	0.45

CT and RN of 0.10 in A_z translates into a difference between a definitive diagnosis for all cases and a definitive diagnosis for just $\frac{2}{3}$ of the cases. That difference would seem large enough to be of practical importance, in advance of gaining a studied and full impression of the various probabilities and utilities involved in the diagnosis and treatment of brain lesions.

2.2.2 Ratios of False-Positive Probabilities

Another way to interpret ROC data in the interest of a preliminary impression of the practicality of a given accuracy difference is to examine the false-positive probabilities for two systems throughout the range of true-positive probabilities.

For an illustration, let us consider hypothetical ROCs having slopes of unity on a binormal graph, and ask whether a reliable difference in A_z of 0.10 is of practical import in a particular diagnostic setting. In Table 6 the cell entries are $P(FP)$ at values of A_z separated by 0.10, at various values of $P(TP)$. The line connecting two cell entries indicate instances where a difference in A_z of 0.10 corresponds to a factor of approximately 2 or more in $P(FP)$. We see that a difference in $A_z = 0.10$ yields differences of a factor of about 2 or more in $P(FP)$ for values of $P(FP)$ less than about 0.30.

If $P(FP) = 0.30$ is about the upper limit on values of $P(FP)$ that could be tolerated, the difference of a factor of 2 or more holds throughout the range of interest. In many diagnostic settings, a difference of that

Table 6

$P(FP)$ AT GIVEN VALUES OF $P(TP)$, FOR VALUES OF A_z DIFFERING BY 0.10[a]

		A_z				
		55	65	75	85	95
	90	87	82	64	44 ————————	15
	80	75	62	46	28 ————————	7
	70	64	49	34 ————————	18 ————————	4
	60	53	38	25 ————————	12 ————————	2
$P(TP)$	50	43	29	17 ————————	8 ————————	1
	40	34	22 ————————	12 ————————	4	
	30	25 ————————	14 ————————	7 ————————	3	
	20	16 ————————	8 ————————	4 ————————	1	
	10	8 ————————	3 ————————	1		

[a] Decimal points are omitted.

magnitude might easily be seen to be important, even in the absence of precise statistical data on incidences or of tight consensus on the cost of an *FP* decision. One may need only a vague notion of the cost of an *FP* decision, and the numbers of negative cases to be exposed to the diagnostic systems under test, to be rather certain that a difference in $A_z = 0.10$ connotes an important difference in efficacy.

2.2.3 Inverse (A Posteriori) Probabilities

Still another way to lend additional meaning to ROC data is to calculate the inverse probability of a true-positive response, namely, the probability that a case is positive given that the diagnostic system says it is. We have pointed out in Section 1.3 that such inverse probabilities will not provide an index of accuracy that is independent of the decision criterion, or of prior probabilities, but they may be useful in interpretation after we have obtained an ROC curve and are ready to consider various decision criteria. Bayes's rule can be applied to the forward probabilities of the ROC (of response conditional upon the stimulus) to calculate the inverse probabilities (of stimulus conditional upon the response). The formula for a true-positive case, expressed in the notation of Section 1.2, is

$$P(a|A) = [P(A|a)P(a)]/P(A),$$

where $P(a|A)$ is the probability of a case being abnormal if the diagnostic system says it is, $P(A|a)$ the probability of the system calling a case abnormal when it truly is, $P(a)$ the prior probability of a case presented to the system being abnormal, and $P(A) = P(A|a)P(a) + P(A|n)P(n)$ the probability of the system's calling a case "Abnormal."

The data of Figure 11, showing the performance of one of the modalities in detecting a localized abnormality in our mammography test (Chapter 11), can be used for illustration. Consider the decision criterion defined by *PFP*) or $P(A|n) = 0.10$. We see from the figure that the corresponding $p(A|a)$ equals 0.65. For a high prior probability of localized abnormality, namely $P(a) = 0.80$, $P(A)$ equals 0.54, and the inverse true-positive probability $P(a|A)$ equals 0.96. For a moderate prior probability of localized abnormality, namely $P(a) = 0.50$, $P(A)$ equals 0.375 and $P(a|A)$ equals 0.87. For a relatively low prior probability of localized abnormality, namely $P(a) = 0.10$, $P(A)$ equals 0.155, and the inverse true-positive probability $P(a|A)$ equals 0.42. Thus, in high-probability cases, or in a referral situation, where the prior probability might be 0.50 to 0.80, from 87% to 96% of the cases called positive on the basis of the modality in

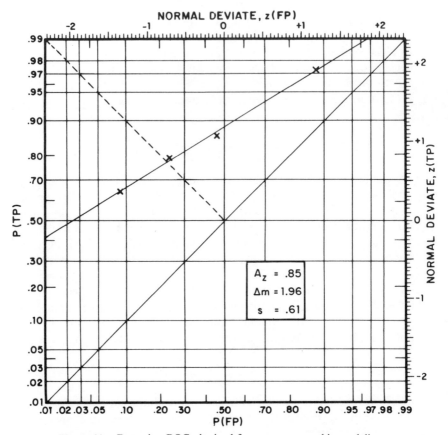

Figure 11. Detection ROC obtained for a mammographic modality.

question would in fact be positive according to biopsy. In a screening situation or for a class of patients not at high risk where the prior probability of localized abnormality might be 0.10, for example, about 40% of the cases called positive on the basis of the image would be called positive at biopsy.

We should not consider these numbers as reflecting absolutely the accuracy of the modality without a careful review of the conditions of our test and the qualifications of interpretation that stem from them. However, we can determine the effect of a change in A_z of some amount, and let us choose 0.10 again. For the moderate prior probability of 0.50, where $A_z = 0.85$ led to $P(a|A) = 0.87$, a value of $A_z = 0.75$ leads to $P(a|A) = 0.83$. Four fewer cases out of 100 called positive on the basis of the image would be confirmed by biopsy for the less accurate system. For the low prior probability of 0.10, where $A_z = 0.85$ led to $P(a|A) = 0.42$, a value of $A_z = 0.95$ leads to $P(a|A) = 0.49$. Hence, 7 more cases out of 100 called positive would be confirmed by biopsy for the more accurate system. It strikes the authors again that a reliable difference of 0.10 in A_z has practical consequences that are substantial enough to be taken into account in a choice between systems.

2.2.4 Use of Multiple Systems

Preceding pages have focused on the evaluation of single diagnostic systems and on a choice between competing systems. One may also wish to determine the accuracy afforded by two (or more) systems used together, either in parallel or in sequence. Rating-scale data collected separately for different systems can be merged to show how the combination would perform under conditions in which each yields its own diagnosis without knowing of the others' diagnoses.

How two or more systems in combination will perform in practice depends on just how they are to be combined in practice. As discussed in detail elsewhere (Green and Swets, 1966/1974, Chapter 9), there are two basic methods of combination of separate, noninteracting judgments. One method is appropriate (in fact, optimal) when each of the systems yields finely graded outputs, that is, confidence ratings, or, better, a posteriori probabilities of the existence of one of the stimulus alternatives considered. An appropriate integration of these outputs yields a new decision variable, and a decision criterion may be adopted to cut that new decision variable into ranges of positive and negative decisions.

The second basic method of combining separate judgments is based on binary outputs (positive versus negative decisions) from each. The two or more individual decisions are combined according to some rule into one overall decision. One simple rule is to make an overall positive decision when any one of the systems gives a positive decision (*disjunctive rule*). At the other extreme is the *conjunctive rule:* The overall decision is positive only when all individual systems give a positive decision. The first rule represents a lenient criterion, and the second represents a stringent criterion in the ROC space. Intermediate rules (e.g., a majority vote) are possible.

If graded outputs are available and used, two assumptions enable prediction of the upper bound on the combined performance. One is that the systems are statistically independent, and the second is that the

ROCs are linear and of unit slope. Specifically, the combined value of the accuracy index d_a will equal the square root of the sum of the squares of the individual values of d_a. In the case of equal individual values of d_a, this equation implies that the combined d_a will grow as the square root of the number of systems (Green and Swets, 1966/1974). Thus, for example, two systems each yielding $d_a = 1.0$ will together yield $d_a = 1.4$.

Combining systems by combining separate binary decisions from each yields a gain in accuracy in an amount that depends on the specific rule used to combine the decisions. The conjunctive rule, for example, gives an ROC of lesser slope than the disjunctive rule. (Since the two ROCs cross at the minor diagonal, one would prefer the conjunctive rule at low false-positive rates and the disjunctive rule at high false-positive rates.) On the average, the combination of binary decisions yields a potential gain about half that possible when graded outputs are used (Green and Swets, 1966/1974).

We stress that the upper bound on the improvement afforded by the use of two separate systems over one system is 40% in d_a, and that this amount of improvement is gained only when (a) rather finely graded diagnoses are issued by both systems, and (b) the systems are statistically independent—two conditions not generally met. Furthermore, the maximum improvement when binary decisions are combined is only about half the upper bound or about 20% in d_a.

This realization is important because it has been common practice to combine binary decisions in a theoretical way that is unjustified and yields much larger estimates of the gain afforded by two systems over one. Specifically, the common model has been to multiply values of the false-negative probability, under the assumption of statistical independence, and subtract their product from unity to yield a predicted true-positive probability. Thus for systems having $P(TP) = 0.50$, two systems are presumed to have $P(PT) = 0.75$, three systems are presumed to have $P(TP) = 0.875$, and so on. The promise—unjustified because of the assumption of statistical independence and because it ignores what is happening to the false-positive probability—is a gain in $P(TP)$ from 0.50 to near 0.90 simply by parallel use of three systems. It may well be that parallel use of two or three particular systems is justified in certain diagnostic settings, but that justification should be properly and quantitatively determined in each setting.

In our study of CT and RN brain scans, combination of the two modalities via separate binary decisions yielded no improvement over the performance of CT alone when the disjunctive rule of combination was used, and yielded a decrement from the performance of CT when the conjunctive rule was used. However, our analysis of data collected by others (Turner *et al.,* 1976) indicated a near optimal gain when an Anger multiplane tomographic scanner and a conventional scintillation camera were combined. In the latter study, a given reader read the two sets of images separately and then together, whereas in our study the two sets of images were read separately by different readers, and their judgments were combined after the fact. This difference between the two studies highlights the fact that the theory and analysis presented here pertain to separate, noninteracting readings. How much gain is obtained by using the same or interacting readers with multiple modalities is, we believe, largely an empirical matter.

We simply mention that an alternative to combining two systems in parallel fashion is, of course, to use a contingent, sequential combination. One could decide to use system A, and, if A is positive, to use system B. Or to use system A, and, if negative, to use system B. The sequential use of two systems has been treated by Metz *et al.* (1975).

2.2.5 Use of Multiple Observers

The considerations that apply to the use of multiple, separate, noninteracting readers with one modality are precisely those that apply to the use of multiple modalities as discussed in Section 2.2.4. Again, rating-scale data for individual readers can be merged in analysis to show how they would perform as a noninteracting team. Again, as a first consideration, combining the judgments of separate readers will enhance the single performances to the extent that the readings are statistically independent, and we have reasons to believe that readers' judgments may often be highly correlated (see Chapter 11).

Analysis of our CT/RN data was conducted by constructing three-reader teams in each modality. Three decision rules for a team's binary response were considered; a team response was positive (*a*) if any one reader was positive, (*b*) if any two readers were positive, and (*c*) only if all three readers were positive. With positivity of response determined in relation to each of the category boundaries of the rating scale, three 4-point ROCs were obtained for each modality. The different decision rules moved the ROC points up or down the curve, of course, since they represent three degrees of stringency of the decision criterion. However, the team ROCs did not exhibit greater accuracy (higher A_z) than the individuals' ROCs. How much gain would have been obtained had the three readers convened to discuss each case is an open question.

2.3 COMBINING INDIVIDUAL RESULTS INTO A GROUP OR AVERAGE ROC

It is desirable to combine the test results of individual test observers in order to give an overall summary measure of a system's performance—one based on all the observers and describing an average observer typical of the class of observers selected for the test. This motivation for combination differs from that discussed in Section 2.2.5, where the emphasis was on predicting how combined observers would perform in practice. Here we are concerned with characterizing the observed test performance and in doing so with the most stable estimate of that performance available. There are two ways to combine individual data to serve these concerns, both of which are used throughout this book, and we take this opportunity to make them explicit and to discuss their relative merits. One method is to "pool" raw data (response frequencies) to obtain an ROC curve for a group of observers; the second method is to "average" (take the mean of) some transformed values of the individuals' raw response frequencies (such as the values of their corresponding normal deviates) or some index values derived from individual ROCs (such as the accuracy parameters A_z, d_a, Δm, and s, and the variances of any of those parameters).

2.3.1 Pooling

In pooling raw data, we merge all the rating-scale judgments made for all cases and all observers. With five observers, for example, we treat each case as if it were five cases read by one observer, and we proceed as if we had just one observer. Thus, a single matrix as in Table 3 (a matrix showing two states by five rating categories) contains all the cases and observers. A single (group) ROC is then calculated from that matrix. Our CT/RN data are represented in that manner in Figures 9 and 10, and data representative of our mammography study in Figure 11. Combination by pooling may be the method of choice when data are relatively scarce and when the desire is to gain a greater stability for the estimates of performance indices. We indicate in Chapters 3 and 4 how sampling variance is reduced by replication of observations over observers.

The assumption made when pooling observers is that they come from the same population, and therein lies a problem. Although the assumption that they come from the same population may be reasonable with respect to their discrimination capacity (accuracy), the assumption that they have near identical decision criteria is less palatable. Moreover, it happens that pooling observers with different criteria will depress the combined index of accuracy.

To see how combining different decision criteria will yield a lower estimate of accuracy than is associated with any one criterion, refer to Figure 1. Visualize an ROC point at approximately (0.05, 0.35) and another at about (0.40, 0.90), both on the ROC curve of the figure. Now it can be shown that the average of those two points will lie somewhere along a straight line connecting them—not on the concave curve connecting them. Just where on that line it will lie depends on the number of observations associated with each point; if they are based on an equal number of observations, the average point will lie midway between them. Thus, the average point would have coordinates (0.20, 0.60), rather than the coordinates of the point indicated on the curved line (0.15, 0.65). The difference in the index d_a between the original points and their average is roughly the difference between 1.4 and 1.1, which represents a depression of about 20%.

Of course, test observers may not differ by as much in their decision criteria as in this illustration. And the risk of a depression of the accuracy index may not be great, particularly if two systems are being compared only with each other.

2.3.2 Averaging

The second method of determining a performance representative of several observers is to calculate the average, rather than pooled, performance. One approach under this heading is to average the coordinate values of ROC points so that the typical performance is represented by data points as well as by a curve fitted to them, as in the case of pooling. An alternative approach is to average index values derived from individual curves: The indices Δm and s yield a curve without data points; the indices A_z and d_a yield a number without a curve.

If a way of averaging ROC points is desired such that the resulting group curve has the correct average d' (or Δm or d_a when the slope $s = 1$), the proper calculation is to average normal-deviate, or z, values that correspond to the observed points (McNicol, 1972, pp. 111–113). Averaging the coordinates of the points expressed as probabilities, which is tantamount to pooling the raw response frequencies, will not achieve that objective. We note, however, that the objective is not met by averaging z values to the extent that the ROC slope s departs from unity. And for practical purposes, the difference between averaging z values and pooling raw frequencies is small when the individual performances to be combined are similar—when, say, individual values of d' or d_a have a range less than 1.0. In determining a representative performance for localization and classification, of course, we have no z values to work with, and a pooling of raw response frequencies (or averaging of probability values) is the only way to obtain data points on a joint ROC representing a group of observers.

Under the alternative averaging approach, which does not preserve the data points and may not preserve the curve either, one simply takes the mean of any of the various ROC indices of accuracy and the mean of the corresponding standard error. In this case, one need not assume that the observers come from the same population, and the risk noted earlier of depressing the average index, by failing to combine individual estimates in a bias-free way, does not exist. Pooling raw frequencies and averaging ROC indices yielded similar results in our CT/RN study. And, of course, although ROC points are lost when averaging accuracy indices, one can proceed to average some index of each point, for example, Z_k or β as described in Section 1.7.

Our recommendation is to design the test so that observers of similar capability are to be combined; to take averages of the normal-deviate coordinate values of data points, rather than their probability coordinate values, when working with the detection ROC; and to establish the consistency of two or more ways of combining individual performances or attempt to account for any inconsistencies.

2.4 SUMMARY

A general ROC solution, for more than two alternatives, does not exist at present, but it may not be terribly missed. One can treat multiple alternatives for localization and classification, along with detection, by means of the "joint ROC." This curve plots $P(FP)$ along the abscissa and therefore takes into account the decision criterion for detection, but it ignores decision tendencies relative to the site and type alternatives. The ordinate of the curve is the joint probability of a correct positive decision, defined with respect to site or type or both, and the value of that probability at some selected $P(FP)$ can serve as an index of accuracy.

We need single indices such as A_z and β to treat test performance in a rigorous way, as is further illustrated in the succeeding two chapters. However, with a full ROC curve or curves available, we can derive several other numbers that are more directly meaningful for the practical setting of interest. These numbers can give a preliminary assessment of the efficacy of a system.

A common desire is to represent in a summary fashion the performance of a group of diagnosticians or of one diagnostician typical of the group. Pooling the raw response data of individuals yields ROC points as well as a single curve, but they will be sensitive to any large differences among individuals, especially in decision criteria. Averaging accuracy indices derived from the curve, such as A_z, gives more reliable group estimates of accuracy but not a typical curve.

CHAPTER 3

Statistical Design of a Performance Test

We wish to remind our audience that this chapter, dealing with the size and logical design of a performance test, and the next chapter, dealing with the reliability of generalizations from test results, are largely statistical in nature. Furthermore, none of the chapters in Part II, which considers experimental methods used in such tests, depends on Chapters 3 and 4. We believe that it will be in the interests of some to proceed to the substantive material in Part II and save the more abstract ideas of Chapter 3 and 4 until later.

As another prefatory note, we point out that although the discussion in this chapter and the next is general to tests of any diagnostic system, we adopt here the terminology appropriate to medical images interpreted by human diagnosticians. Thus we refer to imaging modalities, image readers, and reading tests rather than somewhat more generally to diagnostic systems, observers, and performance tests. This specific terminology is a convenience in coordinating these chapters with Chapter 11. Chapter 11 describes a medical imaging study that we undertook largely to examine empirically the theoretical statistical issues that we treat here.

The structure of the reading test will depend on four basic factors:

1. the particular questions to be answered by the test,
2. various logistic and cost constraints,
3. the nature of the statistical procedures to be applied, and
4. the degree of statistical power required.

We discuss each of these factors here only in general terms, sufficient to suggest the issues in designing the test. More detailed discussions occur in other chapters.

3.1 QUESTIONS TO BE ANSWERED BY THE READING TEST

We generally assume in this book that the primary question to be answered by the reading test is whether one modality mediates more accurate reading than another. But that question will usually have to be refined—for example, by specifying the conditions under which the comparison is to be made. In laying out the study plan, the fundamental condition (i.e., the diagnostic context) will have been decided upon already, but the need for more refined specification will often be ignored until the reading-test design is begun. Should the comparison be made with or without the readers having access to case background information for each test case? Should the reading be done by the most highly qualified readers or by "typical" readers? Decisions such as whether to add a reading condition or to conduct the test with more than one type of reader, will expand the size of the test and thus affect its cost. A complex design involving blocking of the reading trials and counterbalancing of test conditions may be needed to ensure that comparisons across conditions are not biased by reader fatigue or learning.

Where study resources permit, the reading test might be designed to answer one or more of a variety of secondary questions. For example, one might like to know not just whether one modality is better than another, but how much better it is and why. One specific question in this connection is how much of recorded error for a modality is due to unreliability of the reader rather than due to noise in the imaging process. Measuring the reliability of a particular component of a diagnostic system requires repeated application of that component to the same cases. Thus, to measure the reader's reliability, readers must read the same cases at least twice. Measuring the reliability of the imaging process would require, were it medically appropriate, imaging the patient at least twice and running each of those images through the reading test. Another possible question is whether or not combining information across modalities increases diagnostic accuracy. Answering that question would require imaging the same case in each modality, a rather fundamental requirement affecting how the cases are originally collected and also how the results are statistically analyzed.

3.2 LOGISTIC AND COST CONSTRAINTS

The number of test cases available that fit the various test requirements, for example, for truth and case background data, is often the major logistic constraint on test design. Another important constraint is how much of the reader's time one can demand. The number of hours it is reasonable to spend per session and the number of sessions it is reasonable to schedule without seriously disrupting the reader's other activities are often severely restrictive. Also, if each case is to be read twice by the same reader, the session involving the second reading might have to be separated by, perhaps, several weeks from the session involving the first reading, to reduce the probability that the reader will recognize the case on the second occasion. Recognition of a case previously read might compromise the reader's ability to find new information on the second reading.

The cost of the reading test will also be a major constraint. The researcher will have to weigh the costs versus the benefits of adding a reading-test condition or of increasing the amount of reading to generate more precise results. In many situations, of course, the cost of the reading test will be relatively small in comparison to the cost of the overall study, and to reject moderate expansions that might make the reading test much more informative would be inappropriate. But certainly there will be situations for which the desired design has to be trimmed to save money or fit logistic constraints. One possible approach is to simplify study questions and pare away entire test conditions. This alternative depends wholly on scientific judgment. The arithmetic of such savings is straightforward. Another approach, simply trimming the amount of reading in each condition, is discussed at greater length in Section 3.3. Also described there are approaches to case and reader matching. These approaches, when medically and logistically feasible, can achieve substantial savings in the cost of the reading test.

3.3   GENERAL APPROACH TO STATISTICAL ANALYSIS OF ACCURACY DATA

The general approach we prescribe for testing the statistical significance of a difference in accuracy is the familiar one of computing the critical ratio (C.R.), the ratio of the difference in accuracy between two modalities to the standard error of that difference. Although the approach can be extended to cover tests comparing more than two modalities (Section 4.6), we shall limit this general discussion to the two-modality situation.

We present here a general formula for computing the C.R. that accounts for two commonly varied aspects of reading-test design. The first of these is replicated reading: having each case read by more than one reader or more than once by the same reader. The second aspect covered in the general formula is matching cases and readers across the modalities being compared. Replicated reading and matching are commonly employed in reading studies for the purpose of increasing the "power" of the reading test in the face of shortages of cases. Power is the probability of correctly rejecting the null hypothesis, that is, the probability of finding a real difference between the modalities. Power is always expressed in relation to some acceptably low probability of incorrectly rejecting the null hypothesis.

The main control over power is n, the number of cases being read, but when adequately sampled or documented cases are in short supply, as they often are, and when additional power is needed beyond what those limited cases can provide, replication and matching can provide considerable additional power. Replication is, of course, employed for reasons other than boosting power: for example, to increase the generality of findings that would be suspect if based on just one reader, or to provide information of interest in its own right on the variability of reading between and within readers.

3.3.1   General Formula for Computing the Critical Ratio

We present the general formula first in contracted form and then develop an expanded formula for the denominator. In contracted form, C.R. is given by

$$\text{C.R.} = (\text{Mean } \Theta_1 - \text{Mean } \Theta_2)/\text{S.E.}_{\text{(diff)}} \qquad (\text{Eq.1})$$

The numerator is assumed to be obtained in the following way. A sample of n cases is assembled for each modality and read independently by each of ℓ readers on each of m independent occasions. For each reader on each occasion, we obtain some index, call it Θ, of each reader's accuracy on the sample. For each reader we take the mean of Θ over the m reading occasions, and for each modality we take the mean of those individual reader means over all readers. The difference between those grand means for each modality constitutes the numerator in Eq. 1.

Turning now to the denominator of Eq. 1, S.E.$_{(\text{diff})}$, we note first that, without certain simplifying assumptions, this expression is rather complex. The problem is that a large part of this expression is the merger of the standard error (S.E.) of Θ_1 and the S.E. of Θ_2, and each of those terms, although we have not shown them, consists of three components of variance: variance due to case sampling, reader sampling, and reader inconsistency in reading the same case on different occasions. The main simplifying assumption we make is that the S.E. of Θ_1 equals the S.E. of Θ_2. This requires two subassumptions: that ℓ, m, and n each be the same in the two modalities, and that the three variance components each be the same in the two modalities. Given those assumptions, S.E.$_{(\text{diff})}$ is given by:

$$\text{S.E.}_{(\text{diff})} = \left[2^{1/2} S_c^2 (1 - r_c) + \frac{S_{\text{br}}^2}{\ell}(1 - r_{br}) + \frac{S_{wr}^2}{\ell m} \right]^{1/2}, \qquad \text{(Eq. 2)}$$

where

S_c^2	=	variability in Θ due to case sampling; proportional to $1/n$,
r_c	=	the fraction of S_c^2 common to the two modalities; the correlation between cases across modalities,
S_{br}^2	=	variability in Θ due to reader sampling,
r_{br}	=	the fraction of S_{br}^2 common to the two modalities; the correlation between readers across modalities,
S_{wr}^2	=	variability in Θ due to reader inconsistency.

The details of how to compute S.E.$_{(\text{diff})}$ are reserved for Chapter 4, where we present a computational formula, and for Chapter 11, where we illustrate its application to data from the mammography study. Here we are concerned mainly with the meaning of each term and how its impact can vary, depending on characteristics of the reading-test design. Our ultimate concern in this section is how the researcher can use that understanding, albeit in conjunction with estimates of these terms, to predict the cost and effectiveness of alternative reading-test designs.

3.3.2   Case and Reader Matching

As a general rule, the researcher will want to take advantage of case and reader matching to enhance the power of the statistical test. In principle, matching can be accomplished in two ways, either by using the same cases and/or the same readers in the two modalities or by using cases and/or readers which, although different, are matched on some variable relevant to the accuracy of diagnosis. Using the *same* cases and/or the *same* readers is the most direct procedure, of course, and in our view is the preferred alternative whenever it is possible. Using the same cases is not possible, for example, when multiple imaging is not medically justified, and using the same readers is not appropriate when in practice the readers of the two modalities have different characteristics, such as different kinds of training or experience. In our opinion, the amount of statistical power that is gained by attempting to match *different* cases and/or *different* readers does not usually justify the costs. For one thing, matching different cases (e.g., on size of lesion) and matching different readers (e.g., on level of training or years of experience) bring with them an attrition of available cases and readers, both of which tend to be in short supply. Thus, in the remainder of this discussion we consider explicitly only the relatively high degree of matching that can be achieved with the same cases or the same readers versus no matching at all.

Although use of the same cases can achieve a high degree of matching, observe that a near-perfect degree of matching will be achieved only when the two modalities are highly similar in terms of the correlation of image characteristics with the underlying pathophysiology. One would expect that correlation to be very close, for example, if the modalities being compared were essentially the same except for some small shift in an imaging or processing parameter. Thus, provided the same cases were used in both modalities, one would expect to achieve near-perfect matching if one were comparing, let us say, the effect of two slightly different algorithms for processing CT images. The same would be true for a comparison of X-ray imaging for two slightly different dose levels, provided all other aspects of the imaging process were carefully controlled. As a counterexample, we observe that CT and RN images would probably be a considerably less than perfect match, because they do not display the same pathophysiology.

Near-perfect matching of readers will usually occur only when the same readers are used and the modalities are highly similar so that the reader expertise in the one modality is essentially the same in the other.

Note that there is no restriction that cases be the same or in any way matched to achieve near-perfect reader matching.

We note that when cases are unmatched, the term r_c in Eq. 2 goes to 0, and the correction for communality of variance due to case sampling goes to 1. Thus, the full impact of variability due to case sampling is felt in the computation. Similarly, when readers are unmatched, r_{br} goes to 0, the correction for communality of variance due to reader sampling goes to 1, and the full impact of variability due to reader sampling is felt. On the other hand, when the correlations are as high as 0.90, say, the variances are reduced by 90%.

3.3.3   Effect of Matching and Replication on Statistical Power

The aim in this section is to convey some feeling for the effects of matching and replication on the size of the S.E.$_{(diff)}$ and, consequently, on the size of the C.R. and the power of the test.

For convenience, let us assume that

$$S_c^2 = S_{br}^2 = S_{wr}^2 = \tfrac{1}{6}.$$

Thus, in the worst situation, with no matching and no replication, S.E.$_{(diff)}$ = 1.0. Let us also assume that near-perfect matching of cases is achieved, and that $r_c = 0.90$. Similarly, let us assume near-perfect reader matching and $r_{br} = 0.90$. We can examine the combined impact of matching and replication on size of the S.E.$_{(diff)}$ in Figure 12. There we see S.E.$_{(diff)}$ as a function of ℓ for $m = 1$ and $m = 2$ for two conditions: both cases and readers unmatched, and both cases and readers near perfectly matched. It is clear in this illustration that replication and matching can have significant effects on the S.E.$_{(diff)}$ and, attendantly, on the power of the statistical test. Replication alone without matching accounts for nearly a 40% decrease in S.E.$_{(diff)}$, or equivalently, a 1.7-fold increase in the size of the C.R. Replication with near-perfect matching leads to almost a 5-fold increase in the C.R.

To look at these illustrative effects of replication and matching in terms of the power of the statistical test, we first have to set the probability of incorrectly rejecting the null hypothesis, which we shall set at 0.05. Then let us consider the impact on the C.R. for a situation in which, with no matching or replication, the actual differences between the modalities is of a size that would cause the null hypothesis to be correctly rejected only 10% of the time. The 1.7-fold increase in C.R. due to replication alone would increase the power to 24%. The 5-fold increase,

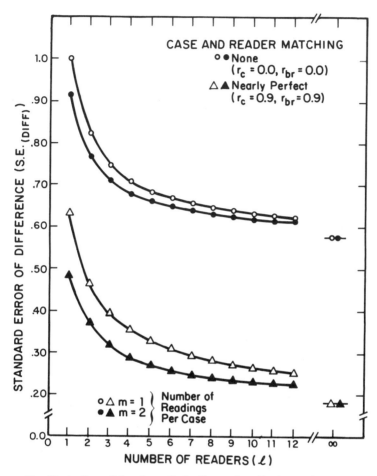

Figure 12. Illustration of the theoretical effects of replication and matching on the standard error of the difference. Types and degrees of replication and matching are indicated in the figure. For convenience here, the assumption is made that $S_c^2 = S_{br}^2 = S_{wr}^2 = \frac{1}{6}$.

due to the added impact of near-perfect matching, would raise the rate of correct rejections to 96%. Looked at another way, if we were to hold power fixed, the 1.7-fold increase in the C.R. due to replication would mean that we could detect a difference 1/1.7 the size we could detect without the benefit of replication. In general, for a q-fold decrease in S.E.$_{(diff)}$ (or increase in the C.R.), we could detect at a fixed level of power a difference $1/q$ as large.

Clearly, the specific properties of functions such as these, their relative height and shape, will vary depending on the particular values of the variance and correlation terms. Because we set those values arbitrarily for the convenience of this illustration, it would be inappropriate to dwell on effects specific to these functions. We can, however, make certain general observations. The impact of replication will clearly depend on the relative values of the variance terms. If S_c^2 is large relative to S_{br}^2 and S_{wr}^2, replication will have little effect. The impact of matching will similarly depend on the relative size of the variance terms. When variation due to case sampling is relatively large, matching of cases will have a potentially large effect, and the same is true for reader matching. How much of that potential can be realized depends on how successfully the cases or readers can be matched.

One other general observation to make is that increasing the number of readers or readings will always have diminishing returns. How quickly one reaches the point where the returns are negligible will, of course, depend on the situation. We can see that in this illustration very little is to be gained in going beyond about seven readers. Similarly, the effect of increasing the number of readings per reader will depend on the relative size of S_{wr}^2, but as a practical matter, m will usually be limited to 2 or 3 at most, so, in any event, one cannot hope to gain a great deal from increasing m. Moreover, it can be shown that unless $r_{br} = 1$ (which cannot occur unless the modalities being compared are identical), $S.E._{(diff)}$ is always reduced more by a fractional increase in the number of readers than by the same fractional increase in the number of readings per reader. This suggests the principle that for a fixed total number of readings ($R = \ell \times m$) of each case, $S.E._{(diff)}$ is smallest if one uses $\ell = R$ readers and $m = 1$ reading per reader. However, as we discuss in Chapter 4, there is a practical need to estimate within-reader variance (S_{wr}^2), and this need requires, at least, that some readers read some cases twice.

3.4   THE DEGREE OF STATISTICAL POWER
REQUIRED

The size of the case sample and the amount of replication required will depend on two main factors: (a) the size of a difference between modalities that the researcher decides would be of practical interest, and (b) the degree of confidence that the researcher considers necessary in concluding that the critical difference has or has not been exceeded. The number of cases, readers, and readings required to achieve this statistical power will in turn depend upon the inherent variability of the data, which

the researcher will have to estimate from prior studies of similar modalities, from a pilot study, or in the first part of a study with an optional
termination. How to use such prior data to determine the desired number
of cases and readers is illustrated in Chapter 11 (Section 11.9) with data
from the mammography study. We can observe—although without suggesting a rule of thumb, because available experience is limited—that
(a) quite adequate power was achieved in our CT/RN study with 136
cases (the same cases in the two modalities), six readers in each modality
(differing across modalities), and a single reading of each case; and (b)
quite inadequate power was achieved in our mammography study with
62 cases (the same cases in the three modalities), three readers in each
modality (the same readers in one experimental condition and different
readers in another), and a single reading of each case.

   The size of a difference of interest will depend wholly on the context
and aims of the overall study in which the reading test is undertaken.
The required level of confidence in the test results will also depend on
the situation: on the benefits of drawing one or the other correct conclusion and on the losses from drawing one or the other incorrect conclusion. The researcher will presumably have considered both of these
requirements carefully in early stages of planning the overall study and
at this point will have to settle on specific values of difference and
confidence in difference on which to set the power of the reading test.

3.5   SOME PRACTICAL RULES FOR STUDY DESIGN

   Although the process of designing the reading test (and, specifically,
deciding which factors should be considered first or weighed more heavily
than others) will depend on the situation, we suggest the following as
a general guide. The first main consideration is the size of the case
sample; the rule is that, independent of power considerations, the case
sample should be large enough to ensure credible generalization of the
study results to the case population and large enough for valid application
of whatever statistical tests one plans to apply. As regards the size of
the case sample to ensure credible generality of the reading-test results,
that is a matter of scientific judgment which we leave to the investigator.
As regards the size of the case sample needed to ensure valid application
of particular statistical procedures, we offer two comments. First, we
remind the investigator that the procedures recommended in this book
are based on large-sample statistics. As a rule of thumb, then, we rec-

ommend that a minimum of 50 to 60 cases be read in each modality; otherwise, small-sample statistics should be used. Second, we point the reader to a discussion in Section 4.3 on the minimum size of a case sample for a credible estimate of case correlation when case matching is to be exploited.

The second main consideration, again to ensure credible generalization of the study results, is that the reading test be conducted, as a rule, on at least several readers. Also, when reader matching is to be exploited, a minimum number of readers is needed to obtain a credible estimate of reader correlation (see Section 4.3.2). Again, these considerations are independent of power requirements.

The third consideration is that for a complete analysis of the sources of error in reading performance, at least some of the readers should read at least some cases independently at least twice. As we explain in Chapter 4, if this minimum amount of rereading of cases is not done, then there is no basis for estimating within-reader variance, with the result that the statistical interpretation is weakened and considerable statistical power may be lost.

Finally, when consideration shifts from ensuring validity and completeness of the statistical tests and credible generalization of the results to controlling the power and cost of the test, the trade-offs of several alternative mechanisms must be considered. Probably the most important mechanisms to consider first are case and reader matching, because they can deliver considerable increases in power, often at relatively low cost. If case matching and reader matching are not feasible, or if yet more power is needed, increasing the number of cases should be considered. If cases are in short supply, increasing the number of readers will be the next most important consideration. If for some reason the number of readers is limited, some gains in power might be achieved by increasing the number of readings, but as a rule that would be the direction of last resort.

An algorithm could presumably be developed for finding the combination of numbers of cases, readers, and readings that would maximize power at a fixed cost, or minimize cost at a fixed degree of power. But rarely will the design options be so unconstrained and the parameters of reading variability and cost be so precisely quantified as to make such an algorithm of more than academic interest. For all practical purposes, we think, the researcher will do better simply to keep in mind these various options for controlling power and to use them as a general guide in designing the reading test. A graphic aid can be helpful, as illustrated in Chapter 11, Figure 24.

3.6 SUMMARY

The structure of a performance test depends on which questions it is to answer, and how precisely it is to answer them, in relation to the various resources available. The investigator will have some control over the numbers of test cases, test readers, and readings per reader. The first two should be large enough to permit credible generalization to their respective populations of interest, large enough to justify application of the statistical tests to be used, and large enough to supply the desired reliability. The number of readings per reader will necessarily be small, but obtaining more than one may be desirable to provide an estimate of within-readers variance. When two or more systems are compared, advantages accrue to using the same cases and the same readers with each system, although such duplication is frequently impossible. In comparing systems, manipulation of the various parameters just mentioned is undertaken to provide a desired level of confidence in a difference of a specified size.

CHAPTER 4

Statistical Treatment of Accuracy Results

In this chapter the statistical analysis of accuracy results is described and illustrated. We discuss (*a*) how to obtain the standard error of the accuracy index for a given modality, (*b*) how to determine the confidence interval for the index, and (*c*) how to test for a statistically significant difference between two modalities. Then two brief sections follow, one summarizing the assumptions underlying these analyses and the other showing how to extend statistical tests to differences among more than two modalities.

For simplicity, we work out specific examples only in terms of the accuracy index A_z. But the general approach we present here is also applicable to statistical analyses of other indices of the entire ROC curve, including d_a, Δm, and the slope s. It is also applicable to analyses of indices of performance at selected points on the ROC curve that would be required, for example, if the slopes were found to be materially different. Thus, in Section 4.4 we show how the approach applies in statistical analyses of the point index $P(TP)$ at a fixed value of $P(FP)$.

An assumption basic to all applications of this general statistical approach is that the indices are normally distributed. This requirement is met for the indices d_a, Δm, and s, simply by employing a reasonably large case sample. For A_z and for $P(TP)$ at fixed $P(FP)$, situations may arise in which the normality assumption is less easily met, and then corrective steps may be in order, as discussed briefly in Section 4.5.

4.1   STANDARD ERROR OF THE ACCURACY INDEX

The first step in statistical analysis is to determine for the chosen accuracy index, call it Θ, its standard error (S.E.). To explain most simply what the S.E. is, we first present the basic formula for it and define the pure variance terms that comprise it. We then point out certain complexities in working with the basic formula and describe and illustrate application of an alternative formula that gets around those complexities.

The basic formula for S.E. is

$$\text{S.E.} = \left[S_c^2 + \frac{S_{br}^2}{\ell} + \frac{S_{wr}^2}{\ell m} \right]^{1/2}, \qquad \text{(Eq. 3)}$$

where

S_c^2 =   case-sample variance, the component of variance in Θ due to differences in mean difficulty of cases from case sample of size n to case sample of size n,

S_{br}^2 =   between-reader variance, the component of variance in Θ due to differences in diagnostic capability from reader to reader,

S_{wr}^2 =   within-reader variance, the component of variance in Θ due to differences in an individual reader's diagnoses of the same case on repeated occasions,

ℓ =   the number of independent readers,

m =   the number of times the case sample is read independently by each reader.

In pointing out the complexities of applying this basic formula, we note first that the pure variance terms S_c^2 and S_{br}^2 cannot be estimated directly from the observable variance in Θ, because the observable variance inevitably includes S^2_{wr}. Thus, to apply the basic formula one must first correct the observable variance by subtracting out S^2_{wr}. Rather than suggest such a two-step procedure, we prescribe a direct computational formula that includes the required corrections. We also note that considerable notational simplicity is achieved here, and much more when we get to the corresponding formula for the S.E. of the difference (Section 4.3), if we also relinquish some of the generality of the basic formula. The prescription is to compute S.E. as if the number of readings m is equal to 1—in essence, to leave m out of the formula. With that small reduction in generality, the meaning of which we will explain next, the direct computational formula for S.E. becomes simply

$$\text{S.E.} = \left[S^2_{c\,+\,wr} + \frac{S^2_{br\,+\,wr}}{\ell} - S^2_{wr} \right]^{1/2} \qquad \text{(Eq. 4)}$$

where

$S^2_{c\,+\,wr}$ $= S^2_c + S^2_{wr}$, the observable variance in Θ that would be found by having one reader read once each of a set of different case samples,

$S^2_{br\,+\,wr}$ $= S^2_{br} + S^2_{wr}$, the observable variance in Θ that would be found by having one case sample read once by each of a set of different readers,

S^2_{wr} $=$ the observable variance in Θ that would be found by having one reader read one case sample on two or more independent occasions.

Some comments now on the meaning of leaving m out of Eq. 4. The main point to make is that we are not suggesting that all rereading of the case sample be dropped; in that event no empirical basis would exist for estimating S^2_{wr}. Rather, we are suggesting two things. First, it will generally be a waste of study resources, unless ℓ is necessarily very small, to have every reader reread the case sample. A reasonably good estimate of S^2_{wr} can often be obtained on as few as three or four readers, and unless $S^2_{br} = 0$, one can always expect a greater reduction in S.E. from adding a reader than adding a rereading by any one reader. Thus, as a general rule, one should strive to apply those study resources available for reading to getting more readers. For calculations shortly to be illustrated, one has to have $\ell > 2$, and as a practical rule, ℓ should be substantially larger whenever study resources permit. Second, the generally very small reduction in computed S.E., which would come from factoring in the relatively little rereading required just to estimate S_{wr}^2, is not worth the notational complexity.

4.1.1   Illustration: Determining the Standard Error of A_z in the Mammography Study

We consider first how to obtain the within-reader variance S_{wr}^2. This is the variability in Θ among the m ROC curves obtained when an individual reader reads the same case sample m times. That variability is computed for each of the few readers that are selected to do the rereading, and the arithmetic mean of the resulting terms, taken over all of those rereaders in a modality, constitutes S_{wr}^2 for that modality. Thus, for each modality one determines for each rereader the mean of the squared deviations of Θ's from the rereader's mean Θ, and then takes the mean of the resulting terms over all the rereaders. (Note that we are recommending here that a maximum-likelihood estimate of a variance be obtained for each rereader—that is, that the sum of the squared deviations be divided by the total number of observations m. This recommendation is made because m will be extremely limited in size (usually to $m = 2$), and unbiased estimates of variance, as would be obtained by dividing by one less than m, could lead to an inflation of S_{wr}^2 relative to the other two variance components of Eq. 3. Our solution to that potential problem is to obtain maximum-likelihood estimates of all of the variance terms.)

We illustrate the computation of S_{wr}^2 with data, shown in Table 7, from the unmatched-readers condition of our mammography study (Chapter 11). In this condition, each of three readers read in only one of the three modalities under study, and read each case twice. For this illustration, we consider only modality X.

Taking the average of the squared deviations, the within-reader variance in modality X for reader X1 is $[(0.785 - 0.81)^2 + (0.785 - 0.76)^2]/2$, or 0.000625. Similarly, for reader X2 the value is 0.000025, and for reader X3 the value is 0.000625. Now, taking the mean of these terms as our estimate, we find that for modality X, $S_{wr}^2 = 0.00043$.

Consider next how to compute the observable between-reader variance, $S_{br + wr}^2$. The general approach is to compute the variability in Θ over all readers, working with only the first reading occasion of any rereaders. Thus, for modality X, $S_{br + wr}^2$ is $[(0.823 - 0.81)^2 + (0.823 - 0.88)^2 + (0.823 - 0.78)^2]/3$, or 0.0018.

Last, we come to the $S_{c + wr}^2$ term. Ordinarily, the repeated testing needed to compute this variability would not be feasible, and some other practical approach to estimating $S^2_{c + wr}$ is needed. Such an approach is implemented in the computer program of Dorfman and Alf (1969) as listed in Appendix D. The variance terms, which appear in the variance–covariance matrix of the program output, are theoretical, multinomial probability estimates and can be shown to be maximum-likelihood estimates of $S^2_{c + wr}$. Such theoretical estimates of $S^2_{c + wr}$ for each value of A_z are given in Table 7. To compute $S^2_{c + wr}$ for a given modality, one takes the mean of $S^2_{c + wr}$ over all ℓ ROC curves obtained in that modality, using the ROC curves from the first reading occasions of the rereaders. So, for modality X, $S^2_{c + wr} = 0.0034$.

We can now put the three estimates of observable variance that we have obtained into Eq. 4 and compute the S.E. for modality X as follows:
S.E. $= [0.0034 + 0.0018/3 - 0.00043]^{1/2} = 0.060$.

4.1.2 Obtaining a Combined Estimate of the Standard Error

In most circumstances, and specifically, we think, for our mammography study, it is appropriate to compute the S.E. for each modality and then to take the average of these terms, over all of the modalities being studied, to generate a combined, overall estimate of the S.E. This procedure is appropriate whenever there are insufficient data to test whether the S.E. varies significantly among the modalities, *and* when there is no compelling argument that they would differ. Combining into an overall value provides a more stable estimate of the S.E., and the statistical procedure is conceptually and notationally simplified.

4.2 CONFIDENCE INTERVAL OF THE ACCURACY INDEX

Whereas the main thrust of statistical analysis will usually be to test the statistical significance of differences between modalities, it will often be of interest to determine the confidence one can place in the obtained value of the accuracy index for an individual modality. This is the familiar need for expressing with a specifiable degree of confidence how far the obtained value might be from the true value of the index. We assume in all of these discussions of statistical procedures that the reading test is conducted on a sufficiently large sample of cases in each modality that

Table 7

VALUES OF A_z and S^2_{c+wr} FROM THE MAMMOGRAPHY STUDY: UNMATCHED-READERS CONDITION

		Reading occasion				
		1		2		
Modality	Reader	A_z	S^2_{c+wr}	A_z	S^2_{c+wr}	Mean A_z
X	1	0.81	0.0040	0.76	0.0053	0.785
	2	0.88	0.0020	0.87	0.0026	0.875
	3	0.78	0.0042	0.83	0.0032	0.805
	Mean	0.823	0.0034	0.820	0.0037	0.822
Y	1	0.72	0.0055	0.89	0.0019	0.805
	2	0.86	0.0025	0.81	0.0056	0.835
	3	0.82	0.0032	0.80	0.0044	0.810
	Mean	0.800	0.0037	0.833	0.0040	0.816
Z	1	0.87	0.0030	0.84	0.0033	0.855
	2	0.79	0.0042	0.84	0.0035	0.815
	3	0.90	0.0020	0.84	0.0035	0.870
	Mean	0.853	0.0031	0.840	0.0034	0.847

large-sample statistics apply. With that assumption the sampling distribution of Θ is normal, and we can find in a table of the cumulative standardized normal distribution that range of scores around the obtained value that would bracket the true value on a specifiable percentage H of test occasions. We determine the z score that would be exceeded on $[(100 - H)/2]\%$ of testing occasions. We then multiply that $\pm z$ value by S.E. to determine the upper and lower bounds of the confidence interval.

For example, let us compute the 95% confidence interval for the mean value of A_z in modality X of the mammography study. The mean value of A_z over the three ROC curves is 0.823. We have already determined that for modality X, S.E. = 0.060. The $\pm z$ value that includes 95% of the sampling distribution is 1.96. The 95% confidence interval is, therefore, $0.823 \pm (1.96 \times 0.060 = 0.118)$. Thus, we can be 95% confident that the true value of A_z for modality X lies between 0.705 and 0.941. (Because 1.96 is close to 2.0, a common procedure is simply to double the S.E. Thus, at a glance the interval is 0.82 ± 0.12 or from 0.70 to 0.94. Two significant figures are usually adequate and appropriate for the estimates.)

4.3   STATISTICAL SIGNIFICANCE OF A DIFFERENCE BETWEEN MODALITIES

The general and familiar procedure for conducting a test of the significance of a difference between modalities has already been explained in Section 3.3 in connection with designing the reading test. Briefly, the approach is to divide the obtained difference, (Mean Θ_1 − Mean Θ_2), by the standard error of the difference, S.E.$_{(diff)}$. For large case samples, this ratio can be treated as a critical ratio (C.R.), which scales the obtained difference in units of the normal deviate z. Thus, the probability under the null hypothesis that the observed difference could have been obtained just by chance, can be determined by looking up the z value in a table of the cumulative standardized normal distribution. We focus attention first on how to compute S.E.$_{(diff)}$.

The investigator may wish to review the basic formula for S.E.$_{(diff)}$ that is given as Eq. 2 in Section 3.3. Here, for the same general reasons discussed in Section 4.1, we substitute for the basic formula one that is more practical for actual computation. The direct computational formula we present is a̶s̶ ̶f̶o̶l̶l̶o̶w̶s̶:

$$
\text{S.E.}_{\cdot(\text{diff})} = 2^{1/2} \left[S^2_{c\,+\,wr}(1 - r_{c\,-\,wr}) + \frac{S^2_{br\,+\,wr}}{\ell}(1 - r_{br\,-\,wr}) - S^2_{wr} \right]^{1/2}
\tag{Eq. 5}
$$

where

$r_{br\,-\,wr}$ = the observable correlation between the Θ's obtained when each of a set of at least three different readers reads the same case sample in the two modalities,

$r_{c\,-\,wr}$ = the observable correlation between the Θ's obtained when a single reader reads each of a set of at least three different case samples in the two modalities.

By comparing Eqs. 2 and 5, the investigator may be satisfied that we have done the same thing here as with the formula for S.E. We have replaced the pure variances S^2_c and S^2_{br} and the pure correlations r_c and r_{br} by their observable counterparts. Also, and again for considerable notational simplicity, we have left m out of the formula.

Consider first the approach to obtaining an estimate of $r_{br\,-\,wr}$. If the readers are unmatched, the pure correlation r_{br} is 0, and so by definition

$r_{br-wr} = 0$. If the readers are matched, r_{br-wr} must be estimated empirically. The procedure is to calculate the product–moment correlation between the Θ's obtained by the readers in one modality and the Θ's obtained by the same readers in the other modality (using Θ's from the first reading occasions for the rereaders). If more than two modalities are being compared, this operation is repeated for all possible pairings of modalities, and the mean is taken of the resulting terms.

Now consider the approach to obtaining an estimate of r_{c-wr}. If the cases are unmatched, the pure correlation term r_c is 0, and by definition $r_{c-wr} = 0$. If the cases are matched, an empirical estimate is in order. An empirical estimate of r_{c-wr} requires that the case sample be broken into three or more equal parts. One then conducts ROC analyses on each of those subsamples. For each reader (using Θ's from first reading occasions for rereaders), calculate the product–moment correlation between Θ's for the three or more subsamples in one modality and the equivalent Θ's in the other modality. If more than two modalities are being compared, repeat that operation for all possible pairings of modalities and take the mean of the resulting terms. Then take the mean of the resulting product–moment correlations over all readers.

For this approach to be reasonable, one has to have enough cases in the full reading-test sample to provide a sufficient number in each of the subsamples to ensure reliable curve fitting. Clearly, the more cases one has the better, but we can offer no definite rule on what a minimum reasonable number might be. In the *User's Guide* (Appendix D), Dorfman and Alf suggest alternative procedures to use when, due to small samples, the computer program fails to converge on a maximum-likelihood fit. The ultimate fallback position they suggest is to use the least-squares fitted curve that the program uses as its starting point. The slope and intercept of the least-squares starting point are part of the program output, and from them, following procedures given in Chapter 1, one can derive any one of the accuracy indices. Thus, one can obtain objective estimates of ROC curve parameters even on very small samples. At issue when samples are very small, however, is whether such estimates are credibly reliable. We view that issue as a matter of scientific judgment best left to the individual investigator. We can offer as an example our judgment that with respect to the presently examined mammography study, the full sample is really too small to divide sensibly even into three parts. Part of that judgment reflects our concern that each subsample would contain only eight positive cases. Thus, we adopt the conservative option of not trying to estimate r_{c-wr} in the mammography study, and we proceed in the following illustrations as if r_{c-wr} were 0. The investigator will no doubt appreciate that taking this option can lead to a substantial loss in power. If one wants to take advantage of case matching, one has to have enough cases to permit obtaining a credible estimate of $r_{c - wr}$. Otherwise, one might be better off being free of the constraint of multiple imaging, and then compensating for the losses in power from not matching by increasing the number of unmatched cases.

4.3.1   Illustration of Determining Significance of a Difference in A_z in the Mammography Study: Unmatched-Readers Condition

Taking modalities X and Y, the first main step is to determine the numerator of the critical ratio (C.R.)—the mean difference between the respective values of A_z. Using the data in Table 7 for just the first reading occasion we find Mean $A_z(X)$ − Mean $A_z(Y)$ = 0.823 − 0.800 = 0.023.

The second main step is to compute S.E.$_{(diff)}$. We first obtain a combined estimate of the variance components, $S_{c + wr}^2$, $S_{br + wr}^2$, and S_{wr}^2. Taking data from Table 7, again for just the first reading occasion, and combining over all three modalities, we find $S_{wr}^2 = 0.0012$, $S_{br + wr}^2 = 0.0025$, and $S_{c + wr}^2 = 0.0034$.

We then determine the correlation terms, $r_{br - wr}$ and $r_{c - wr}$. Here, because readers are unmatched, we assume that $r_{br - wr} = 0$. We have no adequate empirical basis for estimating $r_{c - wr}$, and therefore we proceed as if $r_{c - wr} = 0$.

The third main step is to compute the C.R., and we find that

$$\text{C.R.} = z = \frac{0.023}{2^{1/2} [0.0034(1 - 0.0) + (0.0025/3)(1 - 0.0) - 0.0012]^{1/2}}$$

$$= \frac{0.023}{0.078} = 0.29.$$

Consulting a table of areas under the normal curve, we find that a difference with $z \geq 0.29$ would occur given the null hypothesis on about 77% of testing occasions; thus we conclude that the difference is not statistically significant.

4.3.2   Illustration of Determining S.E.$_{(diff)}$ for A_z in the Mammography Study: Matched-Readers Condition

In the matched-readers condition of the mammography study, three readers ($\ell = 3$) read the same cases in all three modes, but they read each case just once. The data are shown in Table 8. As is evident in

Table 8

VALUES OF A_z AND S^2_{c+wr} FROM THE MAMMOGRAPHY STUDY: MATCHED-READERS CONDITION

Modality	Reader	A_z	S^2_{c+wr}
X	1	0.79	0.0035
	2	0.76	0.0045
	3	0.83	0.0032
	Mean	0.793	0.0037
Y	1	0.79	0.0037
	2	0.75	0.0062
	3	0.82	0.0036
	Mean	0.787	0.0045
Z	1	0.80	0.0034
	2	0.69	0.0055
	3	0.88	0.0025
	Mean	0.790	0.0038

Table 8, we found essentially no differences in A_z among the three modalities, hence we focus this illustration just on computation of the S.E.$_{(diff)}$.

The first step is to determine the observable variance components. Since no rereading was done in this condition (something one would not ordinarily let happen except in a purely methodological exercise), we shall take as an estimate of S^2_{wr} the value 0.0012 obtained in the unmatched-readers condition. Taking data from Table 8, we find that $S^2_{br+wr} = 0.0026$ and $S^2_{c+wr} = 0.0040$.

The second step is to determine the correlation term r_{br-wr}. We compute the product–moment correlation in the values of A_z obtained for the three readers between each possible pairing of modalities. Taking data from Table 8, we find r_{br-wr} between modality X and modality Y = 0.96, r_{br-wr} between modality X and modality Z = 0.99, and r_{br-wr} between modality Y and modality Z = 0.99. Taking the mean of the three terms, we find that $r_{br-wr} = 0.98$. [That value is obviously an overestimate. For an explanation of why it is obvious, see Section 11.8. It is a sampling oddity of a kind one has to expect to get occasionally with extremely small samples (here $\ell = 3$). We emphasize again that one should strive to work with a reasonably large sample of readers.] For r_{c-wr} we again have no adequate basis for an empirical estimate, and so consider that term to be 0.

Substituting these figures in Eq. 5 we have

$$\text{S.E.}_{\text{(diff)}} = 2^{1/2} [0.0040(1 - 0.0) + (0.0026/3) (1 - 0.98) - 0.0012]^{1/2}$$
$$= 0.075.$$

It is of interest to compare the findings obtained here with matched readers to those obtained in Section 4.3.1 with the unmatched readers. Were we dealing with readers from the same population in both conditions, we would expect the variance estimates to be the same in both conditions and to gain from reader matching ($r_{br - wr} = 0.98$) a reduction in S.E.$_{\text{(diff)}}$ of about 15%. The reduction in S.E.$_{\text{(diff)}}$ that we see, from S.E.$_{\text{(diff)}} = 0.078$ with the unmatched readers to S.E.$_{\text{(diff)}} = 0.075$ with the matched readers, is considerably less than that expectation. The explanation is that the variance estimates, and particularly the estimate for $S^2_{c + wr}$, are higher in the matched-readers condition, and those increased variances largely offset the gains from reader matching. With a larger case sample, and in turn more stable estimates of the variance terms, we would probably have shown the effect of reader matching more clearly.

4.4   STATISTICAL ANALYSIS OF TRUE-POSITIVE PROBABILITY AT A FIXED FALSE-POSITIVE PROBABILITY

Two issues arise in applying the general approach described above to statistical analysis of the point index $P(TP)$ at a fixed $P(FP)$. The first arises in making the normality assumption. For large case samples, in the range of 50 cases or more, and for true values of $P(TP)$ at or near 0.50, the sampling distribution of $P(TP)$ can be shown to be a very close approximation to the normal distribution. For true values of $P(TP)$ relatively distant from 0.50, larger case sample sizes and perhaps a skewness-reducing transform may be needed to retain the validity of the normality assumption, as discussed in Section 4.5.

The other issue is how to obtain an estimate of $S^2_{c + wr}$. The reader will recall that an estimate of this term for each of the other indices we have previously discussed is available as a by-product of the curve-fitting procedure of Dorfman and Alf. (See the discussion in Section 4.1.1 and Appendix D.) The equivalent theoretical estimate of $S^2_{c + wr}$ for $P(TP)$ is obtained by the following formula:

$$S^2_{c + wr} \text{ [for } P(TP)] \approx \frac{1}{2\pi} \exp\{[-(A + B Z_k)^2]\} [\text{Var } (A)$$
$$+ (Z_x)^2 \text{ Var } (B) + 2Z_k \text{ Covar } (A,B)] \qquad \text{(Eq. 6)}$$

where the terms Var (A), Z_x, Var (B), and Covar (A,B) are generated by the program of Appendix D.

4.5 ASSUMPTIONS UNDERLYING THE RECOMMENDED STATISTICAL PROCEDURE

In developing the recommended approach to statistical analysis, we have been willing to forsake a certain amount of generality for some rather large gains in conceptual and notational simplicity of the procedure. In all, we made three simplifying assumptions.

The first assumption is that we are always dealing with normally distributed indices. This assumption allows us to use the z statistic and to apply the C.R. test. For the indices d_a, Δm, and s—and for other than high true values of A_z and other than extreme values of $P(TP)$—the only requirement for meeting this assumption is that we employ large case samples, in the range of at least 50 cases per modality. As the true value of A_z approaches high values and as the true $P(TP)$ approaches either extreme, the sampling distributions become distinctly skewed with values bunching near the limits. One unquestionably good corrective step if this problem is faced before the fact, is to increase the case sample size. At all true values, normality is more closely approximated the larger the case sample size. Another procedure often recommended in statistical texts and one applicable after the fact, is to apply a skewness-reducing transform. McNicol (1972, pp. 117–119) discusses this option for reducing skewness in A_z, and suggests its more general use in reducing skewness of probability measures. His suggestion is to apply the arcsin transform. Specifically, one would work with values that are 2 arcsin $A_z^{1/2}$ or 2 arcsin $P(TP)^{1/2}$ as taken from a published table, for example, from McNicol (1972, Appendix 5).

The second assumption of our general approach is that the numbers of cases and readers are constant across the modalities. This is a rather trivial requirement in two senses: First, it will frequently be easy to meet, and, second, if it is not met, the investigator simply has to expand the statistical formulas to keep track of all terms with unequal frequencies of replication.

Our third simplifying assumption is that each of the several components of variability and correlation is constant across the modalities. This assumption permits the use of combined variance and correlation terms in the statistical formulas. We think this simplifying assumption is usually reasonable in that it is likely to be essentially correct for similar modalities and readers. Moreover, there will often be insufficient power to prove that these terms are unequal. According to statistical theory, when the terms are equal, a combined estimate is superior.

4.6 TESTS COMPARING MORE THAN TWO MODALITIES

Our basic approach to testing for statistically significant differences in accuracy has been presented in the context of comparing just two modalities. We now consider how that basic approach can be extended to cover situations in which more than two modalities are to be compared. The extension, on the surface a simple one, is to apply the C.R. test to all possible pairings of the modalities. Thus, if three modalities (A, B, and C) are to be compared, the approach is to apply the C.R. test on each of three pairs, AB, AC, and BC. In general, for K modalities, the test would be on each of $K!/2(K-2)!$ pairs. There is, however, one complication to extending the approach in this way. It requires the investigator to consider how best to protect against errors in drawing conclusions from the set of comparisons as a whole.

The investigator will want to control properly the probabilities of concluding that a difference exists for any given pair when in truth it does not (type 1 error) and of concluding that there is no difference for a given pair when in truth there is (type 2 error). The issue of how best to protect against type 1 and type 2 errors, even in situations with one comparison, is certainly not simple. One can define a rational approach, which is to estimate the cost of each type of error, and set α (the probability of a type 1 error) and β (the probability of a type 2 error) so as to maximize the expected value of the decision. Occasionally, the investigator may be in a position to approximate that strategy and then should certainly attempt to do so. More often than not, however, the investigator will have to proceed without the refined specifications of costs that permit a fully rational approach. In those situations one may adopt certain conventional criteria. Frequently, for example, investigators will set α at a level that seems comfortably low, for example, 0.05 or 0.01, and will leave β completely unspecified. Independent of how one might arrive at the setting of α and β for a single comparison, however, some rethinking about the adequacy of those settings will be required when multiple comparisons are to be made.

When multiple comparisons are made, the probability of making a type 1 error on the set of comparisons will increase as the number of comparisons increases. It can be shown, for example, that if one conducts a C.R. test with $\alpha = 0.05$ on each pairing of five conditions, which in truth do not differ, the probability of rejecting the null hypothesis on at least one of the ten possible comparisons is far greater than 0.05. It is actually about 0.29 (see Snedecor and Cochran, 1967, p. 272).

Aware of this striking degree of inflation of α for the set of comparisons as a whole, the investigator may wish to select α not for an individual comparison, but rather for the set of comparisons as a whole. One might even consider it reasonable, for example, to choose $\alpha = 0.05$ for the set of comparisons as a whole, in which case the setting of α for each individual comparison would have to be much smaller. Exactly how much smaller would depend on which one of several alternative methods for conducting the multiple tests is followed. The main difference among those alternative methods is how β changes with α, and the investigator may indeed wish to take effects on β into account and thus to choose one of those methods over another. For a comprehensive review of these alternatives, see Winer (1962, pp. 85–89).

If the investigator wishes simply to concentrate on α and accept whatever value of β results, Fraser (1958, pp. 85–86) presents a rather simple way of determining how to set α' for an individual comparison so that α for the set of comparisons is at a desired level. He shows that for K modalities

$$\alpha' = \frac{\alpha}{\binom{K}{2}}.$$

We offer no position on exactly what the investigator should do. We simply want to urge that these issues be kept in mind, that α and β be set as rationally as possible, and that one explain, in reporting the study results, whatever rationale was followed.

4.7 SUMMARY

Discussed in this chapter are statistical procedures for obtaining the S.E. of an accuracy index, a confidence interval for such an index, and the statistical significance of an obtained difference between indices. Basic and computational formulas for the S.E. of a single index take into account the portions of total variance due to case-sample, between-reader, and within-reader variance. The formulas for the S.E. of a difference consider also the correlations between cases and between readers. Examples of computations are drawn from the imaging study of Chapter 11. Concluding sections list the assumptions of the formulas and suggest a way to protect against an incorrect conclusion when comparing several systems and obtaining several differences.

CHAPTER 5

Forms of Efficacy Analysis

The fact that a system yields highly accurate diagnoses does not mean that it will have a positive impact in a particular diagnostic context. For one reason or another, the information provided by the system might not influence the diagnostician's thinking about the cases examined. Even if it did, a careful auditing of all the risks and costs as well as benefits might well show that application of the system led to no real gain and perhaps even led to a net loss. Such possibilities provide the reasons for carrying evaluation of a system beyond the point of measuring diagnostic accuracy.

This chapter is written with a considerably different aim than that of the rest of the book. Rather than provide a comprehensive discussion of how to conduct an efficacy analysis, which could require a long treatise, we attempt only to present the general logic and rationale of efficacy analysis and to show certain fundamental difficulties and various options for getting around them. For the details of how to conduct particular types of analysis, we shall point to several sources for expanded explanation and guidance. As we pointed out earlier, the content of this chapter is derived from the medical context.

By efficacy analysis we mean a range of possible assessments of the effect or impact of the diagnostic modality under study. We say range because assessments will vary in several ways, depending on the particular aims of the analysis, on the time and resources available, and on numerous medical, logistic, and methodological impediments. One way efficacy analyses can vary is in the type and number of dimensions assessed. Some analyses may only consider health benefits, whereas others may extend the analysis to include various economic costs. Analyses can also vary with respect to how far they look into the future. Some look at only the first few steps into the diagnostic–therapeutic process; others follow patients through to the end of all possible differential impacts of the modalities under study. Measures of effects can also be taken with different degrees of resolution. For example, impact on patient health can be assessed very crudely in terms of whether the patient lives or dies; or very precisely in terms of whether the patients who live suffer various degrees of disability, discomfort, or loss of livelihood.

Finally, efficacy analysis can take different approaches to merging the different types of impact. Different types of health benefits may be merged into "quality-adjusted" years of survival. In cost–benefit analyses, which we take here as a point of departure for characterizing and contrasting alternative analyses, all impacts are transformed into value in a common currency, usually dollars, and added together into a unitary measure of net expected benefit. In cost-effectiveness analysis, a practical and very often fully adequate alternative to cost–benefit analysis, health benefits are audited in some convenient and meaningful health currency, and the expected value of the process is expressed as a ratio of dollar costs to number of health units achieved.

In this chapter we (a) develop the concepts and main steps of cost–benefit analysis, (b) describe those characteristics of diagnostic–therapeutic processes that complicate and impede a full cost–benefit analysis, and (c) outline various available alternatives when a full cost–benefit analysis is either not feasible or not needed.

5.1 COST–BENEFIT ANALYSIS: A CONCEPTUAL STARTING POINT

We develop as the starting point of this discussion a brief and highly simplified description of cost–benefit analysis. We present it as a model of what might be called a complete efficacy analysis. By complete, we mean it treats all relevant dimensions of impact, cumulates effects through the full diagnostic–therapeutic process, and merges all of those impacts into a single index of net dollar benefit. In taking this point of departure, we are not suggesting that cost–benefit analysis is the appropriate or necessary goal for analysis in all decision contexts. We do suggest, however, that it is an appropriate place to start when thinking about the kind of efficacy analysis that is needed and how it should be tailored to the particular situation.

Conceptually, cost–benefit analysis is rather simple to describe, though its practical application can be very complicated and plagued with significant logistic and methodological problems. The procedure begins with the construction of decision flow diagrams and ends with a determination of efficacy in terms of net expected value. We briefly characterize the approach here; for a detailed description see Raiffa (1968).

5.1.1   Decision Flow Diagrams

To measure the impact of a diagnostic technique within a particular diagnostic–therapeutic context, one must first determine what costs and benefits of the process might be affected. Decision flow diagrams, discussed shortly in Chapter 6 and illustrated in Figures 13 and 14, serve this fundamental purpose. These diagrams show the alternative paths a case might take through the diagnostic–therapeutic process, depending on decisions about which tests and treatments will be administered and on what outcomes of those tests and treatments are forthcoming.

The decision flow diagram has to characterize only that part of the overall diagnostic–therapeutic process conceivably affected by inclusion of the diagnostic technique under study. It is often reasonable to assume that introduction of the technique does not affect stages prior to the one at which it is introduced. In such cases, the diagram starts with a node representing the diagnostic alternatives issued by the diagnostic technique.

How the diagram is drawn forward—what nodes of the process it must include and what fineness of distinction at each node must be preserved—depends on the costs and benefits to be taken into account in the efficacy analysis. The decision maker for whom the efficacy analysis is being conducted must specify what the important costs and benefits are.

Efficacy analysts will usually first consider the dimensions of terminal health status on which benefit is to be measured. They will design terminal nodes of the diagram that sort cases into all significant degrees of status on those dimensions. Each branch of the diagram is then drawn forward from the diagnostic node for the modality under study, preserving only those subsequent nodes and that fineness of distinction at each node necessary to achieve the required sorting according to benefit at the terminal nodes.

Two diagrams are drawn, one representing the process in its original form and the other representing the process when adapted to include diagnosis by the imaging system under study.

5.1.2 Full Cost–Benefit Analysis

To conduct a full cost–benefit analysis, probabilities and values (with all values in fully commensurate units) must be assigned to each path in the diagrams. Then, as we describe, the expected value of each diagrammed process is computed (with and without the imaging system under study) and the net expected value is determined by taking the difference in expected value between the two versions of the process.

Probability of Traversing Each Path. For the process in its original form, branching probabilities can sometimes be obtained from long-term records. For the process in its adapted form, some amount of data collection will be required, at least for the node representing the diagnostic technique as described in Chapters 6 and 8. At that node, as we have stressed, the idea is to trace out an ROC curve and to choose the balance between probabilities of paths in a deliberate manner.

Note, however, that if the introduction of the technique could conceivably affect raw probabilities *upstream* in the process, the decision flow diagram would have to be redrawn to include the immediately preceding node, and data would have to be collected to establish the new probabilities there. Again, if it is suspected that the diagnostic technique will affect conditional probabilities *downstream* in the process, as might occur, for example, if the new technique allowed some significant fraction of cases to proceed along a less invasive path—data must be collected to establish the new conditional probabilities. Otherwise, probabilities established in records of the original process could be used for equivalent nodes of the adapted process.

If new estimates are required and empirical studies are not feasible, it may be possible to obtain estimates from studies in similar diagnostic–therapeutic contexts. Failing that alternative, one might base the estimates on expert opinion.

Value of Traversing Each Path.   The costs incurred in taking each leg along each path are measured and combined with the health benefit derived at the end of each path to produce an index of that path's overall value. To combine those terms into a single index, the critical requirement is that they be commensurate. The measure of each cost and each benefit has to be transformed into units on a common scale of value—for instance, monetary value.

Many of the dimensions of cost and benefit that the decision maker considers important will be directly computable in dollar terms—for example, fees for tests and treatments or income that the patient gains or loses. Other costs and benefits, such as patient discomfort or quality of life, may require special scaling procedures like those described by Keeney and Raiffa (1976) and by Edwards (1977).

5.1.3   Net Expected Value

Expected Value of Each Path and for the Diagrammed Process as a Whole.   The expected value for each path is obtained by multiplying its probability times its value. Expected value for the diagram as a whole is determined by summing expected values over all paths.

Efficacy of the Imaging System in Terms of Net Expected Value.   The final step in this ideal approach is to subtract the expected value of the diagrammed version of the diagnostic–therapeutic process in its original form from that of the process in its adapted form. That difference is called the *net expected value* of the diagnostic test, and it serves as a measure of efficacy.

5.1.4   Advantages of Net Expected Value

The primary advantage of measuring efficacy in terms of net expected value is that it merges costs and benefits on all dimensions. Another important advantage is that, under certain conditions, it permits an analytical approach to calculating optimal diagnostic performance. That is, one can establish the value of the decision criterion used in diagnostic judgment that will maximize the expected value of the process.

Capabilities of Relating Benefits and Costs on Various Dimensions.   If two or more dimensions of cost or benefit must be taken into account in the efficacy analysis, the decision maker will frequently face ambiguous findings, in which increased benefits or decreased costs on one dimension are accompanied by decreased benefits or increased costs on another. Unless there is some mechanism available for determining trade-offs across dimensions, it will often be unclear whether there is a net gain or loss. The more complex the analysis (i.e., the more dimensions of cost and benefit included in it) the more likely such ambiguities will be encountered and the more troublesome they will be to resolve. By forcing all measures into commensurate terms, the cost–benefit approach avoids such ambiguities. Whether or not such forcing does violence to the true values of costs and benefits in any particular context is, of course, a matter worthy of concern, which explains the interest of many investigators in the cost-effectiveness approach as opposed to the cost–benefit approach.

Potential for Determining Maximum Net Expected Value. The second advantage of a full cost–benefit approach to efficacy analysis is that it provides, in conjunction with ROC analysis, an analytic approach for determining the maximum net expected value to be derived from diagnostic tests as a function of how one sets the decision criterion for interpreting the results of the test. An article by Metz *et. al.* (1975) can be consulted for details. The critical requirement of the analysis is that one be able to determine the expected value of the diagnostic decision. This requirement can be met easily once the decision flow diagram is complete with probabilities and with values in fully commensurate form. Folding back the tree to obtain these upstream expectancies is described by Raiffa (1968).

This same approach can be extended to handle a sequential combination of tests. Metz *et al.* (1975) work out the extension for independent tests. They also point out that the extension could be made to a combination of dependent tests.

In computing maximum net expected value, one has to assume that conditional probabilities downstream remain constant when detection criteria are changed.

5.2 IMPEDIMENTS TO COST–BENEFIT ANALYSIS

At the level of detail sketched here, cost–benefit analysis is conceptually simple. But in practice, a full cost–benefit analysis can quickly grow into a task of inordinate size and complexity fraught with significant logistic and methodological problems. Our goal here is to convey some feeling for those impediments, and we focus on four main aspects. First, the dimensionality of significant costs and benefits is usually far too high to handle. The decision flow diagram tells the tale most dramatically, because the permutations and combinations of all the different shades of cost–benefit combinations have to be represented in the branching structure. The decision flow diagram becomes what Raiffa (1968) would call "a bushy mess." Second, many of the important life dimensions, such as pain or quality of life, will be resistant to quantitative measurement of any kind, particularly in terms commensurate with dollar costs. Third, some important dimensions, even if conceptually easy to measure in commensurate terms, will be very difficult if not totally infeasible to assess within the budget and schedule of the analysis. Fourth, benefits and costs may be distributed widely over time, and the value of the impacts will have to be corrected to take the time of their occurrence validly into account. Let us briefly consider these four impediments.

5.2.1 High Dimensionality of Costs and Benefits

Many dimensions of cost and benefit can emerge as important for an adequate efficacy analysis. One will often be able to see several important dimensions when looking at a given situation from the standpoint of just one party (such as the patient) with respect to just one main function (such as improvement of the patient's health). Trying to consider costs and benefits from the standpoint of more than one party or with respect to more than one function, can greatly increase the dimensionality of the analysis.

Costs and Benefits in the Views of Different Parties. Often several different parties will have a stake in whether or not a diagnostic technique should be adopted. Depending on the decision context, the impact of the technique on the benefits and costs as seen by each party might potentially be important for the analysis. Consider the different perspectives of the patient, the attending physician, the supporting institution (insurer, hospital, or health maintenance organization), and society as a whole. Patients' primary concerns about their health status at the end of the diagnostic–therapeutic process—about the out-of-pocket expenses they accrue, the discomfort they endure, the days lost from work—will be shared in certain ways by all the parties. The physician adds his or her own particular concerns for the welfare of the patient and for the efficiency and effectiveness of his or her own performance. See Wulff (1975, 1976) for helpful discussions of the evaluation of diagnostic techniques from the standpoint of the practicing physician. Institutions and society as a whole add concerns about large-scale cost accounting and medical resources allocation.

There is no practical way to take all of these perspectives formally into account in an efficacy analysis. However, one can never overlook the fact that every agent in the diagnostic–therapeutic process will try to optimize impact of the modality from its own perspective. Thus, even when evaluating from a societal perspective, the decision trees defining the analysis should realistically reflect optimizations from other perspectives.

Costs and Benefits With Respect to Different Functions. Further complicating matters is the fact that the benefits of imaging systems can be measured at three levels of function: research, prognostic, and therapeutic (McNeil and Adelstein, 1976).

In the research function, benefits of the imaging system are measured in terms of contribution to research and teaching about the underlying pathophysiologic process. In the prognostic functions, benefits are measured in terms of the impact of accurate prognosis—independent of therapeutic benefit—for example, a true-negative test that allays the patient's anxiety about having a dread disease or helping terminal cancer patients plan and cope with their untreatable disease. In the therapeutic function, benefit is measured in terms of impact on the patient's state of health.

5.2.2 Incommensurate Costs and Benefits

Many aspects of cost and benefit will be readily translated into commensurate terms, generally monetary value. Even some aspects of health benefits are unarguably if not easily translated into dollar values—for example, increase in projected income because of increased survival or decreased disability (see Barnoon and Wolfe, 1972). But it is the important residual costs and benefits on such dimensions as endured pain or quality of life that pose a problem for measurement on any scale, particularly on a scale of monetary value.

Two problems must be recognized. First, many decision makers will reject the notion of trying to quantify such values. It is hoped that they will become more receptive to the idea as they become more aware of the well-developed techniques now available to do the job. For a review of classic methods for quantifying subjective feelings, see Torgerson (1965). For a review of methods for obtaining measures of subjective utility for various costs and benefits, see Keeney and Raiffa (1976) and Edwards (1977). We can also point to empirical studies in medical contexts that illustrate different approaches to obtaining utility estimates:

1. Weinstein and Stason (1977) took the approach of attaching arbitrary utility values to various states of health in hypertensive patients;

2. Pauker and Pauker (1977) obtained actual estimates of utility of various outcomes from patients in genetic counselling; and
3. McNeil, Weichselbaum, and Pauker (1978) obtained actual utility estimates of alternative therapeutic strategies from lung cancer patients.

Second is the problem that even among those who might accept the general idea, there may well be some resistance until a reasonably well-defined, standard procedure has evolved. It is encouraging, therefore, that a substantial effort along these lines has already been mounted in medicine (see e.g., Berg, 1973, and papers grouped in a recent issue of Health Services Research, by Torrance, 1976, and others).

5.2.3   Costs and Benefits That Cannot Feasibly Be Measured

The third impediment is the fact that some important aspects of costs and benefits, particularly health benefits, cannot be feasibly measured within the time and budget constraints of the efficacy analysis.

The classic problem is with long-term follow-up, which is often required to establish the full health benefit of the diagnostic–therapeutic process. In some situations epidemiological data may be available to fill the gap, but problems are encountered even when the data have been obtained on a presumably well-matched population. Note, for example, the kinds of bias problems that have plagued the use of survival data to measure the effectiveness of cancer control efforts (Enstrom and Austin, 1977).

If budget and time constraints are severe enough, it may not be feasible to follow the process to the point where therapy is complete. If the problem were purely budgetary, it might be resolved. But often, and particularly with respect to obtaining follow-up, the problem is time. For example, diagnostic imaging devices may be evolving so rapidly that there is not time to await adequate follow-up before the measure of efficacy must be used to steer decisions about the next generation of devices.

5.2.4   Costs and Benefits Distributed Widely over Time

In some situations, significant components of cost or benefit may occur rather far into the future, and the schedule of impact may not be the same for the different modalities being compared. Care must be taken to audit these time-distributed components in a valid and comparable fashion across the modalities. Inflation is one factor to be considered, and certainly all costs and benefits should be adjusted for inflation. But future costs should be weighted less heavily than present costs, because resources not spent until a point in the future could conceivably be invested and yield a return in the interim. That potential interim return must be subtracted from the delayed cost by an appropriate discounting formula. Similar adjustments are necessary to correct for delayed benefits, which are worth less than immediate benefits because one cannot enjoy them in the interim, and one risks never seeing them at all. The rationale for these corrections is relatively straightforward, but they lend significant complexity to the analysis. Moreover, the appropriate inflationary projections and discounting rates are highly debatable. For illustrations of discounting see Schoenbaum *et al.* (1976), Schoenbaum, McNeil, and Kavet (1976), and Weinstein and Stason (1977).

5.3 TAILORING THE ANALYSIS TO SUIT THE SITUATION

For the reasons previously mentioned, a full and finely detailed cost–benefit analysis may not be feasible. Moreover, in many situations an extensive analysis may not be necessary. A cost–benefit analysis tells the decision maker whether or not the modality under study will pay for itself. But for the decision maker with money already earmarked for the modality eventually chosen, the question will be simpler. Which modality will give more for the earmarked money? As we show below, a cost-effectiveness analysis can answer that simpler question.

5.3.1 Cost–Benefit Analysis with Reduced Comprehension or Resolution

If the complexity of the task impedes making a full cost–benefit analysis, steps can certainly be taken to reduce complexity while retaining a cost–benefit approach. One does this (*a*) by reducing the dimensionality of costs and benefits—at some risk to maintaining a valid analysis or (*b*) by giving up some fineness of distinction of costs or benefits within dimensions—at some risk to maintaining adequate resolution of the analysis.

Reducing Dimensionality of Costs and Benefits. There is little specific that can be said here. Implicit in trying to choose the dimensions to retain is the requirement that they can somehow be ordered in importance. Short of that, one would at least have to say which dimensions could be dropped without qualitatively altering the meaning of the analysis.

Making Coarser Distinctions Within Dimensions of Cost or Benefit. Assume that in the original view of a problem, distinctions are considered important among three levels of disability in the nodes that represent terminal health outcome. When pruning of the decision tree is clearly needed, one might review that initial assumption and question whether the analysis can still detect a significant net expected value if measures on that dimension were collapsed, to say, two instead of three levels. It may become apparent from the review that resultant loss in sensitivity would be trivial and, thus, that many details of the analysis related to that distinction could be dropped.

5.3.2 Cost-Effectiveness Analysis

Some situations may not permit a cost–benefit analysis, because benefits and costs resist commensuration. In other situations this type of analysis may simply not be required. One can then turn to cost-effectiveness analysis. We characterize this approach here, but the reader can consult McNeil *et al.* (1975) and Weinstein and Stason (1976, 1977) for detailed descriptions and illustrations.

The procedure in cost-effectiveness analysis is the same as in cost–benefit analysis in all respects except that health costs are kept separate from financial costs. The performance of each diagrammed process is measured in the form of a cost-effectiveness ratio. For example, in the numerator one might put the total cost of operating the diagnostic–therapeutic process on the presenting population for some unit of time. In the denominator one might put the average increase in quality-adjusted months of life experienced by that sample. If the total cost of operation of the process with modality A were $1 million and the average saving in quality-adjusted months of life were 4, the cost–benefit ratio would be

$$\frac{C}{E_A} = \frac{\$1,000,000}{4 \text{ quality-adjusted months of average increased life expectancy}}.$$

A basic inadequacy of this approach is that it does not provide a basis for choosing the best process in all analyses. One can tell which process is best from examining the cost-effectiveness ratio if, for example, one of the ratios has a numerator that is smaller and a denominator that is equal to or larger than the other. But what is to be the decision if the ratio for one process has, for example, a larger numerator and denominator than the other? Consider having to choose between test A and test B, where for test B,

$$\frac{C}{E_B} = \frac{\$1,500,000}{5 \text{ quality-adjusted months of average increased life expectancy}}.$$

Nothing short of a *cost–benefit* analysis can make that an obvious choice. The choice may be made a bit more easily, however, if the decision maker considers the *marginal cost* of that additional month of benefit. The marginal cost is obtained by taking the difference between the two ratios. In our example, the marginal cost of gaining an additional month of benefit from using test B comes to $500,000. The decision is still not by any means obvious for the decision maker, but such a measure may often be very helpful.

On top of this basic limitation on comparing two systems, a cost-effectiveness analysis does not entirely solve the problem of value commensuration. For example, getting all health benefits squeezed into an index such as *quality-adjusted months of life* is a problem in itself.

5.3.3 Cost-Effectiveness Analysis with Shortened Horizons

If it is not feasible to measure health benefits in the long term, an analysis on much shorter horizons may still be much more helpful than no analysis at all. McNeil *et al.* (1975) nicely illustrate how informative cost-effectiveness analyses can be even with greatly shortened horizons. They faced the problem of evaluating the efficacy of alternative diagnostic techniques in managing patients presenting symptoms of renovascular disease. Unable to conduct long-term follow-up sufficient to determine impact on so distant a horizon as quality-adjusted life expectancy, they settled for measuring the *cost per diseased patient found* (case finding) and the *cost per surgical cure*. Their analysis showed, for example, that one technique found 8.5 out of 10 diseased patients at an average cost of $2,000, and that the marginal cost of another technique, which found 9.1 out of 10 diseased patients, was $18,000. That kind of comparison, although incomplete, would presumably be of value to a decision maker.

The analysis may suffer, of course, from not taking long-term benefits and costs into account. However, if one can assume that conditional probabilities downstream in the process are independent of the diagnostic techniques under study, short-term impact is all that is important for a *comparative* analysis. Also, many situations will exist (e.g., in the management of appendicitis) where all the action may take place within a short horizon.

5.3.4 Potential Efficacy Analysis: Impact on Diagnostic and Therapeutic Choices

If it is not feasible to obtain information for any nodes of the decision flow diagrams other than the initial diagnostic node, one can still measure some impact that would be of potential interest to a decision maker. After all, if there is no striking impact on diagnostic or therapeutic choices, that fact in itself would be very valuable to know. There certainly will be no downstream effects to be measured if none are detected at the initial node.

Lusted *et al.* (1977) have discussed analysis at this level as a practical alternative in situations in which cost–benefit or cost-effectiveness analyses are deemed infeasible. They lay out a three-stage hierarchy of efficacy analyses. What they call *Efficacy-1* is a measure of impact of the alternative diagnostic techniques on diagnostic choices: essentially, whether the physician has greater or less confidence in the diagnosis. Efficacy at this level they characterize as *diagnostic-thinking efficacy*. They report in the same article a pilot study in which impact of the skull X ray in the emergency room is measured at the Efficacy-1 level.

Efficacy-2 in this scheme is a measure of the extent to which the physician's decisions about treatment are affected by the diagnostic techniques and can be characterized as *therapeutic-thinking efficacy*. Although Efficacy-2 does not require knowledge of long-term patient outcomes, it does require knowledge of whether the physician would have prescribed the same treatment if the modality had not been available.

Efficacy-3 in this scheme is equivalent to what we have called *cost–benefit analysis*.

5.4 SETTING THE EFFICACY ANALYSIS AT AN APPROPRIATE LEVEL

The preceding discussion indicates that one can back away considerably from a full cost–benefit analysis and still provide information on efficacy of potential use to a decision maker. It would be inappropriate, however, to leave the impression that backing away to the point where one feels comfortable is the thing to do. Each step backward weakens the analysis. Reduced comprehension, reduced resolution, inability to trade across dimensions of cost and benefit, reduced horizons—each takes its toll, and each reduces the ability of the analyst to make complete comparisons among the alternatives.

One should not, for example, always back away to the point at which the information required for the analysis can be obtained in an unquestionably valid and highly precise form. It may be that critical distinctions between alternative diagnostic procedures can be made by using only rough estimates of some factors. As Weinstein and Stason (1977) point out, one can always conduct sensitivity analyses, which check what would happen to the efficacy measure if the estimates of a particular factor were in error by varying amounts.

Some efficacy analyses will be commissioned to provide information useful in making particular decisions, and the analyst will be able to work closely with the decision maker to set the analysis at the most appropriate level. More often than not, however, efficacy analyses will be undertaken for a more general purpose, and the level of analysis will be set according to the good judgment of the analyst. In the latter circumstance, we urge the analyst to consider that the higher one sets the level of analysis, the more likely its results will be of interest and use to decision makers who come upon it after the fact.

5.5 SUMMARY

We urge the investigator to determine with care and foresight the level at which an efficacy assessment is to be made. Some preliminary indications of efficacy are described in Chapter 2 (Section 2.2). More ambitious assessments bring into play the considerations described in this chapter. We suggest that a full cost–benefit analysis should be a good starting point in thinking about any particular study. The nature of the difficulties it presents may indicate whether to use a limited form of cost–benefit analysis or a cost-effectiveness analysis. Conceptual, logistic, and methodological difficulties haunt such an assessment, but a few ways to cope with some of them are being developed. In any evaluation study, an efficacy assessment will have to be tailored to suit the situation.

PART II

Experimental Methods

Chapter 6 treats the planning of an evaluation study, emphasizing the relationship of study goals and constraints to the structure of a performance test. The structural details of such a performance test are discussed in Chapter 7. Particular attention is given to formatting the response of the system to the test cases and to considerations in presenting background information on each case. Chapter 8 treats the functions and form of an original sample of potential test cases, and Chapter 9 treats the further selection from that sample of the cases that are adequate for a performance test. The stress here is on the degree to which the test-case sample represents the proper population. The selection of test observers is briefly discussed in Chapter 10. Our focus throughout Part II is on tests of medical imaging systems involving human observers; a concrete setting is necessary, we believe, to guide an examination of experimental methods, and a setting as complex as this one should produce a discussion that contains most others.

CHAPTER 6

Elements of Study Design

Designing an evaluation study is, in part, a matter of *formulating a plan for collecting and analyzing data.* Here we suggest that formulating such a plan is best regarded as the fourth activity to occur in the process of study design. Three earlier activities are, in sequence: *developing the goals of the study, determining the time and cost constraints,* and *outlining the end product* required to satisfy the study goals. The value of giving care initially to these activities cannot be overstressed; however, it must be acknowledged that they will also continue in varying degrees throughout the study. Goals and plans can be modified, and in complex clinical research they frequently must be; desired end products may not materialize; and constraints on resources may change.

The determination of available resources is comparatively straightforward, and it falls outside the scope of this book; this chapter characterizes the other three activities listed.

6.1   DEVELOPING STUDY GOALS

Goals must be developed, clarified, and refined for four aspects of the study specifying: (*a*) the imaging systems to be compared, (*b*) the diagnostic–therapeutic context for the comparison, (*c*) the performance criteria to be applied to the systems under comparison, and (*d*) other analyses. One must determine the dimensions and range of variation of each of these aspects of the study to establish what options exist for shaping goals and narrowing them to fit the constraints of money and time.

6.1.1   Specification of the Imaging Systems

A new imaging technique under study (and existing competitive techniques) may span broad classes of systems, and much variation may exist within a given system. For example, if the initial goal is to determine the value of CT compared to RN scanning, a first clarifying step is to determine the existing varieties of imaging devices of each class and their relative numbers in the field. Variations in the adjustments that can be made (according to local practices), even within types and models, should also be determined. The objective is to establish which systems should be represented in the study and which may be excluded in the interests of economy.

The mode of operation of the systems chosen must also be specified. After deciding to collect computed tomograms from several medical centers, for example, one might establish the number of slices required and whether or not contrast-enhancing agents are to be used. Moreover, it would be appropriate to specify a standard phantom or test pattern that would be sent to all machines at regular intervals to help ensure that they are all functioning above a certain minimal standard. One might further require that a single physicist clear each machine periodically for further participation in the study.

6.1.2   Specification of the Diagnostic–Therapeutic Context

The medical contexts for the use of an imaging system, existing or potential, may include screening and referral centers, or large teaching hospitals and small community hospitals. Producing results that can be generalized validly across a large range of situations could require a very complex and extensive study. (Indeed, the results obtained with test images secured from a teaching hospital or screening center often cannot be generalized to a community hospital, because of characteristic differences in procedure in those two settings.) The particular contexts in the total spectrum that are to be considered must be designated so that the study can be designed to represent them adequately. As in other fields of research, an iterative process will usually be necessary to arrive at an adequate and feasible study effort.

6.1.3 Specification of Performance Criteria

Asking which system is "better" covers many possibilities that must be made explicit. Is the system better in terms of detection accuracy, accuracy of differential diagnosis, impact on overall cost of diagnosis, impact on cost of care, or impact on medical outcome? Specifying the performance criteria will serve to justify a complex and costly study or to make clear the need to narrow the study goals.

6.1.4 Specification of Ancillary Analyses

The primary goal of the evaluation study is presumably to determine which of the modalities under study is best in some sense. But the evaluation study may have other, ancillary goals. For one thing, it may be of great value to know *why* one modality is better than another and to understand what potential there is for improving a particular modality. Questions may also arise about the potential value of combining modalities for improved diagnosis. To answer such questions, analyses of the components of error within modalities and of correlations in performance across modalities may be required. Such analyses may add requirements for the methods of collecting the original case sample and designing the reading test.

Sometimes the evaluation may focus on the effect of manipulating a particular parameter of a modality, such as radiation dose or field of view. Questions may then be asked about the trend of performance over the range of parameter settings.

6.2 OUTLINING THE END PRODUCT

At every stage of study design and execution, the investigator should have in mind a preliminary outline of the required end product. The outline may not be fully developed until after several stages of design have been accomplished or even until some stages of execution have been accomplished, but even rough outlines are helpful at the beginning.

6.2.1 Constructing Decision Flow Diagrams of the Diagnostic–Therapeutic Process

If an analysis of efficacy is desired, the end product of an evaluation study should be anticipated in the form of decision flow diagrams— probabilistic descriptions of the way patients can be expected to move through the diagnostic–therapeutic process, starting with presenting signs and symptoms. Each branch of the process will have assigned to it a probability value and one or more measures of the values and costs of entering that branch. These decision flow diagrams are the bases for computing the various performance measures in terms of efficacy on which the systems will be compared.

Even if the evaluation is restricted just to accuracy of diagnosis, de- cision flow diagrams will still be helpful in such aspects of study design as establishing appropriate diagnostic response alternatives for the reading test and guiding the analysis, interpretation, and qualification of reading-test results.

Simple illustrations of decision flow diagrams are given in Figures 13 and 14. Figure 13 shows a diagram that might be developed and quantified

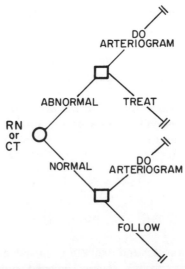

Figure 13. Decision flow diagram for comparing monetary cost in the diagnosis of structural disease of the central nervous system, starting with RN or CT imaging in a particular hypothetical context; see text.

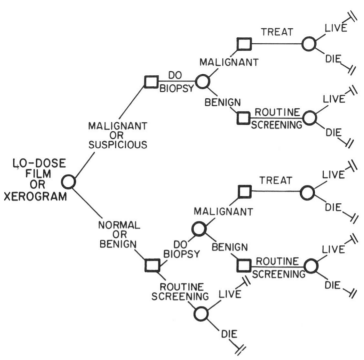

Figure 14. Decision flow diagram for comparing overall cost of diagnosis of breast disease and effectiveness of subsequent treatment, when either Lo-Dose film or Xerography is used initially; see text.

for a limited study of CT versus RN scanning. In this hypothetical study, the diagnostic–therapeutic context includes hospitals in which only one of the systems will be used—for diagnosing patients with symptoms of structural disease of the central nervous system, with arteriography for backup—and where the single criterion of interest is the dollar cost of diagnosis. Estimates must be obtained of the fixed and variable costs of processing patients through each system. Branching probabilities have to be established for two nodes: first at the "chance" node (circle), where the initial diagnosis is made by either the CT or RN system, and next at the "decision" nodes (squares), where the choice is made whether or not to go into a second stage of diagnosis via the arteriogram.

Figure 14 shows the decision flow diagram for a hypothetical study to evaluate Lo-Dose film mammography versus Xerography in the detection of breast cancer. The context is screening, and the performance criteria include 10-year survival rates in addition to dollar cost of diagnosis. Adding the criterion of medical efficacy to the cost criterion makes the second diagram clearly more complex than the first, and one can begin to appreciate here the need to sketch such diagrams early in the design process. They serve as a means to inventory the various pieces of information that will have to be collected in order to compute the desired indices of performance.

6.2.2   Other Ways of Viewing the End Product

Sketching the decision flow diagrams will help in shaping a study with appropriate logic and scientific validity. In addition, one should also anticipate in as much detail as possible the form and substance of the required reports of the study, along with the background and interests of the community expected to use them. Such outlines will help in determining the necessary background material to be developed and the level of detail and sophistication at which the report should be written.

In addition to the decision flow diagrams, outlines of study requirements will also help initially in gauging the time and cost of the study effort. When the estimates of time and cost clearly exceed the amounts allowed, the initial outlines provide a basis for judicious adjustments of goals or resources. When the feasibility of the study is unclear, these previews of study requirements can motivate timely and well-aimed analyses—to establish, before resources are heavily invested, whether or not the study should be attempted.

6.3   PLANNING THE COLLECTION OF DATA

Equipped with refined goals and an outline of the end product, the investigator can lay out a plan for collecting the information required. Again, if system efficacy is to be evaluated, a detailed analysis of the decision flow diagrams will lead him to a listing of the specific data required at each branch and to a specification of data collection and processing procedures.

The need for an image-reading test to establish the various possible branching probabilities at the first node (the image-based diagnostic node) will be evident. Determination of the data to be collected in that test and the collection and analysis procedures are the primary subjects of this book.

The information desired at all subsequent branchings of the diagram and the various steps required to obtain it must also be particularized. For some branches, one may obtain estimates of probabilities, costs, and values from previous epidemiological studies. For other branches, one may have to provide for generating the information within the evaluative study.

What is termed here the study's "original case sample" serves as both the pool from which cases (including images) for the reading test are selected and the data base for any further determinations of probabilities, costs, and values that one desires to generate within the evaluation study. The assembly and use of the study's original case sample are described in Chapter 8. First we treat the procedures of a reading test.

6.4 SUMMARY

In any evaluation study, we suggest that three steps precede the formulation of a plan for collecting and analyzing data. The first is to develop the study's goals with respect to the precise forms of the systems to be compared, the diagnostic–therapeutic context for the comparison, and the performance criteria to be applied. The second step, not discussed here, is the determination of time and cost constraints. The third is to outline the desired end product, a process that may be aided by sketching decision flow diagrams if an assessment of efficacy is to be made. The results of these steps should reveal what information must be obtained in a performance test and what from the diagnostic context of the study.

CHAPTER 7

Procedure of a Performance Test

In a performance test (in this discussion, an image-reading test) a carefully selected sample of cases, consisting primarily of images, is presented in a highly systematic fashion to selected readers, usually taking cases one at a time and readers individually. A few simple considerations attend the presentation of cases. Difficult problems face us in designing the format of the reader's response and in deciding how to handle the background information that may be given the readers on each case. Additional issues are more common grist for the experimental psychologist's mill: reader orientation, viewing environment, timing of trials and sessions, investigator–reader communications following the test, and the role of the test administrator.

7.1 CASE AND IMAGE PRESENTATION

Cases might well be arranged in a different random order each time they are presented, if that is not too cumbersome or expensive. The objective is to reduce possible sequential effects of one case, or of a series of cases, on the next; and of one response, or a series of responses, on the next. A different order would then be used for each reader and for each viewing of the set of cases by a given reader. If arranging different orders does present problems of convenience or expense, the use of fewer orders with some repetition is probably adequate, particularly with large numbers of cases. One might also choose to use the same set of random orders for different groups of readers being compared, that is, groups reading different modalities.

Counterparts, which are images of the same patient taken by different modalities under study, should also be mixed randomly in the set of cases; they should not be identified to the reader as counterparts. (An exception occurs when an explicit objective of the experimental design is to determine the diagnostic accuracy provided by a pair, or set, of imaging modalities. Then one must realize that one type of image may provide cues for interpreting another.) *Repetitions* of sets of images may or may not be identified as repetitions; see Section 7.3 on background information given readers and Section 7.7 on reader orientation.

We believe that images should be presented and handled only by a test administrator. If the readers are allowed to handle films, for example, then a way must be found to ensure that the collection of fingerprints on the films will not serve as cues to later readers. Experienced readers know that more fingerprints accumulate on abnormal images and that fingerprints often collect at the site of a suspected lesion.

Of course, readers must be allowed to manipulate images in ways that they and the investigator consider necessary for a legitimate test. The readers in our study of CT, for example, were able to manipulate the usual variables of window width and window level.

7.2 RESPONSE FORMAT

Section 7.2.1 immediately following identifies the various possible levels of reader responses to presented images (cases). Sections 7.2.2 and 7.2.3 consider the general need to obtain reader responses according to some format, and then recommend a general format. Also considered are the relative ease or difficulty of defining a response ensemble of diagnostic alternatives as a function of the level of response desired, and the ease or difficulty of defining an ensemble appropriate to all modalities being evaluated. Our treatment of responses in Section 7.2.5 concludes with a few comments on the response medium.

7.2.1 Basic Levels of Response

The three basic levels of response that may be obtained in an image-reading test are *detection* (abnormal versus normal), *localization* of abnormality, and *classification* of abnormality (differential diagnosis). Detection is relatively simple, given that the types of abnormality under consideration are constrained to some appropriate domain; localization can range from a relatively simple spatial definition to a complex anatomical definition; and, similarly, classification can vary widely in complexity from a few coarsely defined alternatives to many finely defined alternatives at various hierarchical levels. The simplicity of our terms and definitions, of course, does not deny the fact that these "basic levels of response" depend, often in undetermined ways, on complex perceptual judgments about factors such as size, shape, and profusion of features, structures, or shadows. Nonetheless, we propose formatting the responses in these terms to gain a workable description of judgment dimensions.

In the interest particularly of an efficacy analysis, another kind or level of response may be desired: one that suggests next steps, either in terms of further diagnostic tests (perhaps with other imaging modalities) or in terms of treatment. One can imagine securing such a response from the test reader under certain conditions or from a person outside of the image-reading test under other conditions.

7.2.2 Need for Formatting the Response

In an assessment of diagnostic accuracy at any level, the reader's responses need specifically to be constrained to ensure that they can be matched up against the "truth" about the patients' conditions, that is, to ensure that they can be scored as right or wrong. This is not to say that the truth about patients' disorders comes in categories that are convenient for reader responses. The results of brain biopsy, for example, may be far too specific to match with diagnostic categories sensibly based on brain scans, and the pathologist's categories may well have to be collapsed into cruder categories for an image-reading test.

Responses must also be formatted to ensure that they are comparable across the modalities in competition. This matter is fairly straightforward at the level of detection. To what extent comparability can be achieved for localization and classification is an open question, depending on the diagnostic context as well as on the imaging modalities under study. In some situations, a small and mutually compatible set of responses may allow a fair and adequate comparison of the accuracy and efficacy of each modality. Just the pair of responses "benign" and "malignant" might suffice in a comparative study of mammographic efficacy, for deciding whether or not to obtain a biopsy. However, if the task were to find high-risk patients by analysis of the entire breast pattern (Wolfe, 1976), one would have difficulty finding a small but comprehensive set of responses that is mutually compatible for the modalities under consideration. The problem is magnified as the diagnostic task is more complex and as the disparity among modalities in terms of tissue–image correlates is greater.

How far the test designer should go in soliciting responses in categories not usually used in connection with a given modality in the interest of comparing two or more modalities, is probably limited by what finally makes sense to the test reader. A request for some secondary information about characteristics of the image that is not usually reported (perhaps about one or another of the dimensions of number, size, shape, and sharpness of lesions) may make sense to the test reader when such characteristics are acknowledged to affect the diagnosis.

Whether or not the test design should include provision for free, open-ended comments in addition to the formatted response probably also depends on the diagnostic complexity of the situation at hand. A pilot study should reveal the usefulness of such comments in any instance— usefulness to the test designer or test reader or both.

7.2.3 General Response Format

A rating-scale response is recommended here for detection and for those aspects of localization and classification that may be treated in terms of two alternatives. When more alternatives are desirable, a simple choice of any number of them is probably best. One might also gain some indication of the readers' confidence in their choices.

Detection. For all practical purposes, the rating response for detection is fundamental to the accuracy and efficacy analyses described in Chapters 1 and 5. As described in Chapter 1, ratings of the relative confidence in the existence of an abnormality serve to produce in the most economical way the relative operating characteristic (ROC). The ROC shows the trading relationship between two types of errors (strictly, between false-positives and the complement of false-negatives, namely, true-positives) for a constant level of perceptual or diagnostic accuracy.

In our experience, a five-category rating scale, which produces four points on the ROC curve, is a good balance between the fineness of distinction that the reader feels can be made and the degree of definition of the curve that the evaluator seeks. One workable set of labels for the rating categories is

1. definitely, or almost definitely, abnormal,
2. probably abnormal,
3. possibly abnormal,
4. probably normal,
5. definitely, or almost definitely, normal.

These particular category labels are similar to those used at the various sites of the collaborative study of CT and are exactly the ones used in our central, retrospective analysis of the data from that study.

One might prefer the symmetrical, six-category scale obtained by inserting "possibly normal" between categories 3 and 4 in the previous example. However, some readers feel that normality does not really come in that many degrees. There is little value, of course, in supplying response categories that will be little used. (The evaluator's objective is good spacing of ROC points, and a little-used category will produce a point very close to the point determined by the adjacent category.) Note that we have avoided the term "equivocal" as a label for category 3, on the grounds that the label chosen should not encourage use of that category for "difficult" or "lazy" trials.

Localization. The appropriate number of location categories depends on the imaging modality and on the structure imaged, as does the labeling of the categories in spatial or anatomical terms. A designation only of the suspected location(s) (or distribution) of the abnormality appears to be adequate for most studies, although a second choice will convey some additional information. Indications are that localization performance can be accurately predicted from detection performance, at least in some situations (Starr *et al.,* 1975). The reader may also be allowed to specify in his or her own terms a more precise location than that permitted by the categories provided.

Classification. As a standard procedure, the test reader can choose one of the types of abnormality under consideration, that is, make a permissible differential diagnosis, and may follow that response with a second choice and maybe a third choice. The test reader might be asked to estimate the probability, or the odds, that these choices will prove to be correct (see, e.g., Lusted *et al.,* 1977). In some studies, readers have been asked to convey intensity of belief by distributing 100 points over the several alternatives (see, e.g., Fineberg, 1977). Our own experience is that this task is rather difficult, and we do not feel very confident about interpreting the results. We have asked test readers to give their percentage confidence in their first choice, but have not found the analysis of those data particularly helpful.

Again, the reader may be given an opportunity to state a more precise diagnosis than is permitted by the categories supplied. Special instructions may be required, such as "if multiple abnormalities, indicate (first, second, or third choices of) the most significant" or "if complex abnormality, indicate (first, second, or third choices of) the primary process."

7.2.4 Two Specific Examples

Several of the foregoing comments are made concrete in the response form used in our analysis of CT compared to RN brain scans. This form is shown in Figure 15.

RESPONSE FORMAT FOR CT/RN STUDY

1. This examination is   Check One
   (1) Definitely, or almost definitely, abnormal   ☐
   (2) Probably abnormal   ☐
   (3) Possibly abnormal   ☐
   (4) Probably normal   ☐ ⎫
   (5) Definitely, or almost definitely, normal   ☐ ⎬ [go to Item 6]
                                                              ⎭

2. Site of lesion(s):
   If solitary or diffuse, indicate site(s) of significant anatomic involvement, or if multifocal, indicate sites of major anatomic lesions.

   EXTRA AXIAL   LEFT   MID   RIGHT   L or M or R

   (1) Skull or scalp   ☐   ☐   ☐
   (2) Cerebral convexity or meninges   ☐   ☐   ☐
   (3) 1 or 2 (above)   ☐   ☐   ☐
   (4) Interhemispheric; Parasaggital   ☐   ☐   ☐   ☐
   (5) Sellar region   ☐   ☐   ☐
   (6) Cerebellopontine angle   ☐   ☐

   INTRA AXIAL

   (7) Cerebrum   ☐   ☐
   (8) Frontal lobe   ☐   ☐
   (9) Parietal lobe   ☐   ☐
   (10) Temporal lobe   ☐   ☐
   (11) Occipital lobe   ☐   ☐
   (12) Corpus callosum; Thalamus/basal ganglia   ☐   ☐   ☐   ☐

Figure 15. Response format for CT/RN study. (Continued on next page.)

(13) Brain stem; Cerebellum

(14) Lateral ventricles

(15) Third ventricle

(16) Fourth ventricle

3. The abnormality is: Check One

   (1) Definitely, or almost definitely, a neoplasm

   (2) Probably a neoplasm

   (3) Possibly a neoplasm

   (4) Possibly a non-neoplasm

   (5) Probably a non-neoplasm

   (6) Definitely, or almost definitely, a non-neoplasm

4. Differential diagnosis: Rank up to four choices

   NEOPLASM

   (1) Primary, malignant

   (2) Primary, non-malignant

   (3) Secondary, metastatic

   (4) Secondary, direct spread

   NON-NEOPLASM

   (5) Infarction

   (6) Intracerebral hemorrhage (any etiology)

   (7) Arteriovenous malformation (unruptured)

   (8) Infectious/inflammatory process (e.g., abscess)

   (9) Extracerebral collection (e.g., subdural hematoma)

   (10) Encephalomalacia (e.g., atrophy, degeneration,
        porencephaly)

   (11) Hydrocephalus (any etiology)

   (12) None of the above

   Give your percent confidence in your first choice: ____%

5. Using the information available from this study, can you be more explicit
   about any diagnosis checked above? If so, specify, referring to the number
   of the diagnosis as checked. Example: (1) glioblastoma, (8) abscess.

6. Comments.

Figure 15. Response format for CT/RN study. (Continued from previous page.)

The form begins with a rating for detection (item 1), then gives several choices concerning location (item 2), and then provides for a rating of two classification alternatives (item 3). More extensive information regarding classification is solicited in items 4 and 5. The open-ended item 6 permits comments about inadequate presentations (e.g., too few CT slices, no RN flow study), restrictions imposed by the response format (e.g., permitting a right–left choice for thalamus and basal ganglia combined), cases seen before, and so forth.

Our item on location is no doubt on the high end of the scale of intricacy, because of the combination of a complex organ and a high-resolution technique. It also carries most of the burden for being both adequate and fair to both modalities. Thus, for example, an inclusive, uncertain "or" was added to the tacit "and's" for the various structures: specifically, line 3 under item 2 serves to combine lines 1 and 2. Lines 4, 12, and 13, moreover, allow inclusive, uncertain "or's" for left–mid-right position. In the interest of gaining some economy, a "mid" check on those three lines is taken to mean the central structure (interhemispheric, corpus callosum, brainstem), and a "left" or "right" check indicates the lateral structures (parasaggital, thalamus/basal ganglia, cerebellum).

The item on location is also the one most difficult to score. It requires a mapping of the pathologists' systematized-nomenclature-of-pathology (SNOP) code onto our alternatives, and it requires conventions about scoring errors of omission and commission on the way to a single accuracy score in terms of percentage correct.

We have scored item 4 on classification in terms of the percentage of first choices that were correct. We also examined the percentage of correct choices when all choices were considered and looked for any substantial difference that might exist relative to the confidence in the first choice.

The notation seen in item 1, instructing the reader to proceed directly to item 6 if he or she rated the case as "normal" (category 4 or 5), indicates our decision in the CT/RN study to ask for a judgment about lesion location or class only for cases rated at least as "probably abnormal," that is, rated in categories 1, 2, or 3. The obvious reasoning is that we could hardly ask the reader to make the highly refined distinctions about an abnormality sought in items 2 and 4 when he or she believed no abnormality to exist. A price is paid, however, for taking that course; different readers pass on different cases, and different numbers of cases, to the items beyond item 1. To point up the difficulty, consider that a reader who is relatively conservative about declaring the existence of abnormality, in item 1, will be responding in later items to fewer cases—and, on the whole, to less ambiguous cases—than the reader less conservative in item 1. There is a way to take the decision bias in detection into account in estimating the accuracy in localization and classification, in the so-called "joint ROC," as discussed in Chapter 2, but the possibility of using a simple ROC, which would be obtained from item 3, is degraded.

In an assessment of mammographic modalities, the issues of localization and classification are far less complex than for brain scans. This fact permits a far simpler response format and leads us to a different decision about pursuing cases beyond the detection item. The response format used in our assessment of Xeromammography compared to conventional and Lo-Dose film mammography is shown in Figure 16.

In this instance we encouraged and required the reader to go on to classification (in item 4), no matter what detection response was made (in item 3). A fuller discussion of our reasoning in this regard is given

RESPONSE FORMAT -- MAMMOGRAPHY

1. The <u>technical quality</u> of this image is:

    High

    Satisfactory

    Low

2. The <u>extent of obscuration</u> of possible localized abnormality by parenchymal pattern or diffuse disease is:

    Great

    Moderate

    Small

3. Given the fact that approximately 50% of the cases in our study have a localized abnormality, rate your confidence that the present image is of a case having a localized abnormality. <u>Localized abnormality</u> is:

    1. Definitely, or almost definitely, <u>present</u>

    2. Probably present

    3. Possibly present

    4. Probably absent

    5. Definitely, or almost definitely, <u>absent</u>

4. Assume for the moment that the case imaged here has a localized abnormality, even if not apparent in the image. Given the fact that approximately 80% of the localized abnormalities in our study are malignant, rate your confidence that the present image is of a case with malignant localized abnormality. The <u>localized abnormality present</u> is:

    1. Definitely, or almost definitely, <u>malignant</u>

    2. Probably malignant

    3. Possibly malignant

    4. Probably benign

    5. Definitely, or almost definitely, <u>benign</u>

5. Comments :

Figure 16. Response form for mammography assessment.

in the context of our technical report of the study in Chapter 11 (Section 11.2). The net result was that we could confidently analyze the two-alternative classification response in terms of a simple ROC, as well as plot the joint ROC, which combines detection and classification. Were we to do the CT/RN study again, we would ask the readers to take every case on to the two-alternative classification response (item 3 in Figure 4), but not to the more complex localization and classification items (items 2 and 4).

7.2.5 Response Medium

The reader should no doubt be given a guide to follow whenever sequential responses of different types at different levels are requested. The guide could be, as in the preceding figures, a single-page form for each case, which one fills in as one proceeds through the case. If image-reading tests are conducted often, data entry directly into a computer may be warranted. In studies conducted at BBN, the test reader calls out the responses as they are recorded on the paper-and-pencil form, and the test administrator simultaneously keys them into a computer via a terminal with a full keyboard and an alphanumeric CRT display. The display serves to cue the successive types of response for the test administrator and to supply an immediate visual confirmation of the key presses; the reader's paper form is available for an additional check if later desired.

7.3 BACKGROUND INFORMATION GIVEN READERS ON EACH CASE

7.3.1 General Considerations

Should background information (such as history, presenting signs and symptoms, and results of other diagnostic tests) be presented along with each image viewed in a reading test? Our impression is that no standard practice has evolved to date. Indeed, we have heard of a group of readers at a famous university hospital, X, who suffered embarrassment at performing far less accurately with a particular imaging technique than readers in an earlier published study at another famous university hospital, Y, until the readers at X, who based judgments exclusively on images in their study, learned that the test readers at Y used all available background information and consulted with the referring physician on each case.

One might conduct the test both ways, that is, with and without background information. Readings without other information may be viewed as the purest means of assessing the information supplied by the images themselves, unaffected by differences among readers in using clinical information. It seems clear to us, however, that a full determination of the efficacy of a technique must come from a representative, realistic diagnostic context, which includes all available background information.

Indeed, from the standpoint of efficacy, the question of whether to present background information along with the image is inappropriate. In a study of efficacy one condition will almost surely present background information along with each image. However, if an absolute measure for a single imaging system is desired, then another condition will present not the image alone but the background information alone (to a clinician). A comparison of a background-information-alone condition with a background-information-plus-image condition provides an absolute evaluation of the efficacy of the imaging technique. The same comparison, we may note, provides a better estimate of the incremental accuracy of diagnosis afforded by an imaging system than does simply presenting the image alone.

We imagine that some investigators will aspire to a rather full efficacy analysis of single systems; they will make the comparison just described. Other investigators, no doubt, will settle for an accuracy analysis; they will desire to compare image-reading accuracy with and without background information. The next section discusses the controls appropriate to each kind of study. In the following sections on the implications for case selection of presenting background information, and on the format of the information presented, there is no need to distinguish between the two kinds of study.

We should point out that the following discussion of control conditions is pertinent when absolute measures for individual systems are sought. When relative or comparative measures of the performances of two or more systems are adequate, one may possibly dispense with the background-information-alone condition in an efficacy analysis and with one or the other of the two conditions mentioned in connection with an accuracy analysis. (It is conceivable that system rankings could change between image-plus-background and image-only studies: Information in the images of the system performing better in the image-only study may be highly correlated with background information, and hence redundant, whereas information in the other system's images may be little correlated with background information, and hence complementary.)

7.3.2 Controls

Consider first some aspects of experimental controls for a comparison of images with and without background information and then for the simpler comparison of background information without and with images.

One likely sounding procedure for assessing diagnostic accuracy with and without background information is to present the image first without information, then to supply the information and ask the readers to look again, and then to ask the readers if they wish to modify their first judgment. This procedure can probably be discarded upon further thought on the grounds that the control condition for the impact of the information is inadequate. Given that accuracy may increase with viewing time, a more adequate control condition would be two looks without information, rather than one. However, asking a reader to take a second look at an image just viewed for what was considered an adequate time, without the provision of additional information, no doubt leaves this reader with less motivation for a close second look than the reader who has been given new information prior to the second look.

Perhaps a better procedure is to separate the two viewings of a given case, and not to identify the second with the first, so that the reader is not aware of his or her first judgment while making the second. Using this procedure, one might present the readers a second viewing of half of the cases with information and half of the cases without—in a block or blocks after the first viewings are complete (in a different random order). If there is no practice or learning effect from the first to second reading without information, then second readings with information can reasonably be compared to first readings of the same cases without information, within each reader. A comparison within each reader—deriving a baseline for each reader from that reader's own performance—is, of course, especially desirable when the number of readers is small. Note that the second readings without information of cases not identified as such provide an estimate of intrareader variability or reliability, which is another estimate that might well be obtained in every study.

If a generalized practice or learning effect is of concern during the reader's participation in the test, second views might be randomly interspersed with first views. In either case, blocked or interspersed, we believe that the readers should be informed about the procedure followed. The necessity of rapport with the readers should not be undermined by the desire to obtain a second reading that is not identified as such for the reader.

We now consider presenting background information without and with images; the simple procedure of presenting both conditions successively on each trial is not subject to as obvious a criticism as in the procedure just described. Still, one may wish to avoid asking a reader time after time to consider a change of mind, and so decide to separate the two judgments about a given case. Whether one can use the separate judgments in this study to make an estimate of the intrareader variability in making diagnoses without the imagery depends, no doubt, on how memorable the case backgrounds are. Of course, one might choose to use different types of readers in the two conditions: clinicians in the background-information-only condition and radiologists (or radiologists interacting with clinicians) in the background-plus-image condition.

7.3.3 Interaction with Case Selection

In some instances, the presentation of both background information and images may tend to give quite accurate diagnoses. In these instances one might have to use a substantial proportion of unusually difficult cases in order to avoid extreme response proportions, such as high true-positive and low false-positive proportions. Measures of accuracy are based on such response proportions, which are difficult to measure reliably as they approach an extreme.

Cases may be selected according to some scheme that precludes the possibility of supplying background information, at least as far as detection is concerned, because the information is perfectly predictive of the existence of abnormality. For example, in our study of intracranial disease, we selected all positive (abnormal) cases from a group of patients with signs and symptoms of such disease, given a desire for early histological confirmation of positive cases, and all negative cases from a group of patients with a primary tumor not in the central nervous system and asymptomatic for intracranial disease of the central nervous system, given a desire for the best early confirmation of negatives. In such circumstances, supplying background information to the reader along with each image would make viewing the image unnecessary. This problem can arise when adequate follow-up on an adequately large first-order sample is not available.

We see, then, that cases for the reading test should be selected so that background information is approximately as predictive in the test as in practice. Arriving at the estimate of predictability in practice may be a matter of expert opinion rather than case data. The degree of predictability afforded by background information in the test should presumably be made known to all test readers; differences in self-instruction should be avoided here, since the predictability affects readers' accuracy and not merely their response bias. The fact of an effect on accuracy is perhaps clearer if one views supplying highly predictive background information as tantamount to giving the reader an adviser possessed of greater accuracy than the reader, to coach the reader on each image viewed. The reader's accuracy will then depend both on how accurate the adviser is and on how much the reader chooses to rely on the adviser.

It should be emphasized that background information on each case can do more than facilitate perception or refine judgment. It can be so revealing in itself, so predictive of the existence of abnormality (inadvertently, because of the procedure used in case selection) that the reader can do best with a pure strategy of always believing the coach. The relevant work in the detection literature deals with the performance of a combination of detectors (e.g., Pollack and Madans, 1964; Green and Swets, 1966/1974, Chapter 9). If one detector or source of information is much more accurate than another, decisions may as well be based on the better source alone; combining the two sources contributes negligibly to the accuracy. Also germane to this issue is the work of Metz *et al.* (1975) on sequential combinations of two diagnostic tests.

7.3.4 Format

The items of background information that are available and helpful to readers in interpreting the image should be assembled in a convenient, consistent format. Again, to reduce the potential for bias favoring one or another system, assembling the information should probably be made a clerical task to be performed by a nonradiologist.

Readers may find a tabular form of presentation cumbersome. At least a "one-liner" describing the case might be used to give the presentation something of a familiar flavor.

We should add here that the issue of whether or not case background data are to be presented will often have significant impact on the response format (Section 7.2). If case-background and image-alone conditions are to be compared, the problem of designing a common format that is adequate for both conditions arises—just as it does in comparing modalities.

7.4 TIMING OF TRIALS AND SESSIONS

The length of a viewing session, the spacing of sessions, and the number of sessions per day should be chosen to maintain as high a yield of readings as is compatible with alertness or perhaps with comfort.

For each case we would fix the time allowed for viewing-plus-reporting and leave the image or background information present throughout. Setting that time at the smallest value that makes sense for almost all of the cases is probably adequate. Readers might be asked to indicate any cases they believe to require more time and might be invited to return to those cases for unlimited viewing later.

We have found that 7 minutes is appropriate for a case imaged by CT, read first with either contrast enhancement or noncontrast, and then with views of both kinds interchangeably. On the order of half that time might be appropriate for one reading of RN scans, but our RN films were of several different types, so we used the limit of 7 minutes for them to permit the adjustments that were required. Some other kinds of imagery (e.g., mammograms and electron radiograms) might be appropriately viewed for 1 or 2 minutes.

Our readers read throughout four sessions of approximately 1 hour each per day. On the first and last day, another 2 hours was spent in orientation and interview.

7.5 VIEWING ENVIRONMENT

It may be important in an efficacy study to maintain an environment and schedule highly similar to those in the field setting to which the results will be generalized. If the test is intended to reflect the potential of the system, however, either in terms of efficacy or accuracy, the reader's schedule should be less hectic than usual on the test day, and the environment of the test should be much freer of distractions than is customary for reading images. Each reader should have a separate room with controlled light, temperature, and noise, and with furnishings designed for efficient and convenient viewing and reporting.

We are not suggesting as the best environment, however, one so impoverished and constant that the reader is lulled into insensitivity. The presence of a test administrator helps in this regard.

7.6 ROLE OF TEST ADMINISTRATOR

The test administrator primarily enforces control of the test so that it proceeds in the way that the investigator assumes it does. Additionally, the administrator can make the test more efficient and more convenient for the reader.

The administrator presents the images in the predetermined order for the predetermined length of time. The administrator may also record responses, either alone or redundantly. The administrator should be a good listener and should not answer questions other than those necessary to clarify test procedure.

A double-blind test is to be preferred; that is, the administrator should not know what the correct responses are to any case as it is presented. Otherwise, there is always the chance that the administrator will inadvertently and subtly convey information to the reader about which responses are correct.

7.7 READER ORIENTATION

General orientation of the reader should be accomplished in conversation. Instructions about the reading-test procedure should, we believe, be reviewed orally, but might well also be presented in writing. A practice series of a half dozen or so cases is useful to familiarize the reader with the general protocol.

Most studies will probably not require training the test readers—for the purpose, say, of reducing variation among them. The exceptions are studies conducted to evaluate a newly proposed set of cues, such as tissue–image correlates in mammography, or to evaluate in a preliminary way a radically new kind of imaging or image display.

The main procedural items for instruction are those concerned with the response format and the probabilistic aspects of stimulus presentation. Conveying the proper response format to use is generally straightforward once it has been settled, and the few practice cases usually give readers the required facility with it. Adequate description of relevant probabilities concerning the stimuli may be more intricate.

Although the ROC technique is intended to yield a curve representing the various possible decision criteria, or response biases, that can accompany a given level of discrimination, the reader should at least be informed of the a priori probabilities of abnormal and normal cases. The reader's impression of those probabilities will influence the location of the empirical data points on his or her detection ROC curve, and the investigator would like to have some control over the location of those points. Points near the negative diagonal of the ROC space (roughly equal errors of the two types) give more reliable indications of accuracy than points in the lower left-hand corner (low false-positive and high false-negative proportions), but the latter should also be obtained if they better reflect field conditions. Also, the response data and the resulting

ROC may be distorted if the reader's estimates of the prior probabilities change greatly during the course of the reading test; advance information on these probabilities largely precludes this effect.

Readers are not told that there are exactly m abnormal cases and n normal cases, for if they were they might shy away from one or the other response if it seems that m or n has been reached or is about to be reached well before the end of a series. They may, in other words, exhibit an "end effect." A better practice is to give the reader a predisposition to proceed as if the number, say, of abnormal cases in any group to be presented, is a random variable drawn according to some probability and therefore varying about some average number, $\bar{m}$. For example, a sampling probability of 0.5 could easily lead to a split as wide as 60–40 or 70–30 in a small group of cases, and the reader should be so instructed. If the ratio m/n varies from one session to the next, over several sessions and perhaps over days, the end effect mentioned previously should be avoided.

Informing the reader about the a priori probabilities of the different classes of disease, in a similar manner, is also desirable. Our CT/RN test readers, for example, were told that although our cases were imaged as suspect for tumor, approximately 10–20% of the relevant abnormalities were nontumors (nonneoplasms).

Some care must be taken in instructions about sequential probabilities—specifically, about the lack of any sequential dependency from one case to the next. The reader should be informed that the probability of an abnormal case, and also the probability of a case in any disease category, are the same from one trial to another; the trials are independent of one another. A specific caution to avoid the "gambler's fallacy"—betting on red because black has come up on the last several turns—may be helpful.

It is clear by now that a few comments during the reader's general orientation, concerning the reason for all these little precautions, will be desirable. The precautions are intended simply to help free the reader's mind of extraneous factors that might otherwise affect his judgment *on a given trial*. Nonsensory factors that affect judgment *over a group of trials*—a priori probabilities and the values or costs of decision outcomes—are considered in modern perceptual theory to be fundamental rather than extraneous. The purpose of the ROC analysis is to separate sensory effects from such cognitive and motivational effects and to provide independent measures of sensory and nonsensory effects.

Although the professional reader is thus informed that the reading session will be governed by procedures designed for psychological experiments, there is no need to leave the reader feeling like a subject in an experiment. In general, we believe that the reader can be fully informed about all aspects of test procedure and can come to see the reasons for them, so that the position of professional reviewer and adviser can be maintained.

For example, the reader should be informed if repetitive judgments of the same cases are part of the test design. Such measurement is another way of evaluating the reader, as well as the imaging system, and the reader should know the potential of the test for measuring reader performance apart from system performance. Clearly, a guarantee that measures of individual performances will be held in confidence is part of the general orientation.

7.8 FEEDBACK TO AND FROM READERS

Following the test sessions, the readers can be interviewed along two main lines. First, their opinions may be solicited concerning the adequacy of the test questions and procedures (running the gamut from case selection to displays to response format to data analysis) and specific suggestions for improvement may be solicited. A questionnaire used in our study of CT and RN scans is reproduced in Appendix C.

Second, the investigator might use the opportunity to seek information to improve understanding of the reader's diagnostic technique and criteria. What logic of analyzing the image is employed? What kinds of scanning patterns are followed? What, in detail, are the image features that are assessed? How are they weighted?

Feedback to the readers is undertaken to satisfy their interests and to sustain their motivation. Readers have participated in the study because of their personal interests in the subject matter of the test, their beliefs in the study's social value, and their hopes for its success, and therefore they want to receive information about the progress and results of the study. Such information may also help to sustain their intrinsic motivation through a test that is long, necessarily repetitive, and demanding of attention to detail. To the extent consistent with test design, readers can be informed about their individual performance as well as about overall study results as the study proceeds. A complete briefing as soon as possible after the tests is also desirable.

7.9 SUMMARY

The presentation of test cases involves considerations of order, identification of counterparts or repetitions, timing, and possibly, image handling. The suggested response format obtains detection responses by means of a rating scale, and localization and classification responses when appropriate. A rating scale for two alternatives of localization or two of classification may be useful. Whether it is advisable or not to supply background information on each case will depend on the situation. Several considerations exist in defining control conditions in the comparison of performance with and without background information, or with and without images. More straightforward are procedures relating to timing of sessions, viewing environment, role of test administrator, reader orientation, and feedback to and from readers.

CHAPTER *8*

Drawing the Original Case Sample

What we term the "original case sample" is drawn primarily to serve as the pool of cases from which the reading-test sample is selected. For one reason or another, as will be indicated, not all—or even most—cases caught in the first net are appropriate to or adequate for further examination in a reading test. Three additional functions of the original sample are listed in the first section of this chapter. We then consider the types of data to be collected on each case, the need for a representative sample, potential biases in case selection, and the size of the original sample.

8.1 FUNCTIONS OF THE ORIGINAL CASE SAMPLE

Two functions of the original case sample are to help ensure in specific ways the meaningfulness of the accuracy indices derived from a reading test. A third is to support an assessment of system efficacy.

First, the original case sample can supply a profile of the relevant patient population to ensure that all important categories of presenting history, disease, or outcome (depending on the study requirements) are adequately represented in the reading-test sample. The need to ensure the representativeness of the reading-test sample is implicit in the fact that the test will use a relatively small number of cases, as discussed in Chapter 9. A small sample generated purely by random selection will almost certainly not be representative. We return to this subject in Section 8.3.

Second, the original case sample can supply estimates of the relationships between presenting symptoms and signs, on the one hand, and disease or other outcome categories, on the other. A finding of relatively strong relationships may justify (*a*) selecting a reading-test sample to represent those categories adequately, and (*b*) conducting a separate analysis of performance for each of those categories. One will appreciate that the demonstration of relationships between image-system performance and particular categories of disease or outcome remains academic, unless those categories of disease better handled by one imaging system than another can be identified with some accuracy on the basis of initial signs and symptoms.

Third, the original case sample can supply specific information about the course of diagnosis, treatment, and disease in stages subsequent to diagnosis by the system under study. Such information may be needed to fill in otherwise unfilled branches of the decision flow diagrams that guide an efficacy assessment, as discussed in Chapters 5 and 6.

8.2   TYPES OF DATA COLLECTED ON EACH CASE

The types of data to be obtained on each case depend on specifics of the decision flow diagrams and on data available prior to taking the case sample. The data required depend also on the general approach taken. McNeil and Adelstein (1976) and McNeil, Collins, and Adelstein (1977) have described an approach through modeling that reduces the amount of new data collection by a process of extrapolating from existing data.

In addition to images, types of data to consider include a history, clinical work-up, and results of other diagnostic tests; further stages of diagnosis; autopsy and death certification; treatment; and follow-up studies. Some of these types of data may be presented to test readers as case background; others are used to establish the "truth" about patients' conditions for use in scoring the readers' diagnostic judgments.

8.2.1 Images

Images should be taken of each case by each of the modalities under study. If taking multiple images is medically inappropriate, matched groups of patients may be assembled. Within-patient comparisons, of course, are to be preferred from the standpoints of reading-test efficiency and informativeness as discussed in Chapter 3.

8.2.2 History, Clinical Work-up, and Other Test Results

A history, clinical work-up, results of any prior diagnostic tests, and reasons for requesting the imagery under consideration are required for certain accuracy analyses and for almost any form of efficacy analysis. If the investigator is interested in the possibility of accuracy analyses focused on particular classes of pathology or outcome, or on particular classes of presenting signs and symptoms, all of the usual data available before obtaining the imagery are needed to establish the relationships that justify those focused analyses. A thorough efficacy analysis requires presenting appropriate clinical background to the test reader, so that the test represents a realistic context (see Section 7.3). Included in the clinical background are presenting signs and symptoms, prior history of disease, results of previous diagnostic tests, and any condition that could affect the appearance and interpretation of the image, including prior surgical treatment and past and current medication.

8.2.3 Further Stages of Diagnosis and Autopsy and Death Certification

Evidence that further tests (e.g., arteriograms, pneumoencephalo-grams, biopsies) were ordered could itself constitute data for an efficacy analysis if, for example, the cost of diagnosis were one criterion of interest. Evidence from further tests as well as data from autopsy and death certification may also play roles, varying from one situation to another, in establishing the true condition of positive cases used in the reading test.

8.2.4 Treatment

If the cost of treatment is a criterion of interest, evidence that particular treatments are given can constitute relevant data. If certain aspects of medical efficacy are criteria in the study, the results of the treatment may also be needed.

8.2.5 Follow-up

An evaluation study may permit following the patients for years to determine outcomes. If conclusions are desired sooner, estimates of long-term outcome will have to be made, perhaps based on expert opinion or prior epidemiological studies. Follow-up data are required when the types and values of outcomes are needed for efficacy studies, though existing data may suffice. Follow-up data are also often needed to establish the true condition of negative cases used in the reading test.

8.2.6 Truth Data

The collection of truth data, already mentioned in Sections 8.2.3 and 8.2.5, deserves special discussion here. The data that will serve as truth for scoring the diagnoses issued in the reading test have to be carefully considered and well specified at an early stage in planning the collection of the original case sample. Credibility is the primary consideration, but it cannot be the only consideration. The cost of obtaining truth (such as by histology) and the time required (such as by follow-up) must fit within the cost and time constraints of the study.

The possibilities of introducing a bias in favor of one modality and of introducing certain dependencies among the modalities are fundamental problems, as discussed in Section 8.4. Maximizing the credibility of truth data may also conflict with attempts to obtain a representative sample (see Sections 8.5 and 9.4 and Appendix B). Rather drastic restructuring of study design and goals may be necessary in order to resolve such conflicts, and therefore they should be detected early in the planning process.

8.3   SELECTING A REPRESENTATIVE CASE SAMPLE

As Ransohoff and Feinstein (1978) nicely illustrate, many studies of diagnostic systems are conducted on case samples grossly different in spectrum from any meaningful population to which one might reasonably want to generalize the study results. We presume in this discussion that the investigator has carefully defined a meaningful population, what we call the presenting population, and now seeks to draw an original case sample (and, eventually, a reading-test sample) that is representative of that population.

Distortion in composition of the original case sample when compared to the presenting population can occur at two points: (a) when initial selections are made of those patients who will be asked to participate in the study and (b) when patients, with the advice of their physicians, decide whether or not to participate.

Unless care is taken to prevent it, the initial selection process can be distorted in several subtle ways. The best procedure for avoiding distortion would seem to be to define a sampling interval in time (sufficiently long to cover any real or possible temporal variations in the constitution of the patient population) and to sample randomly from among the patients who arrive during that interval. For example, if seasonal variations in the constitution of the case population were suspected, it would be necessary to sample over an entire year. If 500 patients are expected to appear over that period, and if 250 study cases are needed, one could flip a coin as each patient is registered to determine which patients will be asked to participate. Of course, to adjust the random selection to other proportions (depending on the required sampling interval, expected patient density over that interval, size of sample required, and the expected rejection rate), suitable use can be made of a table of random numbers.

The most significant potential distortion of sampling, and one that cannot be avoided entirely, is the optional agreement of the patient or of the patient's physician. The patient must be an adequately informed volunteer. If the special processing required of study cases is seen by the patient as a significant inconvenience or if the patient's physician judges that it compromises good medical management for that patient, the patient will tend not to volunteer. The question, of course, is whether these selectivity factors will distort the composition of the original case sample, making it unrepresentative of the presenting population.

8.4 BIAS IN CASE DATA

Images for each of the systems under study should be taken independently of each other. The investigator must be on the lookout, and must be especially vigilant in large collaborative studies, for various dependencies that might bias the test in favor of one of the modalities and thus invalidate comparison of modalities.

For example, the radiation dose in mammography is based in part on an estimate of the amount of fatty tissue in the breast. If the amount of fat were estimated by inspecting the image from one system, and if that estimate were used to set parameters for the other system, independence of the imaging would be compromised. The problem, of course, is that good medical care may call for taking the images in such a sequentially dependent fashion. As will be evident in subsequent discussions, procedures for good study design may, as in this example, conflict with good medical practice so that dependencies of this sort may be unavoidable.

Truth data should in no way depend on the images taken; that is to say, the procedures for establishing truth should not be affected by the imaging modalities under study. If, for example, in a comparison of CT and RN scans, the truth used to score diagnoses were based on biopsies that tended to be obtained only if a lesion were revealed by CT, or based on autopsies guided by CT, comparison of the accuracy scores of the two systems would not be valid.

8.5 REQUIRED SIZE OF THE ORIGINAL CASE SAMPLE

The size of the original case sample will depend on the extent to which the processing and documentation of cases required in the reading test can be strictly controlled as patients selected for the original case sample move through the diagnostic–therapeutic process. If one could be sure that every selected patient would end up meeting the reading-test requirements, an original case sample might not even be required. The reading-test sample could be drawn directly from the presenting population. Of course, an original case sample might still be needed for other reasons as discussed in Section 8.1.

If one cannot guarantee that every patient in the original case sample will be processed and documented according to the needs of the reading test, then the original case sample will have to be bigger than the reading-test sample in proportion to the fraction of patients not meeting these requirements.

In practice, reading tests will often impose several strict requirements—for example, for truth data; and it will often be very difficult to meet these requirements except on a small fraction of the patients in the original case sample. Thus, in practice the original case sample will often have to be very large in relation to the reading-test sample. A large component of the cost of an evaluation study is at stake here. Care in setting realistic reading-test requirements, and even more important, care in controlling how patients in the original case sample are processed and documented, could bring very large reductions in the needed size of the original case sample.

The catch here, of course, is that the more one imposes restrictions on the way patients are handled as they go through the diagnostic–therapeutic process, the more likely the original case sample will be distorted in its composition by patient–doctor self-selection. On the other hand, the more one relies on using patients who just happen to come out of the process meeting the reading-test requirements, the more one risks other kinds of distortion in composition from the types of patients who just happened to take this path for various medical reasons.

There are no obvious solutions to the problems of determining the size of the original case sample. Probably the best rule is to try to impose as much control as possible in the way *all* patients are processed, short of the point where they tend to opt out of the study. In any event, one will need to be constantly vigilant about the possibility of assembling a sample with a composition unlike that of the presenting population. Rarely will that possibility be avoided entirely. Where distortion does occur despite the best efforts to avoid it, one should at least know the character of the distortion and be prepared to take it into account in assembling the reading-test sample.

8.6 SUMMARY

An original case sample is drawn from a specified presenting population (*a*) to provide a pool from which reading-test cases are selected, (*b*) to help ensure that the reading-test sample will be representative, and (*c*) to supply additional information about the population needed in an assessment of system efficacy. Types of data collected on each case in addition to images include previous history and events subsequent to the imaging—particularly "truth" data against which reading-test judgments are scored, and treatment and outcome data vital to efficacy analyses. Various potential biases in case selection, often very difficult to avoid, may yield types of cases in unrealistic proportions or samples that are too easy or too hard to diagnose. Other biases may favor one system over another. Attrition of 90% from original sample to reading-test sample is not unheard of, therefore proper resolution of these issues is important to a manageable study.

CHAPTER 9

Selection of Test Cases

This chapter focuses on the selection of a reading-test sample that will give adequate representation of the population of cases to which the reading-test results will be generalized. Having a sample large enough to ensure adequate statistical precision of the reading-test results is treated as a separate topic in Chapter 3.

Clearly, an important objective of a reading test is to generalize the results to a specifiable and meaningful population. We assume throughout this discussion that the objective is to generalize to the presenting population from which the original case sample was drawn.

Three main issues arise in assembling a representative reading-test sample: (*a*) the number of cases needed, (*b*) proportional representation of case types, and (*c*) the screening out of "inadequate" cases.

9.1 NUMBER OF CASES FOR ADEQUATE REPRESENTATION

There are two aspects to consider about numbers of cases needed to represent the population. One is how variable the cases of each particular

144

type are with respect to the basic data on which they are diagnosed and on which the diagnoses are scored. If, for example, cases of a particular type vary widely in pathophysiology, in the images they present, or in other data contributing to the diagnosis, one would want to have more than just a few such cases in the sample. One would want enough of those cases to be confident that the reading test was not conducted on a few peculiar variants of that type. The best approach when there is sufficient information on the population is to construct a stratified sample for each highly variable type of case, as discussed in the next section.

The second concern is with respect to the proportional composition of the sample. If one intends to generalize performance on the sample as a whole to the population, then (except for the proportion of normal and abnormal cases; see Section 9.2.3) the sample must be proportionally representative of the population. These two requirements interact; for example, if one type of case to be represented is relatively rare and highly variable, the size of the overall reading-test sample might have to be enlarged to be in proportion with the minimal number of cases needed to represent that rarity adequately.

9.2 PROPORTIONAL REPRESENTATION
OF CASE TYPES

If one can assume that the original case sample validly represents the population, the safest approach to take in assembling an adequately representative reading-test sample is to pick cases from the original case sample in simple random fashion. The only requirement is that the sample be made large enough for all relevant types of cases to have a high probability of getting into it in valid proportion and with whatever minimal frequency is considered necessary. Occasionally, where the population contains just a few relevant and evenly apportioned types, simple random sampling will be the mode of choice. But often the structure of the population is not so simple. Many types of cases have to be represented, some relatively rare and/or highly variable. Random sampling in those situations will usually be inappropriate, because the required size of a simple random sample that ensures adequate representation will exceed the practical limit on the number of cases that can be read in a reading test, often no more than 100 to 300 cases. Where this is the situation or where the original case sample is not representative, some form of stratified sampling is required.

In stratified sampling, one has to identify each relevant type of case and determine its relative frequency in the population. All of the cases of each type in the original case sample must then be identified, and members must be drawn at random from those sets in sufficient numbers to permit assembly of a reading-test sample containing each relevant type of case in just the right proportion. Again, if any one of these types has to be represented in some minimal number because of its inherent variability, the rest of the sample will have to be apportioned to suit.

The problem with stratified sampling is that the researcher has to specify all relevant types of cases in the population—not always an easy task. As to estimating their relative frequency, if one can assume that the original case sample is representative, the proportions of each type of case can be based on its proportions. Otherwise, the true proportions must be sought from what data are available on the presenting population or from the best available epidemiological data.

9.2.1   Representation of Disease Categories

Often the only required typing of cases will be with respect to their disease category. But relevant disease categories can often be numerous. For example, with patients suspect for brain tumor, one might take into account not only lesion type but also size and locus. Which categories to identify for stratification and which to leave to chance sorting will often be difficult to determine. The choice will depend in part on (*a*) the kinds of modalities being compared and the categories on which critical differences in performance are suspected, (*b*) the diagnostic–therapeutic situation, and (*c*) the type of evaluation—accuracy or efficacy.

9.2.2   Representation of Case-Background Categories

If an efficacy analysis is to be performed, adequate representation with respect to categories of case background will also be required. What categories should be stratified will depend on suspicions about critical differences in strength and weakness among the modalities that would interact with particular ways of partitioning the cases.

9.2.3   Relative Numbers of Normal and Abnormal Cases

Consideration should be given to three factors in determining the relative numbers of normal and abnormal cases in the reading test:

1. To obtain the accuracy (ROC) curve showing the different possible balances of underreading and overreading in the detection of abnormal

cases (Chapter 1), one wants to be able to measure false-positives as reliably as true-positives (or false-negatives)—a factor which, by itself, suggests using as many normal as abnormal cases.

2. Because a larger number of abnormal cases may be required to represent the various classes of disease and presenting symptoms adequately, it will be tempting to have fewer normal than abnormal cases in order to keep the total number of cases in bounds.

3. As it happens, readers are often conservative, yielding a low false-positive rate at the expense of the true-positive rate (or the false-negative or omission rate)—a higher probability of abnormal cases helps to coax the readers toward somewhat more liberal decision criteria and less extreme false-positive probabilities.

The cumulative effect of these three factors seems to us to argue for selecting more abnormal than normal cases (perhaps 2:1) to represent patient classes better; to reduce the degree of reliance on estimates of extreme response probabilities, which require very large numbers of observations; and, in connection with the last, to spread out ROC data points well enough to define the curve throughout the possible range (see Chapter 1). In some diagnostic contexts, a "positive yield" of about 65% is quite realistic.

9.3 SCREENING OUT INADEQUATE CASES

For various reasons, it will be necessary, or perhaps very tempting, to screen out of the reading-test sample certain kinds of "inadequate" cases. The general problem with any kind of screening however well justified it may seem is that it potentially distorts the composition of the sample and in turn jeopardizes generalization of the study results to a specifiable and medically meaningful population. We discuss here inadequacies in three broad areas, but other kinds of inadequacy will no doubt arise from time to time. The important message of this section is for the researcher to screen where necessary but to be wary about the potential effects of screening on generalization of the study results.

Situations will, of course, arise in which screening is necessary. In those situations the risk of distorting the sample must be minimized. One helpful step in that direction is for investigators to take themselves as much as possible out of the act. They might, for example, establish some very simple criteria for weeding out those types of peculiar cases they are worried about, which a paramedical assistant could apply in essentially clerical fashion. In that way the investigators make their selection rules explicit and they can insulate the selection process from any other unspecified biases, particularly those that might favor one system over another if they were doing the screening themselves.

9.3.1 Inadequately Processed or Documented Cases

One of the most common problems with cases is that they do not meet the reading-test requirement for particular kinds of processing and documentation. The reading test will usually require that patients be imaged in certain ways and that certain kinds of examinations and records be maintained on them. Where good medical practice and study requirements conflict, the study requirements will usually not be met. When that happens one has little choice but to drop the case. The problem is that such screening may bias the reading-test sample.

Of course, cases may not be processed in the required way for many reasons other than conflict with good medical practice, and if the researcher can anticipate those other causes he or she may well be able to increase the fraction of patients who meet study requirements. Patients may not be imaged or examined in the required way because it is expensive or inconvenient. Certain other aspects of processing or documentation may be neglected simply through laxity or oversight. Making it easier for medical personnel to meet the requirements (e.g., by providing extra resources for that purpose or simply by motivating them and monitoring their performance) may solve the problem. As we said before, rather large savings in study costs can be achieved by the right amount of attention at this stage.

Finally, we might point out that relaxing reading-test requirements may also be part of the solution. In some situations, it may be better to loosen requirements, for example, for truth data. It may be better to have somewhat questionable truth on a reasonably representative sample of cases than to have highly accurate truth on a grossly distorted sample of cases. For example, requiring histological confirmation of disease may leave the sample heavily biased toward certain restricted types of cases:

1. those cases in which prognosis justifies such definitive diagnosis;
2. those cases that can tolerate the surgery; and
3. those cases where locus of the lesion is well enough defined and sufficiently approachable to justify attempting a biopsy.

It might be better in such situations to set up other procedures for establishing truth, such as by special clinical testing batteries and close long-term clinical follow-up, which, although perhaps less accurate, reach a much more representative sample of cases.

9.3.2 Cases with Inadequate Images

Images might be deemed inadequate for the reading test for a variety of reasons. The patient may have moved or equipment parameters settings may have been inappropriate, for example. In such cases, most interpreters in the clinic might call for retakes. Investigators choosing to reject such images should be quite confident that they are doing no more than would be done in the clinic. They should, however, be sure that in weeding out such cases they are not inadvertently favoring one modality over another. For example, if patient movement is a problem with a particular modality because it takes too much time to build up the image, this kind of screening may make that modality look better in the reading-test sample than in practice.

The investigator may decide that the study's goal is to evaluate images of the highest quality obtainable on each system on the grounds that the technologies are improving rapidly and that an evaluation addressed to potential rather than present performance will have more generality. In this case the criteria applied to rejections are probably more difficult to define completely and fairly than when one is simply looking for images that would be unacceptable practically by consensus.

Some images will be of questionable quality because of limitations imposed by the equipment or the imaging procedure. For example, the system may have a restricted field of view with the result that some lesions are often only partially imaged. The system may add artificial structure to the image, such as lines on a computed tomogram caused by metal clips left in surgery. Whenever limitations of image quality such as these are unavoidable, the case should probably not be rejected; ordinarily, inherent limitations of the imaging systems should be taken fully into account in the evaluation. One should keep in mind that artifacts will be less obvious in some modalities than in others, so that rejection of images risks the introduction of a bias in the test sample favoring one system over another. One should also tabulate the rejection rate to see if it is occurring more frequently in one modality than another. The number of retakes may also be important to consider in an efficacy analysis.

9.3.3 Cases That Are Too Easy or Too Difficult

Situations may arise in which the original case sample contains a large proportion of cases that are either so difficult to read that none of the modalities under study could do better than chance, or so easy to read that none of them would make a mistake. To save resources of the reading test, it may be reasonable to exclude such cases from the reading-test sample. However, to generalize the reading-test results to the whole population, the assumed perfect or chance performance on those excluded cases would have to be factored into the performance scores of each modality.

In general, unless the too-easy or too-difficult segment of the population is rather large and clearly definable, such screening of the reading-test sample should be avoided. Certainly, such screening should never be done on a purely ad hoc case-by-case basis.

9.4 CHECKING REPRESENTATIVENESS OF THE READING-TEST SAMPLE

We have pointed to several potential sources of distortion in composition of the reading-test sample and have observed that it will often be difficult to avoid distortion altogether. The last line of defense will be to check the reading-test sample to see what happened. Whenever one suspects that the sample may not be representative, and certainly where study resources permit, an analysis of representativeness should be conducted. If distortion is found, one might be able to go back and correct the sample. If the sample cannot be corrected, one can at least let findings of the analysis temper interpretation of the reading-test results.

To conduct a check on representativeness, one has to identify all the relevant ways of partitioning the sample, determine the proportion of cases in the population that belong in those partitions, and check to see if the reading-test sample has those same proportions. An illustrative analysis of this sort conducted in our study of CT and RN brain scanning is given in Appendix B.

9.5 SUMMARY

Reading-test cases must adequately represent the population to which the results are to be generalized. Types of cases that are highly variable must be sampled in large enough numbers. Types of cases should be represented proportionally—with respect to the alternative states they may assume and possibly with respect to their backgrounds—and this need may require stratified sampling. Various considerations apply to the relative numbers of "signal" and "noise" cases to be used. Temptations abound to screen out cases that might be regarded as inadequate for one reason or another; such screening will often introduce biases and should be handled with care. A check on the representativeness of the reading-test sample that is provisionally or finally selected, in relation to the original case sample, is in order.

CHAPTER 10

Selection of Test Readers

Two main issues arise in selecting readers: (*a*) the number of readers needed and (*b*) the type of reader to be selected.

10.1 NUMBER OF READERS FOR ADEQUATE REPRESENTATION

We treat here the issue of how many readers are needed for adequate representation of the reader population. The issue of how many readers are needed to ensure adequate precision of the reading-test results was discussed in Chapter 3.

If the readers in the population were identical in all respects, then from the present point of view one reader would suffice. If the population is reasonably homogeneous, as will be the case for certain populations, only a few readers will be needed. If the results of the study must be generalizable to a broad heterogeneous population of readers, then clearly a large number of readers will be required.

Certain circumstances might permit running a reading test on a large number of readers. Occasionally, one can do testing at a professional meeting where perhaps several hundred readers can be tested. Whether the sample of readers so obtained is representative of the population of interest is one problem. Also, the number of cases that can be read will be severely restricted, and control of the reading procedures will be very limited. Occasionally, one might have the opportunity to run tests on fairly large groups of readers in training. In this situation, one might be able to run an extensive and well-controlled test, but generalization of the results would be of rather limited interest.

Generally the aim of a study will be to run an extensive and well-controlled reading test on trained, practicing readers. They will usually have to take time from their practice to be tested for at least several hours under controlled conditions. Limited time and resources of the study will often place severe restrictions on the number of readers that can be run under such circumstances. Often that number will be far below what would be required for adequate representation of a broad population of all practicing readers in all settings.

Some practical compromises between the aims of the overall study and the design of the reading test may be required. It may be necessary to run the test on representatives of some meaningful subpopulation, such as readers in a midrange of experience and training.

In some situations, the aim of the evaluation may be to measure performance of the modalities under the best of circumstances. Then one would select the very best readers. The problem of numbers may then diminish, because the subpopulation thus selected often tends to be highly homogeneous.

10.2 TYPE OF READER

The preceding discussion approaches the question of numbers as if readers varied only in *degree* of training or experience. Unfortunately for the test designer, readers can differ in other significant ways, including having different *kinds* of training and having different preferences and experience with the modalities under study.

In the most straightforward instances, all the readers represent a single, specifiable discipline. An example might be a study comparing conventional and Lo-Dose mammographic films, where it can be assumed that practicing mammographers are generally as familiar with one technique as with the other. A complication would arise if, say, Xeromammography were added to the study in this example. Mammographers might have quite different degrees of exposure to that range of modalities. They might have different preferences among these modalities and perhaps different public or private positions as to the individual accuracy and efficacy of each modality.

Perhaps the most complex situation is one in which two modalities to be compared are ordinarily interpreted by two sets of readers with distinctively different training, or in which a new modality is being interpreted by people from a variety of backgrounds. Consider as an example the comparison of CT and RN brain scans. CT may be largely in the province of neuroradiologists, whereas the RN scans may usually be read by practitioners of nuclear medicine. A further complication in this instance is that the CT scans are being read by neurologists, neurosurgeons, and others as well. In such an instance, fairness to each modality requires employing readers from different populations, at least from the two main populations corresponding to the two modalities.

In some situations it will be appropriate to have the same reader for each modality or modality variant under study, as long as one can be sure that the readers have an appropriately representative ability to read in each modality and are definably unbiased. A situation that would probably be appropriate is one in which the effect of manipulating a parameter of a modality is under study, particularly in which the effect of the parameter on the appearance of the imagery is subtle enough that the readers are unable to tell which variant they are getting on any given trial. As explained in Chapter 3, using the same readers has the advantage of increasing precision in the study results. Using the same readers has the disadvantage, however, that each reader has many more readings to do and may not have the time or motivation to do so many. There is also a limit on how many times a reader can be sure to make each rereading of a given case independent of those that came before.

The level of expertise sought in test readers depends on the goals of the study. If the evaluation is intended to reflect as well as is currently possible the full potential of any modality under study—rather than the various accuracies that are likely to be obtained in various field settings—one should secure the most competent readers available. On the other hand, one may want to generalize to a range of field settings. In any event, recommendations from known leaders in a field should provide the sample desired. If a broadly representative sample is desired, the possibility of distortion of the sample—perhaps because of differences in motivation or ability among individuals who agree to participate and those who do not—should be considered.

10.3 SUMMARY

Test readers must adequately represent whatever population is deemed to be of interest. The population might be defined, for example, in relation to the breadth of diagnostic settings in actual practice or in relation to the capability of the reader. Complexities in representing types of readers arise when systems being compared typically involve readers with different training.

PART *III*

A Methodological Case Study

A comparative study of three forms of mammography used in the diagnosis of breast cancer has helped us to refine, and serves to illustrate, several aspects of evaluation method. Chapter 11 is a report of this study. Included are the selection of test cases and observers, test procedure, and accuracy analysis. Given only in connection with this study are illustrative treatments of newly developed statistical techniques. These illustrations, specifically, show how various components of sampling variance affect index reliability, and how various correlations among observers' judgments interact with sample size to determine the reliability of an obtained difference in accuracy. This study also provides concrete examples of how one can begin to assess the practical significance of any difference in accuracy that might be obtained, and how one might determine the desired size of a full study on the basis of a pilot study.

CHAPTER 11

Illustrative Evaluation
of Imaging Systems

The image-reading study reported in this chapter was conducted to illustrate and refine the general methodology presented in this volume, as was the CT–RN brain scan study previously reported (Swets *et al.*, 1979). And, indeed, both studies serve to illustrate and enlighten us about several aspects of method. Included are the selection of cases for a reading test (Chapter 9), selection of test readers (Chapter 10), reading-test procedure (Chapter 7), and accuracy analysis (Chapter 1). But the present study goes beyond the CT–RN study in considering more fully the statistical aspects of reading-test design (Chapter 3), statistical analysis of accuracy data (Chapter 4), and practical interpretation of accuracy data (Chapter 2).

This study emphasizes the relationship between the numbers of cases and readers in a test and the power of the test to detect differences in accuracy between two modalities. Specifically, the focus is on the respective contributions to the overall reliability of accuracy indices made by its main components: that is, the variabilities across cases, across readers, and within individual readers. Other major considerations are the correlations among cases and among readers across modalities, among readers within a modality, and within readers over time. These correlations determine how much more reliable a given observed difference in accuracy is made by increasing the number of cases and/or readers and of using the same versus different cases and/or readers in both modalities.

This study used cases imaged by three mammographic modalities: industrial film radiography, Lo-Dose film radiography, and Xeroradiography. Collection of the images and other case materials was sponsored by the National Cancer Institute (NCI) in a 3-year collaborative study at three institutions: M. D. Anderson Hospital, Guttman Institute, and Duke University Hospital. NCI's interest was in the potential for decreased dosage or increased accuracy of the newer techniques.

Again, as with the CT–RN study, NCI's second objective for our mammography study was to provide a central, retrospective, objective evaluation of the data of the collaborative study as concerns diagnostic accuracy. However, the collaborative study was centered on variables other than accuracy, and we were not able to acquire enough confirmed cases from it to permit evaluating accuracy in a representative and reliable way. To emphasize, therefore, that we do not present our reading-test data as relevant to a choice among the three modalities, we preserve their anonymity in relation to each other by the designations X, Y, and Z. Also, because of the limited number of adequate cases, we do not regard the general level of performance of the three modalities in our test as representing the state of the art in mammography. On the other hand, the limitations of the clinical materials do not seriously impair our ability to make an informative methodological investigation of statistical aspects of study design and data analysis, and to give a demonstration of the procedures used in statistical analysis of accuracy data.

The first sections are concerned with case selection, response format, experimental design, test procedures, and reader ratings of image quality. Next, we consider the conventional ROCs and associated accuracies for detection alone and for classification alone (benign versus malignant), and the joint ROCs and related accuracies for detection-plus-classification. To illustrate the recommended statistical procedure, we compute the standard errors and confidence intervals of the detection accuracies and the statistical significance of observed differences between modalities.

The next section provides an examination of correlations in the readings—specifically, within single readers reading the same cases on two occasions, across readers within a single modality, across modalities with the same ("matched") readers in each, across modalities with different ("unmatched") readers in each—and a discussion of the various meanings of those correlations. The next section shows how certain variance and correlation estimates may be obtained that are appropriate to some issues of study design—specifically, the numbers and the matching of cases and readers. The concluding section gives a general discussion, with illustrations from the mammography results, of (*a*) how an investigator might interpret an observed difference between modalities of any given size, and (*b*) use of pilot-study data to design a final study that is calculated to achieve statistical significance of a difference of some selected size.

11.1 CASE SELECTION

For a variety of reasons we shall not detail here, we selected cases for our study that were assembled at just one of the three institutions participating in the collaborative study, namely, the M. D. Anderson Hospital (MDAH) of the University of Texas Medical Center. The images contributing to the analyses reported here were taken during the period from June 1975 to September 1976.

The major characteristics of the cases, images, and other case materials were determined by MDAH for the purposes of the collaborative study, a study with goals distinctly different from ours, and, indeed, designed well in advance of our study. Specifically, the focus of the collaborative study was on expert judgment about various aspects of image quality without regard to diagnostic accuracy. To serve the goals of our study, we had to impose certain restrictions on the cases we selected from the MDAH sample, which served to eliminate a large number of MDAH cases. These restrictions mainly have to do with the availability of case data (history and pathology reports) for establishing a reasonably credible diagnosis for each case.

We discuss here the image specifications, other case data, our selection procedures, and the composition of our sample.

11.1.1 Image Specifications

The test images were craniocaudad views taken with industrial film (AA), Lo-Dose I (vacuum pack) film (LD), and Xerography (XR), or with just two of those modalities. Specifics of technique were AA: 4.5 sec, 100 mA, 25–27 peak kilovoltage (kVp), small (1 mm) focal spot; LD: 2.5 sec, 100 mA, 27 kVp, small (1 mm) focal spot; XR: 2.5 sec, 250 mA, 38 kVp, large (2 mm) focal spot. All views were done on a Picker generator with a General Electric tungsten target tube with 2.5 mm of aluminum added filtration. A long, flared-back cone was used for distance and collimation along with balloon compression.

For the present study, all images were of a standard 8 × 10-inch size. Patient identification data were masked by opaque removable stickers to preclude reader identification of the case on repeated presentations.

11.1.2 Case Data

The data on individual cases came principally from a standard patient questionnaire administered at each examination and from variously formatted abstracts of diagnostic reports following breast biopsy.

Included on the questionnaire were items about symptoms (lumps, pain or discomfort, and nipple discharge), about whether the patient practiced monthly self-examination, and about occurrences of prior breast surgery.

The diagnoses following biopsy were mostly in the form of one-line or one-phrase descriptions. As a general rule, the locus of the biopsy was not communicated.

11.1.3 Criteria for Case Selection

The primary determinants for selection of our cases from the MDAH sample were (a) that images have been taken in at least two of the modalities, and that those images be available for use in our reading tests; and (b) that there be sufficient data on each case for establishing a reasonably credible diagnosis, against which to score reader performance.

For negative cases, we required that there be available for our inspection two standard questionnaires: one taken at time of imaging and the other taken at a follow-up examination no sooner than 3 months later. To be an acceptable negative case: (a) both histories had to show that the patient practiced monthly self-examinations and had reported no lumps or other symptoms of breast disease and (b) the patient had to be absent from all lists we received from MDAH of biopsies performed on patients in the collaborative study.

For positive cases we sought those with localized abnormalities, malignant or benign. To approximate the truth on each case, we required access to a diagnostic report based on a biopsy taken after imaging, of breast tissue from the imaged breast. We accepted as sufficient evidence of a malignant localized abnormality all cases with one or another of the following diagnoses: carcinoma, invasive cancer, intraductal cancer, or intraductal carcinoma. We accepted as having a benign localized abnormality (*a*) all cases with a diagnosis of benign tumor, and (*b*) all cases with a diagnosis of fibrocystic disease, provided that the patient reported a lump in the breast at time of imaging.

We set no minimum time after imaging for follow-up confirmation of negatives, nor any maximum time after imaging for biopsy confirmation of positives. This decision was purely pragmatic. We judged it desirable in the interests of our methodological demonstrations to sacrifice some validity of the truth data for a larger sample size in an attempt thereby to obtain more stable performance measures.

11.1.4 Sample Composition

All cases in the MDAH sample were over 40 years of age and at high risk for breast cancer. They were principally referrals with symptoms, or single-breast patients receiving follow-up examinations subsequent to a mastectomy.

A total of 88 cases (43 positive and 45 negative) met our initial study requirements and were read in one or another of our study conditions.* Later corrections to certain inadequacies of our selection criteria (one related to ensuring that the biopsy was of breast tissue, the other related to removing ambiguity about whether or not the visible lesion was a mole) led to dropping 6 of the original 43 positive cases. Of the remaining 82 cases, 62 were imaged in all three modalities and 20 were imaged in just two modalities. Because the extra cases obtained by admitting those imaged in just two modalities turned out not to affect our conclusions, we limit data analysis here to the 62 three-mode cases. Thus, for present purposes our sample was comprised of 62 three-mode cases, 24 positive cases and 38 negative cases.

Table 9 gives the distribution of times between imaging and the confirming follow-up study for the negative cases. Table 10 gives the distribution of times between imaging and the confirming biopsy for the positive cases. Table 11 shows the distribution of diagnoses for the positive cases.

---

* More precisely, we had 86 patients: 43 positive cases and 43 negative cases. For two of the negative patients, images of both breasts were available, and we treated each breast as a separate case.

Table 9

**DISTRIBUTION OF THE NUMBER OF MONTHS BETWEEN
IMAGING AND FOLLOW-UP CONFIRMATION OF NEGATIVE
CASES**

Number of months	Number of cases
1–2	0
3–4	3
5–6	4
7–8	3
9–10	0
11–12	21
13–14	2
15–16	2
17–18	1
19–20	1
21–22	0
23–24	1
Total	38

11.2 RESPONSE FORMAT

To provide a basis for standardized analysis, the readers' reports on
each case were constrained to a reasonably simple format, as shown in
Chapter 7, Figure 16. The first two items provide for the reader to
evaluate the technical quality and the potential diagnostic informativeness
of the image. Item 3 asks the reader to express a degree of confidence
that the patient has a localized abnormality (detection). Item 4 asks the

Table 10

**DISTRIBUTION OF THE NUMBER OF MONTHS BETWEEN
IMAGING AND BIOPSY CONFIRMATION OF POSITIVE CASES**

Number of months	Number of cases
0–1	16
2–3	2
4–5	1
6–7	0
8–9	1
10–11	3
12–21	0
22–24	1
Total	24

Table 11

DISTRIBUTION OF DIAGNOSES IN POSITIVE CASES

Type of tumor	Numbers
Malignant	
Cancer	16
Intraductal cancer	1
Total	17
Benign	
Benign tumor	1
Fibrocystic disease	4
Plasma cell mastitis	1
Fat necrosis	1
Total	7

reader to express a degree of confidence that a localized abnormality is malignant (classification). Item 5 gives the reader an opportunity to mention any aspect of the case or the reading test considered necessary or worthwhile to express at that juncture.

The design of this form—the choice of items, their wording and order—was dictated by four main considerations:

1. the general logic of how a reader would proceed, first to assess the nature of the image and then to abstract and interpret the diagnostic information it contains;
2. the fineness of distinctions that the readers are accustomed to making in a clinical setting and the terminology commonly employed;
3. The type of distinctions on which we could obtain truth data for scoring the responses; and
4. reader needs and limitations—how far in the interests of good study design (standardization, quantification, and specificity) the reader can be required to depart from normal ways of reporting, yet perform in a normal way and retain zeal and interest throughout the test.

In item 1, the reader is asked to assess the technical quality of the image by assigning it to one of three broad categories of quality: high, satisfactory, or low. One purpose is to monitor image quality so that it can be taken into account, if necessary, in interpreting study results. A second purpose is to meet any needs of the reader to express reservations about the usefulness of the image in making a diagnosis.

In item 2, the reader is asked to assess the extent of obscuration of possible localized abnormality by parenchymal pattern or diffuse disease, and ascribe one of three degrees of obscuration: great, moderate, or small. This item has the same two basic purposes as item 1.

In item 3, the reader is required to report the likelihood that the patient has a localized abnormality. Five alternatives are ordered according to a rating scale that ranges from 1: "Definitely, or almost definitely, *present*," to 5: "Definitely, or almost definitely, *absent*." We require a choice among several ordered alternatives—as opposed, say, to a binary choice (Present versus Absent)—in order to generate responses in a form suitable for our accuracy analyses in terms of the ROC. The use of five levels of rating is a compromise between, on the one hand, having a large enough number of data points to define an ROC curve reasonably well (the number of data points is 1 less than the number of rating categories), and, on the other hand, not greatly exceeding the number of distinctions readers would normally make in clinical practice.

In item 4, the reader is asked to assume that there is a localized abnormality present in the image, and to report the likelihood that it is malignant. For the same basic reasons as in item 3, we provide five ordered alternatives. Here the responses range from 1: "Definitely, or almost definitely, *malignant*," to 5: "Definitely, or almost definitely, *benign*."

The decision to have the reader assume in every case, independent of the response to item 3, that a localized abnormality is present was made after considerable methodological debate. The disadvantage of doing so is the potential confusion when the reader is asked to classify a lesion that is confidently reported not present. The advantage is that every case then goes through item 4, and the analysis of item 4 results is therefore based on a fixed sample. The alternative is to allow the reader to skip item 4 for certain cases, say, those rated 4 or 5 in item 3. While possibly relieving the reader of some confusion, taking this alternative means that the set of cases getting to item 4 will then vary depending on several factors. One is where we, the test designers and analyzers, arbitrarily set the cutoff on item 3 for skipping item 4. Another is where the reader sets personal criteria for utilizing the various rating categories. A third is the variability in where a given case will fall relative to the dimension of the rating scale from one presentation of that case to another. The net result of allowing readers to skip item 4 is an inability to compare performances across readers or reading conditions. As one specific problem, we might expect that the reader who passes relatively fewer cases on to item 4 (because of a strict detection criterion in item 3) will do better at classification than a reader who passes relatively many cases on to item 4. All of this was explained to the readers, and they were assured that we would score only those cases having a localized abnormality. Thus, of the 62 cases used in our total analyses, only the 24 with localized abnormality were considered in analyzing responses to item 4.

In item 5, the reader can express diagnoses that were not included among the explicitly specified alternatives, qualify any foregoing responses, comment on the quality or adequacy of the information provided, or comment on any aspect of the study procedure. This item collects comments, on a case-by-case basis and when thoughts arise, that the investigators can use in reviewing all aspects of the study design, procedures, and materials; in so doing, this item may also help to preserve the reader's peace of mind.

11.3 EXPERIMENTAL DESIGN

The reading test was designed to assess and compare the accuracy of performance provided by the three modalities, referred to in the following as X, Y, and Z. A second goal was to examine correlations in readings within and across readers, and across modalities.

The test involved four groups of three readers: three "single-mode" groups reading X, Y, and Z, respectively, and a "tri-mode" group reading all three modalities. The three modes were thus read both by unmatched (different) readers and by matched (the same) readers.

The X readers read 85 X images, and they read each of those images twice, independently. The Y and Z readers also read twice, independently, just the images in their modality, 79 cases with Y images and 79 cases with Z images. (The two readings of an image were "independent" in the sense that the images carried no identifying labels and the second presentation did not designate the image as a particular image presented earlier.) The tri-mode readers read, independently and just once, all available images of every one of the 88 cases in the initial sample. (The readings of the two or three images of a given case were "independent" in the sense that those images were not designated as counterparts; a separate diagnosis was based on each image.)

Each reader worked individually on each of two days separated by at least 2 weeks. The single-mode readers read every case on each of the 2 days, but in a different random order (random, except that runs of more than five consecutive positive or negative cases were precluded). The tri-mode readers read half of the cases in each modality on the first day and the remaining half of each modality on the second day. For the tri-mode readers, the modalities were arranged into blocks of about 30 cases, and the order of blocks across readers and sessions was counterbalanced. Orders of cases within blocks were random, with the exception previously noted.

11.4 TEST PROCEDURES

11.4.1 Apparatus

For the film mammograms, a four-panel illuminator (GE Flouroline, Model E5086C) was provided, as well as a high-intensity illuminator (S&S X-Ray Products Inc., Model 185). For the Xerograms, desk space was provided with light sources that the reader could adjust in brightness and direction to suit individual needs. The reading room was equipped with continuously controllable ambient lighting that the reader could also adjust. A 5-inch magnifying lens (Bausch and Lomb, catalog No. 81-33-05) was available.

11.4.2 Reader Instructions

Each reader was given a brief explanation of the context and goals of the study and a detailed explanation of the response form and the reading procedure. Also provided was general background on the cases (i.e., "high risk, over 40") and information about the proportions of cases in the relevant diagnostic categories (i.e., "about half of the cases are abnormal, and about 80% of those are malignant"). Abnormality was defined as a significant localized abnormality. The readers who would read each case twice were so informed.

11.4.3 Reading Procedure

On the first day, the readers were familiarized with the reading equipment and various lighting controls and then given five practice reading trials (with images not part of the test proper) to ensure that they fully understood the response form and the mechanics of the reading procedure. The actual reading test was the same for both days. The test administrator handed the image to the reader. The reader was free to position, handle, and illuminate the images with the facilities available, but carefully instructed to avoid getting fingerprints on the breast image.

The reader then dictated to the test administrator responses to the various items on the response form for each successive case.

At points approximately one-third and two-thirds through the reading schedule each day, the reader was given the opportunity for a brief break. No time limits were employed. Each session involving the reading of about 80 images took about 2 to 3 hours.

11.4.4 Reader Debriefing

Upon completing the reading of test cases on the second day, each reader filled in a questionnaire that sought comments specifically on the imaging and generally on the test procedures. The readers were also then permitted to review any images, along with truth data, that they had flagged for that purpose during the test. Review and commentary were also sought on certain other cases on which we had found an unusual degree of reader disagreement either with each other or the truth. This commentary provided the basis for our withdrawal of particular problem cases as described above under the heading of "sample composition."

11.5 READER RATINGS OF IMAGE QUALITY

Before considering the methods and results of analysis of the main elements of the reading test—detection (item 3) and classification (item 4)—we briefly set forth the readers' responses to items 1 and 5, concerned with image quality. All readers were asked to rate image quality relative to the state of the art circa 1975. The figures given are based on responses to the 62 cases by the six readers (three single-mode, three tri-mode) for each modality.

The following three figures for each mode are percentages, respectively, of images said to be of high, satisfactory, or low quality in item 1: X—19, 55, 26; Y—15, 44, 41; Z—27, 56, 17.

Item 5 was used to single out images of especially low quality as follows. For X, three readers mentioned one image each, a different image in each instance, and two readers mentioned a fourth image. For Y, nine images were singled out by from one to five readers. For Z, five images were mentioned, each by a different reader.

Roughly, Y fared less well with regard to judged image quality than X, which fared less well than Z. On the whole, we would have preferred a higher opinion of image quality among our readers than was evidenced.

We decided to retain all 62 cases in analysis and let the present findings about image quality stand as a general qualification on the adequacy of our study, rather than to attempt to take them into account in any quantitative fashion.

11.6   ACCURACY RESULTS

We consider first the *detection* performance for the three modalities, in every case based on the combination of the three readers of a given modality. As a technical point, we have pooled the raw rating-scale response of the three readers (as if they were one reader) to yield one ROC curve, rather than taking the average of three individual values of $P(TP)$ and $P(FP)$ for each point, or of the z values associated with those probabilities. The differences in the two procedures for combination are negligible in this study.

Presented here as illustrative are the ROCs obtained with modality X, for (*a*) single-mode readers, day 1; (*b*) single-mode readers, day 2; and (*c*) tri-mode readers. The same order, again for just modality X, is then followed for the *classification* ROCs. The detection ROCs portray the readers' ability to discriminate between presence and absence of localized abnormalities. The classification ROCs represent the readers' ability to discriminate between malignant and benign localized abnormalities, given that a localized abnormality is present. Accuracy indices from all three modalities in both response conditions are given in summary tables. We also report here the *joint* ROCs, which combine detection and classification performance.

11.6.1   Detection Accuracy

Figure 17 shows the detection ROC obtained from *single-mode (unmatched) readers, day 1* in modality X, along with the associated value of the accuracy index A_z. Figure 18 shows the *single-mode (unmatched)* readers, day 2, and Figure 19 shows the *tri-mode (matched)* readers.*

The mean values of A_z over the three readers—for the three modalities and three reading conditions—are shown in Table 12. We see there that

---

*Although we shall not allude to them further, the figures' insets show also the quantities Δm and s, the intercept and slope of the ROCs as defined in Chapter 1 (Section 1.4.3).

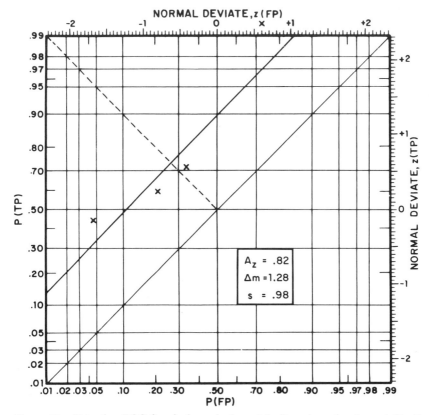

Figure 17. Detection ROC for single-mode (unmatched) readers, day 1: modality X. (In this and some of the subsequent figures one of the four data points lies outside the boundaries of the figure, representing a coordinate of 0 or 1.0.)

Table 12

DETECTION ACCURACY: MEAN VALUES OF A_z

Mode	Single-mode (unmatched readers) day 1	Single-mode (unmatched readers) day 2	Tri-mode (matched readers)
X	0.823	0.820	0.793
Y	0.800	0.833	0.787
Z	0.853	0.840	0.790

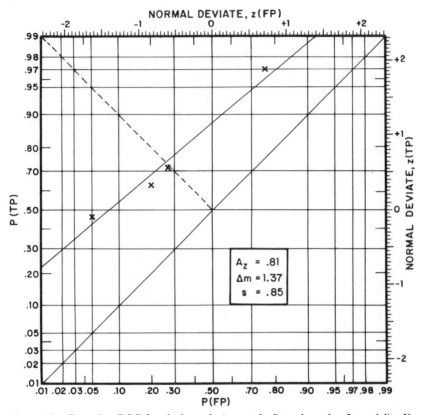

Figure 18.   Detection ROC for single-mode (unmatched) readers, day 2: modality X.

the observed differences within a modality between days, and the differences between pairs of modalities, are slight. We proceed, however, to make some statistical analyses for illustrative purposes.

The general approach to statistical analysis, as described in Chapter 4 of this book is (a) to compute the standard error (S.E.) for each value of A_z and thus the confidence limits on those values of A_z, and (b) to compute the critical ratio (C.R.) of the mean difference in A_z between pairs of modalities and thus the statistical significance of the observed differences.

Applying the formula for the S.E. (Eq. 4, Chapter 4) gives a value of 0.060 for modality X, single-mode readers, day 1, as illustrated in Section 4.1. Then $\pm 2 \times 0.060$ gives approximate 95% confidence limits of ± 0.12. Hence, the 95% limits on the A_z value of modality X of 0.823 are 0.70 and 0.94. The confidence bounds on the other values of A_z in Table 12

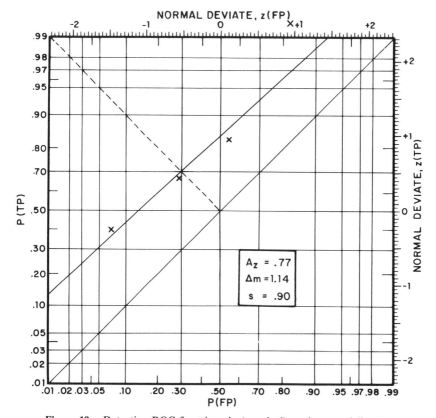

Figure 19. Detection ROC for tri-mode (matched) readers, modality X.

are similarly broad, and it is apparent from them that there are no
statistically significant effects here.

We shall, however, make an analysis of the differences between the
three modalities on day 1 for illustrative purposes. Before computing the
values of the C.R., let us note that the first step is to set the confidence
level for accepting or rejecting the null hypothesis. In the absence of
any precise information on the costs of the two types of error one might
commit in making that decision, we adopt the conventional, largely arbitrary, 5% level. Because this is an arbitrary choice to begin with, it
is for purely methodological reasons that we point out the further possible
need for refinement. Specifically, it may be reasonable to consider that
the adopted confidence level applies not to the individual comparisons,
but to the set of three. Where that is the consideration, an appropriately

smaller criterion is needed for the individual comparisons, as discussed in Chapter 4 (Section 4.6). Following the rule prescribed there, one would need to divide the 5% confidence level for the set by the number of pairwise comparisons being made. Thus, the confidence level for each individual comparison would be 5 divided by 3 or 1.7%.

Turning now to our analyses of the single-mode data for day 1, we first determine the difference between means for each of three pairs of modalities. Taking the data from the first column of Table 12, we see that the difference between modalities X and Y is 0.023, between modalities X and Z is 0.030, and between Y and Z is 0.053. Next, we obtain an estimate of S.E.$_{(diff)}$ for each comparison. As explained in Chapter 4, one will rarely have enough data to prove that S.E.$_{(diff)}$ varies significantly over the various comparisons and rarely have any prior basis for asserting that it does. Such is clearly the case here, and the recommended procedure is to obtain a single, combined estimate of S.E.$_{(diff)}$. A combined estimate of S.E.$_{(diff)}$ = 0.078 for these particular data, as computed in Section 4.3.1, is applied here. To compute the C.R. we divide the mean difference for each comparison by 0.078. For X versus Y, C.R. is 0.29; for X versus Z, C.R. is 0.38; and for Y versus Z, C.R. is 0.68. By chance alone, one would expect to get C.R. = 0.68 (i.e., the largest of these C.R.s) on more than 50% of testing occasions. Thus, even the largest of these C.R.s is very far from the 1.7% confidence criterion, and we are led to conclude that there are no statistically significant differences among the modalities as they are represented in our study.

11.6.2   Classification Accuracy

Figure 20 shows the classification ROC for modality X for *single-mode* (*unmatched*) *readers, day 1*. Figure 21 shows the *single-mode* (*unmatched*) *readers, day 2,* and Figure 22 shows the *tri-mode* (*matched*) readers. Table 13 gives values of A_z for each modality in both reading conditions. We see there that the observed differences between pairs of modalities are not large and in no consistent pattern across the single-mode and tri-mode reading conditions. With n = 24 cases, we can be sure that the differences observed are small relative to their standard errors.

The results shown in Table 13 are "pooled" A_z values rather than means as were shown in Table 12 for the detection data. We reverted to pooling the rating responses to obtain group ROCs and group values of A_z because, with so small a case sample, the computer program failed

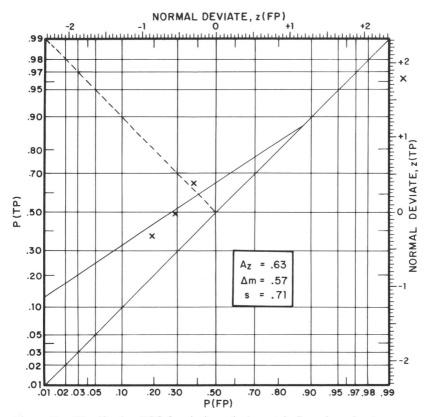

Figure 20. Classification ROC for single-mode (unmatched) readers, day 1: modality X.

Table 13

CLASSIFICATION ACCURACY: VALUES OF A_z FROM POOLED ROCS

Mode	Single-mode (unmatched readers) day 1	Single-mode (unmatched readers) day 2	Tri-mode (matched readers)
X	0.63	0.69	0.78
Y	0.71	0.77	0.77
Z	0.70	0.72	0.80

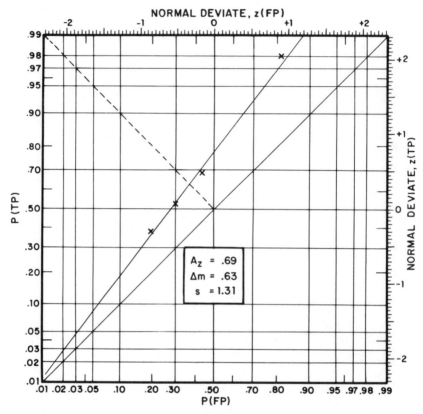

Figure 21. Classification ROC for single-mode (unmatched) readers, day 2: modality X.

to converge to a maximum-likelihood fit for 9 of the 27 readings of the case sample. With that many missing values of A_z, formal statistical analysis is not warranted.

11.6.3 Detection-Plus-Classification Accuracy

Figure 23 shows illustrative joint ROCs for the three modalities, those obtained from the tri-mode (matched) readers. The main result seen here, true also of the single-mode readers on both days, is the similarity of the three modalities. We can reasonably conclude, we think, from visual inspection alone, that there are no appreciable differences among the modalities.

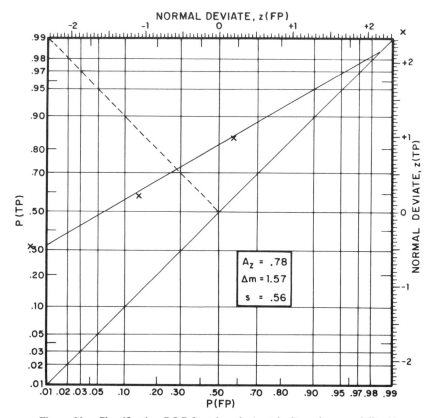

Figure 22.   Classification ROC for tri-mode (matched) readers, modality X.

As discussed in Chapter 2 (Section 2.1.5), one might choose to index the accuracy represented by a joint ROC curve by (*a*) calculating the area under the curve or (*b*) taking the value of the joint $P(TP)$ at some particular value of $P(FP)$. The general approach to statistical analysis of these indices is the same as described in Chapter 4 for other accuracy indices, except for one fairly significant problem. We have no basis for generating for these indices a theoretical estimate of the term $S^2_{c + wr}$ in the computational formula for S.E.$_{(diff)}$. The only way to get that estimate is empirical. The case sample is first broken down into $g > 2$ equal subsamples. For each reader, one conducts the joint detection-plus-classification analysis on each sample and determines the maximum-likelihood estimate of the variability in the index across the g subsamples. The next step is to take the mean of the resulting terms over all readers.

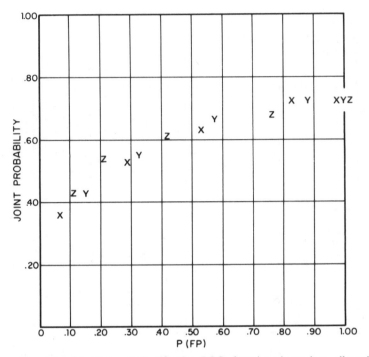

Figure 23. Joint detection-and-classification ROCs for tri-mode readers, all modes.

At this stage of the computation one has an estimate of $S^2_{c\ +\ wr}$ for samples of size n/g. The final step is to divide by g to obtain the estimate of $S^2_{c\ +\ wr}$ for samples of size n.

11.7   CORRELATIONAL ANALYSES

A knowledge of various correlations among readings serves three important purposes. Correlations among cases and among readers, across modalities (as detailed in Chapters 3 and 4) are important factors in determining the desired size and parameters of a reading test and in making an adequately powerful statistical analysis of observed differences between modalities. Those correlations, along with the correlation among readers within a modality and the correlation within a reader over separate reading occasions, are of interest also in their own right because they provide additional information about system and reader performance. We would like to know in any diagnostic setting how well readers, within and across modalities, agree with themselves and with others in detecting, localizing, and classifying abnormalities.

As set forth in Chapters 3 and 4 and illustrated with data from the present study, we have a well-founded procedure for computing the product-moment r between sets of values of a general accuracy index such as A_z. However, this procedure has certain limitations; we have seen that what may seem to be fairly large numbers of cases and readers are needed to give reasonably reliable estimates of the correlation coefficients r_c and r_{br}. And even then we are dealing with something on the order of four to eight pairs of indices, not a large number for correlational purposes. Moreover, this procedure is not as flexible and sensitive as we would like when we consider the use of correlational data to provide ancillary assessments of system and reader performance. When we want to know how well various sets of readings correlate or agree, we should be able to obtain additional information from correlations based on the reports readers make about individual cases.

Some questions arise when we contrast correlations based on reports about individual cases (e.g., raw data in the form of confidence ratings) and correlations based on a value abstracted from an ROC curve (e.g., A_z). We have not worked out the relationship between the two kinds of correlations, and although we believe that power in some sense is lost when moving from raw data to indices that are comparable to mean values, we have so far not characterized the loss in a fundamental way, let alone develop any precise estimates of degree of loss.

Nonetheless, we have proceeded to calculate various correlations based on rating responses in the spirit of an empirical investigation. Our aim is exploratory; we wish to see how the values vary as the focus of the correlation is varied and to get an idea of the absolute magnitudes. The four calculations made we shall term "intrareader," showing the correlation between initial readings and rereadings by individual readers; "intramode," showing the correlation among readers within a given modality; "across modes, same readers," showing the correlation between modalities when the same readers read in each; and "across modes, different readers," showing the correlation between modalities when the readers in each were different.

We have computed the correlation coefficients in two ways. The first is the standard product-moment r based on the responses made in the five categories of the rating scale. In order to reduce the contribution to the calculated correlation of the relative difficulty of our test sample of cases—a very easy sample with clear-cut normal and abnormal cases would show near perfect correlation—we calculated r's for the abnormal and normal cases separately and then took their average. An alternative means of removing the effect of test difficulty is Kendall's (1962) partial tau. For this index, the five categories of the rating scale are collapsed to two (categories 1, 2, and 3 are taken as a response of "abnormal," and categories 4 and 5 are taken as a response of "normal"), and a formula for correlation is used that partials out the correctness of the responses. The partial tau is then converted to an estimate of the product-moment r.

Table 14 shows the four correlations of interest, as calculated both by the product-moment r directly and by Kendall's partial tau—for both detection and classification. The values shown are averages of the values obtained for the three modalities or the three pairs of modalities; differences among modalities or pairs of modalities were generally small and had no discernible pattern. The table also shows combinations of the two estimates that are rounded for the convenience of further reference.

We see, first, that the two types of correlation coefficients agree reasonably well. For detection, their magnitudes give the same order of the four correlations; for classification, there is a reversal of the order of the second and third correlations. We may note also that the correlations for classification are consistently higher than for detection.

Readers are seen to correlate better with themselves than with others, as we might expect, whether working in a single mode or across the three modes. This result is consistent with the benefit presumed to be obtained from matching or using the same readers when possible. Correlation within a mode is higher than across modes, both within and across readers. We would expect that difference to be more pronounced in studies in which the modalities are less similar. We note in passing a suggestion in the table that same readers across modes correlate higher

Table 14

AVERAGE CORRELATIONS[a]

Kind of Correlation	Detection	Classification
Intrareader	0.66 (0.70) 0.70	0.75 (0.83) 0.80
Intramode	0.46 (0.51) 0.50	0.59 (0.52) 0.55
Across mode, same readers	0.49 (0.58) 0.55	0.52 (0.74) 0.65
Across mode, different readers	0.27 (0.28) 0.30	0.45 (0.40) 0.45

[a] Product-moment r's, and, in parentheses, estimates of product-moment r's based on Kendall's partial tau. The underlined values are combinations of the two estimates that are rounded to the nearest 0.05 for the convenience of our illustrative application.

than different readers within a mode. That result, too, might not be expected when the modalities differ more.

As ancillary measures of system performance, we comment only on the "intrareader" correlations, showing the reliability of rereading to be about 0.70 for detection and 0.80 for classification. For one interpretation, consider the percentage of trials on which a reader with that degree of reliability agrees with himself or herself if just two categories of response were used in analysis, that is, when categories 1, 2, and 3 equal "Abnormal," and categories 4 and 5 equal "Normal." Those percentages are 77 for detection and 86 for classification. We are speaking here, of course, about repeatability without regard to accuracy: A high degree of repeatability, though necessary, is not sufficient for high accuracy. We may note that somewhat higher intrareader and intramode correlation, and percentages of agreement, were found in the data of our CT/RN study.

11.8   OBTAINING ESTIMATES OF PURE VARIANCE AND CORRELATION TERMS

Chapter 3 presented a general rationale for designing a reading test. The central idea is first to get a sense for how the design variables n, ℓ, and m (numbers of cases, readers, and rereadings) and possible matching of readers or cases might be expected to impact the size of S.E.$_{(diff)}$ and, in turn, the C.R. Then, the statistical goals of the study should be examined and a decision made as to how best to design the study to meet them.

To get a sense of how particular settings of n, ℓ, and m—and how case or reading matching—could be expected to impact S.E.$_{(diff)}$, one has to work with the basic formula for S.E.$_{(diff)}$ given as Eq. 2 in Chapter 3, and one first has to obtain estimates of the pure variance and correlation terms to be inserted in that basic formula. For simplicity of the discussions in Chapter 3, we did not explain how to obtain those estimates except to say that we would either have to have some good a priori knowledge of them, or that they would have to be estimated in a pilot study. Details on how one would actually compute these terms on data from a pilot study were deferred in Chapter 3 and left to be presented here.

The general approach to computing the estimate for each of these pure terms, except S_{wr}^2, is first to compute their observable counterparts and then to transform each into the pure form by an appropriate correction.

Details on how to compute the observable versions of each of these terms are given in Chapter 4. For S_{wr}^2, the observable and pure variance are one and the same. The following equations show for each of the remaining terms how to convert the observable form into the pure form:

$$S_c^2 = S_{c+wr}^2 - S_{wr}^2,$$

$$S_{br}^2 = S_{br+wr}^2 - S_{wr}^2,$$

$$r_c = r_{c-wr} \frac{S_c^2 + S_{wr}^2}{S_c^2},$$

$$r_{br} = r_{br-wr} \frac{S_{br}^2 + S_{wr}^2}{S_{br}^2}.$$

We proceed now to illustrate how one would use the present study as if it were a pilot study, in order to estimate the various terms of the basic equation, as they are needed to follow the design procedure of Chapter 3. It is instructive first to face the fact that the present study does not provide a full basis for making all of these estimates. That will probably be the situation with many pilot studies. Here we have a reasonable basis for estimating the variance terms, but not the correlations.

We consider first the variance terms. Using the mean values of the observables obtained in Sections 4.3.1 and 4.3.2, we obtain the following estimates of the pure variance terms:

$$S_c^2 = \frac{0.0034 + 0.0040}{2} - 0.0012 = 0.0025 \,,$$

$$S_{br}^2 = \frac{0.0025 + 0.0026}{2} - 0.0012 = 0.0014 \,.$$

To obtain estimates of the pure correlation terms, our approach has to be largely judgmental. As we explained in Chapter 4, where the present mammography data were used in an illustration, we decided that we had insufficient data to make a credible empirical estimate of r_{c-wr}. The conservative option there was to assume $r_{c-wr} = 0$. Here, in this projective design context, we need not be so conservative. Indeed, we think it would be reasonable in this context to assume a value for the pure correlation of at least $r_c = 0.50$. Also, with respect to the between-reader correlation term, we pointed out in the same exercise in Chapter 4 that the obtained value of $r_{br-wr} = 0.98$ was incredibly high, apparently a sampling oddity due to our having so few readers. The reason we asserted that it was incredibly high will now be apparent, because if $r_{br-wr} = 0.98$, the correction for attenuation given above would lead to a theoretically meaningless estimate for $r_{br} > 1.0$. Here we think it reasonable to posit the reasonably high, but meaningful, pure correlation of $r_{br} = 0.90$.

These values can now be inserted into the basic formula, Eq. 2, as follows:

$$S.E._{(\text{diff})} = 2^{1/2}\left[\frac{0.0025}{n/62}(1 - 0.5) + \frac{0.0014}{\ell}\left(1 - 0.90 + \frac{0.0012}{\ell m}\right)\right]^{1/2}$$

where $n/62$ is the size of the case sample, normalized to the size of the sample on which the constants of this equation were generated. With this formula filled in, an investigator would be operationally equipped to follow the general approach to study design laid out in Chapter 4.

11.9 DISCUSSION: SIZING A FINAL STUDY FROM A PILOT STUDY

We have reported this comparative study of three mammographic modalities solely as a methodological exercise. It provides a second exemplar of a reading test following the procedures outlined in the main body of this protocol. The prior sections of this report show (*a*) how we selected cases and readers, (*b*) how we developed the response format, and (*c*) how we designed the reading test—first, to get as much information as possible from the available materials and resources and, second, to explore certain methodological questions. We have also illustrated various aspects of measuring the accuracy of reading performance via ROC analysis and various aspects of statistical analysis of the accuracy data.

Ordinarily at this point in a study report one would discuss the study results, their immediate meaning and generalization, and perhaps their implications for further study of the reading process. Although we have no statistically significant findings of differences among the modalities to discuss, we have acquired considerable quantitative understanding about the general location and slope of the ROC curves and about general aspects of reading variability and correlation. Thus, one might seek to draw some conclusions from these results about the general modality represented by the three specific modalities under test. Because of several limitations of our particular study design, however, drawing even that general a conclusion would not be appropriate here. In addition to having too small a case sample to permit reliable generalization of the findings, our results may well indicate a lower level of performance for mammography than should fairly be ascribed to it. We can list several deficiencies of our study materials that would contribute to an underestimation of mammography's accuracy. Specifically,

1. We had only the cranial-caudad view of each breast (probably not the most informative single view);
2. we could show only one breast (thus eliminating any information in asymmetry);
3. we had limited data on case backgrounds;
4. our truth data were very limited;
5. we worked with dated versions of the modalities; and
6. our readers expressed reservations about the technical quality of a substantial portion of our images.

What we can do productively and validly with these general results is discuss their use in planning a subsequent definitive study. We take this opportunity, therefore, to illustrate such a discussion, which would typically have two concerns. The first concern is how one might use the study results to determine the size of a difference between modalities that one would want the full-scale study to be powerful enough to detect. The second concern would be how the study results might further help in designing the full-scale study to achieve the power required to detect that specified difference.

11.9.1   Determining the Size of a Difference of Interest between Two Modalities

To determine the size of a difference of interest between any pair of the modalities, two steps are required. First, proceeding as if there were no differences in the modalities, one would obtain a single ROC curve representative of all of the modalities being compared. Where does that representative curve lie in the ROC space, and what is its slope? Second, one would ask what the quantitative impact would be if that curve were different in specific ways, say, if it had a particular higher or lower value of A_z.

The first of the two steps is rather straightforward. Following procedures outlined in Chapter 2 (Section 2.3.2), one could obtain a single representative curve, by averaging z scale values of the rating data across all readers and modalities. A much simpler and probably adequate approach would be to average the values of slope and intercept obtained from all the fitted ROC curves across all readers and modalities. Let us assume that the summary curve turned out to have the same slope and intercept ($\Delta m = 1.28$, $s = 0.98$) as the fitted curve in Figure 17.

How would one now gauge the importance of a difference in reading performance if that nominal curve had, say, a different value of A_z? We describe and illustrate here three different measures of the difference in reading performance that would occur if we held other aspects of performance constant and shifted just A_z. Whereas each is far from the ideal measure that one might wish to have, say, from a full-blown efficacy analysis, one or the other of these measures may often provide a very helpful practical understanding of the importance of a particular difference, as described in Chapter 2 (Section 2.2).

One alternative is to measure how the difference in A_z would affect $P(TP)$ at a fixed value of $P(FP)$. For the nominal curve shown in Figure 17, at the value of $P(FP) = 0.10$, the value of $P(TP)$ is 0.48. To gauge whether a difference in A_z of a particular size—say an increase of 0.025—would be of practical interest, one might find it helpful to know that with the fixed value of $P(FP) = 0.10$, $P(TP)$ would rise to 0.57. With an increase of 0.1 in A_z, the corresponding value of $P(TP)$ would rise to 0.75. In the first instance, an additional 9 out of 100 abnormal cases are detected; in the second instance, the gain is 27 of 100. To get a full picture of the impact of differences in A_z from this point of view, one might want to see the whole function of $P(TP)$ at fixed $P(FP)$ over a wide range of values of A_z. One might even want to look at a family of such functions where $P(FP)$ is a parameter.

Another alternative is to fix the value of both error proportions—$P(FP)$ and $P(FN)$—and look at what would happen to the probability of "Equivocal" responses. According to the reasoning given in Section 2.2.1, we can derive the results for a reader in our test who would be allowed to say "Positive," "Negative," or "Equivocal." The key to the derivation is that the proportions of the three responses to abnormal cases must add to 1.0, as for the normal cases. The implication from Figure 17 is that if such a reader were to maintain both error proportions at less than or equal to 0.10, then both of the correct-response proportions would be 0.50, and 40% of the cases would be left as equivocal. If A_z were increased by 0.1, the corresponding correct-response proportions would go to 0.75, and 15% of the cases would be left as equivocal.

Still another view of the performance evidenced in our test is gained by considering certain inverse probabilities, rather than the forward probabilities discussed so far. Although inverse probabilities are not useful in the evaluation of diagnostic systems, because they vary both with the prior probabilities (prevalence) and the reader's decision criterion, they are of practical importance. As indicated in Section 2.2.3, Bayes's rule permits us to calculate from our data the probability, given a positive response, that the case is truly positive. Taking the performance indicated in Figure 17 as an example, and taking an arbitrary point on the curve, we have $P(TP) = 0.50$ at $P(FP) = 0.10$. The prior probability of an abnormal case was about 0.40, and the probability of a positive response at the point indicated was 0.26. According to Bayes's rule, at $P(FP) = 0.10$, the inverse probability is 0.77. In other words, at that false-positive rate, 77% of the cases called positive for localized abnormality would in fact be positive according to biopsy. In this way, the inverse probabilities can be calculated for any other assumed values of A_z or of Δm and s.

In presenting these three ways of looking at the importance of a particular difference in accuracy, we do not wish to imply that they are the only ones that are sensible. We think one or the other will often help, but the investigator should see them, to some extent, merely as examples of alternative views and should be prepared to devise other alternatives that might be more suitable to the particular problem at hand.

11.9.2   Designing a Study to Achieve a Needed Degree of Power

The degree of power required of the study will depend not only on the size of the difference one wishes to be able to detect, but also on the degree of confidence one wishes to have in concluding that such a difference does or does not exist. Let us apply the conventional 5% level of confidence. The required design is then determined in three steps. First, one has to compute the criterion value for the C.R. For a two-tailed test at the 5% level, the criterion would be C.R. $= \pm 1.96$ (see Chapter 3). The next step is to determine what size S.E.$_{(diff)}$ would be needed such that, when divided into the difference of interest, it would yield that criterion value. The third step is to determine the best study design (combination of the number of readers ℓ and cases n) to achieve an S.E.$_{(diff)}$ of the required size.

Using the operational equation of Section 11.8, we find that for a study like the present one with $n = 62$ and $\ell = 3$, the projected S.E.$_{(diff)} = 0.06$. Let us consider how n and ℓ would have to differ to create a study with twice the power (i.e., with S.E.$_{(diff)} = 0.03$). Applying the rule that standard errors decrease as an inverse function of the square root of the sample size, we can see that to halve S.E.$_{(diff)}$ we would have to increase both ℓ and n four times—that is, make $\ell = 12$ and $n = 248$. Thus, we can easily obtain for this particular example one of the designs that meets our goal. The general approach for determining a suitable design to achieve any particular value of S.E.$_{(diff)}$ would be to choose a reasonable value for one of the terms (ℓ or n), substitute it into the operational equation, set the equation equal to the desired value of S.E.$_{(diff)}$, and solve for the other term. It is important to point out that setting one of these terms at any particular value will limit the achievable reduction in S.E.$_{(diff)}$ no matter how big the other term is made. Thus, if one has strict upper limits on, say, the number of cases that can feasibly be obtained, that will put a lower bound on S.E.$_{(diff)}$ no matter how many readers are employed. One of the first steps in designing the study would be to see if any practical limits on the number of cases or readers bound S.E.$_{(diff)}$ to a higher level than one needs for an adequately powerful study. The investigator can get a graphic impression of such bounds, and other useful impressions, from plots like those shown in Figure 24, which we explain next.

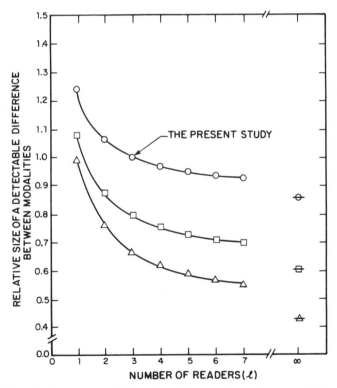

Figure 24. Relative power of different reading-test designs for $n = 62$ (○), $n = 124$ (□), and $n = 248$ (△).

If one could precisely specify and merge all the costs to be incurred in acquiring and adequately documenting cases, and similarly all the costs of having readers read all those cases, one could algorithmically find the optimal study design. Generally, however, there is so much imprecision and complexity in the costing that the design is largely a matter of the individual investigator's judgment. Even so, his or her judgment can be greatly aided by being able to see precisely how S.E.$_{(diff)}$ varies as a function of ℓ and n. An effective approach is to use the operational equation to generate a family of curves showing these effects. Such a visual aid is shown in Figure 24. Taking the operational formula, based on the present mammography data, we have generated curves showing the relative size of a difference in A_z that one could detect as a function of ℓ for three different values of n. The top curve is based on $n = 62$, and the point on that curve for $\ell = 3$ indicates the location of the present study in this space. We have assigned a value of 1.0 to the ordinate at this special point. The investigator can thus determine for other points on these curves precisely how much larger or smaller a difference could be detected relative to the power of the present study.

It is clear from looking at information such as that presented in Figure 24 that one can gain a tremendous advantage in planning a full-scale study from first conducting a pilot study. Without wanting to detract from that important message, we do, however, have to remind the investigator of a caveat stated in Chapter 3. Estimates based on pilot studies will be relatively unreliable, and projections based on such estimates, such as we have illustrated here, will be attendantly unreliable. Whether to stake decisions about a full-scale study on projections from a pilot study will clearly be a matter for the investigator's judgment. How reliable are the estimates? The investigator can compile confidence limits for particular estimates in the operational equation and do sensitivity analyses to see how much S.E.$_{(diff)}$ would shift if the estimate were off by believable amounts. How serious would it be if the projections were off? The investigator can consider the various implications, say, if it turned out that the study was planned to be much bigger or smaller than it should be. Conceivably, one might conclude that further pilot testing is required, or that the full-scale study be implemented incrementally so that early results could influence decisions about how to proceed.

APPENDIXES

Appendix A outlines a sequence of steps to consider in making an evaluation study—the major steps coordinated with the 10 methodological chapters of Parts I and II. Appendix B illustrates with data from the brain-scan study a means of determining the particulars of how faithfully a sample of test cases represents an original case sample, and the ways in which test results may have to be qualified. An example of a questionnaire that might be addressed to participants in a performance test is given in Appendix C. Appendix D gives a listing of the computer program prepared by Dr. Dorfman and Dr. Alf to give maximum-likelihood fits to ROC data. The program produces values of several ROC accuracy indices and their variances, and values of an index of the decision criterion; the appendix provides a user's guide and illustrative calculations. Appendix E gives references to applications of ROC methods and to related discussions of ROC theory in the fields of medicine, military monitoring, industrial monitoring, and information retrieval.

APPENDIX A

Sequence of Steps in Evaluation

The following outline shows the steps that will be taken in a full evaluation as envisioned in this book. Some subset of them will be pertinent to a less extensive evaluation. The first 10 steps are coordinated with the 10 chapters of the book, and so this outline may serve as an index to material covered in detail elsewhere in the book. The sequence of the steps as represented here is meant to follow a logical and chronological order for any particular study and does not correspond to the sequence of chapters.

I. Study design (Chapter 6)
   A. *Develop study goals.* Specify the diagnostic systems to be studied, the diagnostic context of interest, and performance criteria.
   B. *Determine time and cost restraints.*
   C. *Outline the end product.* Analyze the diagnostic–therapeutic process to determine the desirable dimensions of an accuracy analysis, the possibilities for an efficacy analysis, and the time and cost requirements.

D. *Plan the study.*
   1. Determine data to be collected on the case population, the need for and size of an original case sample, and the type of data to be collected on each case in the field.
   2. Sketch the main steps for the collection and analysis of such field data.
   3. Determine the general needs and approach for conducting the performance test.
   4. Lay out the main steps of the performance test and analysis of its results.

E. *Review study goals in light of work required and resources available to accomplish them.* Determine feasibility of accomplishing study goals within available time and resource constraints. Determine need for adjusting study goals or for seeking additional time or study resources.

II. Original case sample (Chapter 8)
   A. *Specify the original case sample to*
      1. serve as a pool of cases from which the performance-test sample is selected.
      2. yield a profile of the relevant case population, and
      3. provide data on diagnostic–therapeutic events subsequent to the diagnostic stage under consideration.
   B. *Specify the types of data to be collected on each case,* for example, images, history, clinical workups, results of other diagnostic tests, further stages of diagnosis, treatment, follow-up studies, and autopsy results.
   C. *Minimize distortions of the sample composition* relative to the case population.
   D. *Determine the size of the original case sample.*

III. Performance-test cases (Chapter 9)
   A. *Specify the performance-test sample* to
      1. give an adequate number of cases, both "signal" and "noise,"
      2. represent categories of signal cases appropriately,
      3. offer an appropriate level of difficulty in diagnosis,
      4. be adequate in image and data quality,
      5. provide credible truth data, and
      6. represent sign and symptom categories appropriately when full efficacy analyses are intended.
   B. *Check to ensure sample is adequately representative,* or to ensure that distortions in representativeness are appropriately considered in interpreting study results.

IV. Test observers, or readers (Chapter 10)
    A. *Specify the observer population.* Determine the frequencies of main types of observers in the population with respect to training and experience.
    B. *Determine an appropriate approach to sampling.* Determine the feasibility of representing the whole population or the need to represent only some subset, say, typical observers or best observers.
    C. *Determine the minimum number of observers required to ensure adequate representation.*

V. Performance-test design (Chapter 3)
    A. *Refine questions to be answered in the performance test.* Specify any secondary questions to be asked, type of observers, and observing conditions for the test.
    B. *Review logistic constraints.* Examine data, time, and cost constraints for a possible need to adjust the performance-test goals and for their impact on statistical approach.
    C. *Choose statistical approach.* Exploit possibilities for use of same cases and same observers across systems.
    D. *Determine power requirements.* Specify practically significant differences among the systems and the degree of confidence required to conclude that those differences exist.
    E. *Determine required numbers of cases and observers.* Work with as large a case sample as is practical and make up remaining need for power by appropriate numbers of observers.
    F. *Make final adjustments in reading test goals or approach to suit data, time, and cost constraints.*

VI. Performance-test procedure (Chapter 7)
    A. *Specify details of case presentation,* concerning, for example,
        1. order of presentation of the cases, and
        2. constraints on reader handling of images or manipulation of display parameters.
    B. *Specify the response format,* to obtain rating-scale data for
        1. two-alternative ROC graphs on detection, localization, and classification, separately, and
        2. joint ROC graphs on detection combined with multiple-alternative localization or multiple-alternative classification or both.
    C. *Specify the background information to be given observers on each case.* Case information may vary from very little if accuracy of image reading is to be assessed with minimal

confounding by level of clinical expertise, to a rather full
set if a full analysis of system efficacy is intended.

D. *Specify timing of trials and sessions, the viewing environment, and the role of the test administrator.*

E. *Specify observer orientation and feedback to and from
observers.*

VII. Accuracy analysis (Chapter 1)

A. *Plot the various ROCs obtained for each system under study.*

B. *Determine the accuracy index* A_z *for all two-alternative
ROCs*. Such ROCs may be based on detection or localization
or classification, and are preferably obtained by means of
the computer program giving maximum-likelihood estimates.

C. *Establish the goodness-of-fit of these empirical ROCs to the
theoretically linear ROC based on normal distributions.*

D. *Determine the slope and intercept of these ROCS for full
description and for comparisons of slopes.*

E. *Determine an index based on a single ROC point*—if the
operating point of interest is known or if the slopes of curves
being compared are materially different.

VIII. Further analyses (Chapter 2)

A. *Determine an accuracy index for any joint ROCs obtained.*

B. *Translate ROC data.* Such translation may be accomplished
in any of several ways to reveal so far as possible the practical import of the accuracy performance observed.

C. *Pool or average ROC data to summarize the performances
of several individuals in each observing condition.*

IX. Statistical treatment of accuracy results (Chapter 4)

A. *Calculate standard errors and confidence intervals of accuracy indices (Eq. 4).*

B. *Calculate the critical ratio for the significance of the difference in pairwise comparisons of systems (Eq. 5).*

C. *Adjust the probability value of the critical ratio when more
than two systems are compared.*

X. Efficacy analysis (Chapter 5)

A. *Conduct a rough overview of requirements for the various
types of efficacy analyses.* Determine the kinds of data and
the kinds of data processing required for each of the main
approaches.

B. *Determine what approach to efficacy analysis might be feasible and meaningful.* Examine the requirements of each
main type in the light of study resources and consider the
knowledge each generates in the light of study goals.

    C. *Where an approach looks feasible and meaningful, consult appropriate guides for detailed planning and execution of analysis.*

XI. Reporting

    A. *Write the report with all potential audiences in mind to the extent possible,* while emphasizing the ones for whom the study was designed and conducted.

    B. *Report the rationale and details of study design* in the interests of proper interpretation of results.

    C. *Highlight the qualifications that must be placed on the results.*

       1. List the ways in which the study was necessarily less than perfect, and inadvertently so.

       2. List all compromises of the best conceivable design and conduct that were made for practical or other reasons.

       3. Gauge their impact on the meaning or generality of the results.

APPENDIX B

Representativeness of a Performance-Test Sample

The objective of a performance test is to obtain results that may properly be generalized to a meaningful population. The population, ideally, is precisely defined and of practical interest. However, the conceptual and practical processes in selecting an original case sample, and then a performance-test sample, create many opportunities for the generalization to be restricted and obscured. Potential problems at these two levels of sampling are discussed in abstract terms in Chapters 8 and 9. The main issues are important enough to warrant concrete illustration, and we provide such an illustration here, to the extent we can, from the study of CT and RN brain scans (Swets *et al.*, 1979). Some of the terminology of this illustration will no doubt appear less formidable to the nonmedical audience if the report of the CT/RN study is reviewed first.

We were not involved in the design of the original case sample and were not on the scene at the medical centers as that design was implemented, therefore we cannot comment very fully on the relationship of that sample to the population of all patients presenting to the collaborative centers with suspicion of tumor. We focus here on the relationship of the reading-test sample to the original case sample. An analysis of the differences between those two samples may help to define the (presumably restricted) population to which the reading-test results can be generalized; otherwise, or in addition, such an analysis may reveal qualifications that should be appended to the reading-test results.

We conducted an extensive analysis of the extent to which proportions of cases in various categories of the original sample were reflected by the proportions in the reading-test sample. For the more important dimensions of variation, we identified the differences that were statistically significant. We then pursued possible causes of those differences in relation to the criteria we had invoked for selecting cases from the original sample for the test sample. Finally, we determined if we could alleviate any of those differences by relaxing any of the selection criteria. We discuss the analytical results here qualitatively, foregoing the quantitative details. Our aim is to sketch the logic of a method of analysis and to give examples of the sampling differences that can occur.

Before examining the particulars, we observe that an important motive for conducting such an analysis is to determine whether the selection criteria usually effected to ensure "harder" or more credible truth in the test sample than is generally available for the original sample serve to create a substantial difference between the two samples. In the study at hand, one may suspect that the sample of cases that have been confirmed (within a reasonably short interval) by autopsy or histology differs in significant ways from the total sample. But herein lies a fundamental and insurmountable problem. In general, the truth data available for the original case sample are not highly credible, and hence one properly hesitates to regard the characteristics of the original sample as the standards that a reading-test sample should match. The tentative diagnoses issued for many of the cases in the original sample, although they are still being actively followed, may well be subject to various kinds of bias that could distort the proportions of that sample from those that would result from perfect, or just better, truth data. Consider that the tentative diagnoses of the original CT/RN sample (e.g., with respect to site and morphology of lesion) could be based largely on the CT image at a time when very little background data existed on the correlation of this new modality with results of autopsy and histology. Furthermore, the fact that the truth data for the test-sample cases could not logically include the CT (or RN) results would immediately induce various discrepancies between the two samples. Therefore, although the language of the analysis described in the following pages holds the CT/RN test sample up to the light of the original sample, we ask the reader to keep in mind that one cannot determine whether any discrepancy results from the selection criteria applied to the test sample or the less adequate diagnostic confirmation available for the original sample.

Also, before reviewing our analyses, we point out that although cases in the original case sample were supposed to be imaged both by CT and RN, approximately 260 (17%) of the cases considered positive in the original sample and included in that sample's descriptive statistics were not imaged by RN, and were hence ineligible for the reading test sample. The nature and size of the distortion that could result from that fact are, as far as we can see, indeterminate. Furthermore, one of the five collaborative centers used an RN imaging device unique to its site and not generally familiar, therefore we excluded from the test sample all cases collected there. Finally, one of the centers was underrepresented in the test sample because of its inability to produce many of the RN scans we requested. These inadequacies of the study are relevant to the present analysis and are mentioned for the purpose of future reference.

We conducted the analysis on the 84 positive cases in the test sample, compared to the approximately 1500 positive cases then in the original sample. We focused on 13 dimensions of variation that fell into three general classes: those general classes that could reveal differences in (a) the type of patient selected (age, sex, race, and presenting clinical group); (b) the type of lesion selected (site and morphology); and (c) the relative readability of the cases for the two test modalities. For each dimension we examined a chi-square goodness-of-fit test in which the expected frequency of each category in the reading-test sample is proportional to its frequency in the original sample.

"Age" was broken into three categories, and "sex" and "race" were broken into two. The categories of the "presenting clinical group" were four: three categories of patients with relatively strong, mild, and weak indications of brain tumor, and one category of patients with extra-cerebral cancer, perhaps with metastases to the brain. "Site" was considered in the three categories: brain coverings plus spaces, cerebrum, and elsewhere. "Morphology" was broken into nonneoplasms and two categories of neoplasms, one including metastatic tumors and one not. "Case readability characteristics" were seven: rating of detection confidence on a 5-point scale for CT; the same for RN; whether or not the CT reader reported site of lesion; the same for RN; whether or not the CT reader reported morphology of lesion; the same for RN; and whether or not an angiogram was reported as done.

On five of the thirteen dimensions, the two samples differed to a statistically significant extent ($p < .05$). In comparison to the original sample, the test sample had

1. a shortage of metastatic tumors and, with respect to other lesions, an excess of those that are more clinically apparent;
2. a shortage of nonneoplastic lesions;
3. a drastic shortage of cases that the RN reader in the collaborative study had falsely classified as negative;
4. a shortage of cases for which the RN reader in the collaborative study failed to give the site of the lesion; and
5. an excess of cases that had been given angiograms.

Further analysis was conducted to determine if the five differences could be related to our main selection criterion—that a case be confirmed by tissue findings—or to a secondary selection criterion—that a case be imaged via both contrast-enhanced CT and nonenhanced CT as well as via RN. Specifically, we chose two subsets of the original sample for comparison with the test sample, one of which contained cases not satisfying the first criterion and one of which contained cases not satisfying the second. The idea in each instance was to pit against the test sample that subset of the original sample that would differ from it most in terms of the particular selection criterion. Here the expected frequencies of the chi-square test are not simply proportional to those of the original sample but are influenced by both samples.

The analysis of these subsets indicated that all five differences noted could be due to the main selection criterion and that four of the five could be due to the secondary criterion. In a third stage of analysis, the two subsets were further refined by subtracting from each the cases that were included also in the other. At this point, the main selection criterion (histological confirmation) was still implicated in all five of the significant differences, and the second criterion was now implicated in one less difference—that is, in the last three of the differences as listed.

Our final concern in statistical analysis was to determine if relaxing either of the selection criteria operating on the reading test would reduce the differences between the two samples, because some relaxation could have been effected without terribly serious effects. Specifically, we might have permitted case confirmation by angiogram as well as histology, and we might have done without the contrast-enhanced mode of CT if either action would have improved the representativeness of the test sample. In this analysis we considered again all 13 of the dimensions first selected.

The first relaxation is examined by comparing the subset of cases in the original sample that met a criterion of either histological or angiographic confirmation, and that did not meet the secondary criterion of imaging in all three modes, with its complementary subset. The second relaxation compares the subset of cases meeting the histology criterion, except for those missing just contrast CT, with its complementary subset. A further selection of appropriate subsets allows examination of results of relaxing both constraints. The outcome was that nothing would be gained by these relaxations; all of the detected differences persist.

Let us consider first some mechanisms possibly underlying the observed differences and then how this evidence should affect generalization of the reading-test results. The question of generalization is, unfortunately, less one of defining precisely a meaningful population to which the results refer than one of how the generalization to the population of the original case sample should be qualified.

Requiring histological confirmation might be expected to lead to differences in the presenting clinical group, because groups with lower probability of brain tumor would tend less to go to surgery. Likewise, that criterion might well produce underrepresentation of neoplasms in the category that includes metastatic lesions, and of nonneoplasms. Again, that criterion might be expected to lead to underrepresentation of cases lacking radiographic evidence sufficiently clear-cut to steer the surgery. Thus, differences on RN detection confidence, RN site, and angiogram (yes or no) are consistent with the idea that test-sample cases had more radiographic study (including angiograms) and more clear-cut radiographic findings. The mechanism of the secondary selection criterion is less transparent, and we shall not speculate on it.

Concerning the generalization of reading-test results, there are the indications that cases in the reading test were, on average, easier to read than those in the original sample. The differences in presenting group mean that earlier and smaller lesions were underrepresented, and hence both CT and RN might have fared better than otherwise. Morphologically, we see possibly counteracting effects on accuracy: an overrepresentation of large neoplastic lesions but an underrepresentation of nonneoplastic lesions. Although the proportionately fewer false-negatives and cases for which site was not given were statistically significant only for RN, the same pattern appeared for CT and might have reached significance in a sample about twice as large.

How large is the sum of these effects? We do not know, of course, but an extension of our analysis gives an estimate of the lower bound of the impact on the detection indices. In particular, we proceeded to analyze about 1200 cases as read at the collaborative centers and scored against the diagnosis most likely at the time. The index A_z for CT was 0.94 (compared to 0.97 in the test sample) and for RN was 0.82 (compared to 0.87 in the test sample). The difference observed is a lower bound, for one reason, because the truth data for the original sample included all accumulated evidence, including results of the two modalities under study. Allowing the two modalities thus to score themselves to some extent can only inflate the accuracy index. Moreover, the readers at the centers had more extensive background information on each case available to them than did the readers in our test.

Potentially more serious than an overestimate of the absolute accuracies of the two modalities is the possibility that one of the modalities was favored over the other, with RN benefiting from fewer difficult cases. Positive cases given a detection confidence rating of 5 (highly confident that the case is normal), by RN readers at the collaborative center, amounted to 35% of the original sample and 11% of the test sample. Cases with sites not indicated by the RN reader at the centers amounted to 42% of the original sample and 19% of the test sample.

The first tack to take in view of such differences is to try to remove their effects by a correction of some sort. In principle, all of the differences observed could be removed by forcing the test sample to assume the proportions of the original sample—necessarily in this instance by subtracting cases from, rather than adding cases to, the test sample. However, that depletion would leave far too small a sample. As an example, correcting the difference on detection confidence for RN would reduce the number of positive cases from 84 to 26. In principle, again, one could obtain accuracy indices on subsets of the test sample and weight them according to population proportions in a merged index. Here, however, the subsets would not be large enough to give sufficient reliability for index estimates.

The investigator's first obligation is to alert the audience about the existence of differences between the two samples; the second obligation is to spell out the most significant of the resulting qualifications that may be in order. The foregoing text provides an illustration. We note again, though, the less adequate diagnoses available for the original case sample and the inability to ascribe all discrepancies to the process of selecting a reading-test sample.

In the technical report of this CT/RN study we advanced certain other qualifications as well, not bearing on the difference in samples. One was that the original case sample was not demonstrably representative of the population of patients presenting to the center as "suspect for tumor"; a noticeable factor was that many patients with extracerebral tumors declined to have the additional diagnostic studies required for entry into the study. A second qualification stemmed from the limited time available for follow-up on negative cases—a common problem. The last qualification concerns a possible effect that would work in opposition to one mentioned earlier as favoring the RN modality: Our RN readers were rather more concerned than our CT readers about the variability in the format of the test images and about the overall technical quality of the imaging studies for some of the cases. It would appear that RN imaging, although older, was substantially less standardized than CT imaging at the time of the collaborative study; that the collaborative study did not effect much standardization of RN imagery for study purposes; and, perforce, that we were comparing the modalities as typically administered (although in major medical centers) rather than comparing their best applications. Additionally, our RN test readers had to contend with a greater range of variability in format than would probably be encountered in a single clinical setting. Our preference in this study, though not necessarily in all imaging studies, would have been to compare the two modalities at their best. Needless to say, we would have liked to have had equally high degrees of standardization.

APPENDIX C

Illustrative Posttest Questionnaire

In Chapter 7 (Section 7.8) we discussed communications with test readers and recommended a posttest interview. In our CT/RN study we used the questionnaire reproduced in this appendix to provide a format for soliciting various kinds of information from the readers. The questionnaire includes sections on the reader's background, adequacy of the physical environment of the test, adequacy of the test procedure, quality of the images, and implications of the study for further work. We attempted to make clear that we desired the reader's critical reaction to all aspects of the study and advice to us concerning the interpretation of results. The questionnaires given CT and RN readers differed to the extent that our questions were specific to the modality; only the form for CT is given here.

COMPUTED-TOMOGRAPHY READERS
STUDY CRITIQUE QUESTIONNAIRE

READER BACKGROUND
Name: _____ Department: _____
Institution: _____
Professional degrees and dates: _____
Which term best describes your background? (check one)
Radiology _____ Neurology _____ Neurosurgery _____
Nuclear medicine _____ Neuroradiology _____ Other (specify) _____
How many years have you been reading CT images? _____ RN images? _____
Where has your experience been gained?

With what CT equipment do you have experience?

With what equipment do you consider yourself most familiar?

What equipment do you currently use?

What is the relative amount of time you spend in research? _____
in clinical practice? _____
In practice, how many CT scans do you normally read in a day of diagnostic reading?
_____

What percent of these are brain scans? _____
What is your best estimate as to what percent of these brain scans are positive? __
What percent of those positives are neoplasms? _____
Approximately how many CT scans of the brain have you read in your total experience?
_____

Briefly, what is your general impression of the relative accuracy of CT and RN, considering
both site and type of cranial lesion?

PHYSICAL ENVIRONMENT
Please comment on how the following aspects of the physical setup of our laboratory may
have affected your reading of images:

Multiple-slice-per-image format (rather than single, larger slices)

Panel setup (i.e., window level, window width, arrangement of knobs, etc.)

Image quality (as determined by the display equipment)

Time limitation per case

Room lighting, noise, etc.

Other

If this study were to be repeated, what changes would you suggest we make in the laboratory set-up?

TEST MATERIALS AND PROCEDURES
Please comment on how the following aspects of the quality of the images presented to you may have affected your reading of images:

Variation in number and location of slices

Patient motion, artifacts

Other

In terms of the over-all quality of the images, what percent would you say fell into each of the following categories:

Good or excellent	————
Satisfactory or acceptable	————
Unsatisfactory	————
Abominable	————
	100%

How did you feel about the case load in our study, i.e., the number of cases you read in a day?

Please comment on whether fatigue and/or boredom might have been a factor in your reading of images, and when it may have occurred.

In what percent of the *cases* where noncontrast was followed by contrast did you feel that the *contrast* scan helped, i.e., either changed your choice of diagnoses or increased your confidence level?

What percent of these *changes in response* do you estimate were due to seeing more or better slices, independent of contrast?

In what percent of the *cases* where contrast was followed by noncontrast did you feel that the *non-contrast* scan helped, i.e., either changed your choice of diagnoses or increased your confidence level?

What percent of these *changes in response* do you estimate were due to seeing more or better slices, independent of noncontrast?

Were the response-form choices for site and differential diagnosis adequate for the responses you wished to make?
Please comment on inadequacies. In particular, please specify any diagnoses you wished to make that you found difficult to fit into the categories provided.

Would you have liked an opportunity, or more time, for detailed comments on specific cases?

Were there additional questions related to reading the images that we should have included in our response form?

How did you use the patient's age in making your differential diagnosis, i.e., what impact did age have on your choice of diagnoses, confidence level, etc.?

Briefly, what was the impact on your image reading of not having clinical background information?

How did the fact that this was a test situation rather than a clinical situation affect your approach to reading the images?

How might it have affected your performance?

Granted that "truth data" were not presented, do you feel that the case sample you viewed represented a realistic distribution of pathologies?
Please comment.

IMPLICATIONS FOR FURTHER STUDY
In what respects, if any, was CT presented in a *less* than favorable light, relative to a *comparison with RN*?

In what respects, if any, was CT presented in a *more* than favorable light, relative to a *comparison with RN*?

In what respects, if any, was the presentation of CT in our study *less* favorable than is typical in *clinical practice*?

In what respects, if any, was the presentation of CT in our study *more* favorable than is typical in *clinical practice*?

Given our study objectives (attached), what problems do you see with the pilot study?

Granted that you viewed only one modality (CT), if we were to utilize performance results from this pilot study in a final report comparing the two modalities, what qualifications or caveats should we include in that final report?

Overall, how do you feel about this study and your participation in it?

What additional advice would you give us concerning any aspect of the conduct of future studies comparing imaging modalities?

APPENDIX D

Computer Program
for Accuracy Analysis

Introduction

The following pages provide a listing for the computer program written by Dorfman and Alf to compute the accuracy indices associated with the ROC. Their (1969) article describes an earlier version of the program that is essentially complete but prints out fewer indices. A *User's Guide* prepared by Dr. Dorfman accompanies the listing here. Prior to both, immediately following, are some text and figures we have prepared to illustrate the program's use.

Figure 25 shows illustrative rating-scale data. Just how these data are entered into the computer will depend on the computer operating system employed. The *User's Guide* assumes that cards will be used, but Figure 26 gives an example of an alternative we have used for typewriter entry. According to Figure 26, our system first calls for the number of response categories less one and a subject number; here, they are "4" and "1," respectively. Then as directed, one enters the column totals and the raw, noncumulated frequencies for each column. ("Noise-only" in our terms

| | Stimulus | |
Response	Abnormal	Normal
Very likely abnormal, 1	350 (0.70)	25 (0.05)
Probably abnormal, 2	50 (0.80)	50 (0.15)
Possibly abnormal, 3	40 (0.88)	75 (0.30)
Probably normal, 4	35 (0.95)	150 (0.60)
Very likely normal, 5	25 (1.00)	200 (1.00)

Figure 25. Hypothetical rating-scale data.

could mean "normal," and "signal + noise" could mean "abnormal.")
The program does the rest, as per Figure 27.

The output, of course, also depends on the particular computer system used. We, for example, edited the original program so that it would work with narrower paper.

Figure 27 shows that the program first puts out "initial values," that is, initial estimates of certain accuracy parameters. A is the parameter we have denoted a, namely, the normal-deviate value of the y intercept of the ROC at $P(FP) = 0.50$. B is the parameter we have called s, the slope of the ROC. $-Z(K)$ is the normal-deviate index of the location of the decision criterion we have termed Z_k, with sign reversed. Not only is the sign of $Z(K)$ reversed, but the value of K in the printout runs in the reverse direction from our notation. (A comparison of the order in the printout with the order in Chapter 1, Section 1.5, will clarify the reversal.) $N1$ and $N2$ are the column totals of the rating-scale data. Here and elsewhere, we have modified the program to print the estimates in decimal rather than exponential format, as suggested under the heading "Output" in the *User's Guide*.

These estimates are followed by the "response frequencies" that had been entered. The detail to note here is that the program numbers the response categories in the reverse of the order used in this protocol. "Chi-square" gives a measure of the goodness-of-fit of a straight line to the ROC points. It is used with $n - 2$ degrees of freedom, where n

```
ENTER (# OF RESP. CAT.-1),SUBJECT #: 4,1

ENTER # OF NOISE-ONLY TRIALS FOLLOWED BY FREQUENCIES.
ENTER 8 NUMBERS/LINE, DELIMITED BY SPACES OR COMMAS.
500,200,150,75,50,25

ENTER # OF SIGNAL+NOISE TRIALS FOLLOWED BY FREQUENCIES
ENTER 8 NUMBERS/LINE.
500,25,35,40,50,350
```

Figure 26. One possible method of entering data to the Dorfman-Alf computer program.

```
         MAXIMUM LIKELIHOOD ESTIMATES FOR RATING METHOD DATA
                                                SUBJECT NO.    1
                             INITIAL VALUES

A=     1.4863            B=      0.5959         NO. OF Z(K)"S =   4

-Z(K)=   0.253     -0.524     -1.036     -1.645

N1=   500.      N2=   500.

RESPONSE FREQUENCIES

              1      2      3      4      5

   N    200.   150.    75.    50.    25.
  S+N    25.    35.    40.    50.   350.

              1      2      3      4      5

   N   .4000  .3000  .1500  .1000  .0500
  S+N  .0500  .0700  .0800  .1000  .7000

CHI SQUARE=     1.301            LOGL= -1205.785




PROCEDURE CONVERGES --   3 ITERATIONS.



                             FINAL VALUES

A=     1.48364           B=      0.59161

-Z(K)=   0.255      -0.525     -1.054     -1.625

CHI SQUARE=     0.675            LOGL= -1205.457

VARIANCE-COVARIANCE MATRIX
 0.0072   0.0030  -0.0016  -0.0015  -0.0012  -0.0004
 0.0030   0.0033  -0.0007  -0.0001   0.0008   0.0025
-0.0016  -0.0007   0.0032   0.0019   0.0014   0.0009
-0.0015  -0.0001   0.0019   0.0032   0.0026   0.0023
-0.0012   0.0008   0.0014   0.0026   0.0043   0.0041
-0.0004   0.0025   0.0009   0.0023   0.0041   0.0078

         A=        1.48364079        VAR(A)=   0.0072
         B=        0.59160558        VAR(B)=   0.0033
  DELTA M=        2.50782082   VAR(DELTA M)=        0.03637032
     D(E)=        1.86433221     VAR(D(E))=        0.00703522
     A(Z)=        0.89918400     VAR(A(Z))=        0.00010827
     D(A)=        1.80583197     VAR(D(A))=        0.00694764
```

Figure 27.   Printout of computations made by the Dorfman-Alf program.

equals the number of ROC points (and one less than the number of rating categories). "Log L," printed next, is as described by Dorfman and Alf in their (1969) article.

The "final values" of the estimates are given next, followed by the "variance–covariance matrix." The columns and rows of the matrix are not labeled in the type-out, but they are (from left to right and top to bottom): A (or a), B (s in our terminology), and the four instances of $-Z(K)$ (or Z_k). In the Dorfman-Alf notation, they are $Z(1)$ to $Z(4)$; in our notation, they are the reverse: Z_4 to Z_1. The diagonal entries thus give the variances of the various estimates.

The program prints out compactly the quantities of major interest to us: a or A, s or B, Δm, d'_e, A_z, and d_a, and the variances of these quantities. These quantities are shown at the bottom of the figure in slightly different, but obvious, notation. They are also mentioned in the last section of the *User's Guide*.

A slightly edited version of Dr. Dorfman's most recent (February 1978) *User's Guide* follows immediately.

RSCORE II

Donald D. Dorfman

This program employs a variant of the Newton-Raphson method, called the method of scoring, to obtain maximum-likelihood estimates of the parameters of signal detection theory for rating-method data. In the method of scoring the expected second-partial derivatives replace the observed second-partial derivatives used in the Newton-Raphson method.

The method of scoring requires a set of initial guesses or preliminary estimates of the parameters. This program does not require a set of initial estimates. The program calculates the least-squares solution for the parameter estimates from the data and uses these least-squares estimates as the initial values for the method of scoring.

Input. The program requires only the absolute frequencies of ratings in each category and the control information shown in the section on data input format. If more than 17 rating categories are being used, the arrays will require redimensioning.

Output. The program outputs: (1) response frequencies and response proportions; (2) initial and final estimates of the parameters, χ^2, and log likelihood for each case; (3) variance–covariance matrix in which both the rows and columns are ordered $a, b, Z_1, \ldots , Z_{kk}$ (the elements of this matrix are useful in the computation of confidence intervals about the population parameters); (4) common measures of sensitivity and their variances.

Some users may find the exponential format in which the parameter estimates are printed inconvenient. The initial estimates and the final estimates of the Z_k's can be changed to decimal format simply by commenting statements 6001 and 6002 and decommenting the alternative versions. Converting final estimates of a and b to decimal format requires simply replacing the two E15.8 specifications in statement 6005 with F10.4 specifications.

Final values are printed out when the sum of the absolute corrections becomes less than 0.001. If the procedure converges, a message will be printed out stating that convergence occurred, giving the number of iterations to convergence. If convergence does not occur within 200 iterations, a statement will be printed that the procedure does not converge.

The program is written in FORTRAN-IV G for the IBM 360/65, but should be easily adaptable to other FORTRANs. It is in single precision and uses the on-line functions EXP, ABS, and ALOG.

DATA INPUT FORMAT

Card 1	Col.	Variable
	1–2	number of Z_k's (cutoffs)
	5–9	subject number
	All are right justified	

Card 2	1–10	N_1
	11–20	f_{11}
	21–30	f_{12}
	.	
	.	
	.	
	etc.	

where f_{1j} are the observed response frequencies for the noise (noncumulated), and N_1 is the number of noise only trials. Use as many cards as needed for f_{1j}, and begin in 1–10 of new cards.

Note that confidence that the stimulus was signal + noise (S + N) increases with the numerical value of j.

New Card	Column	Variable
	1–10	N_2
	11–20	f_{21}
	21–30	f_{22}

where f_{2j} are the observed frequencies for the signal + noise, and N_2 is the number of signal + noise trials. Use as many cards as needed for f_{2j}. The numbers on cards 2 and following must be right justified. If one response category, for example, definitely yes, has zeros for both stimuli, then exclude this category, and assume one less cutoff.

LIST OF MAJOR VARIABLES

For those who may wish to change the program, a list of the major variables is provided.

Variable	Refers to	Variable	Refers to
AA	a	KK	Number of $-Z_k$'s
A1	$N1$	KKK	Number of response categories $(KK + 1)$
		NDTR	Subroutine used to calculate normal integrals and densities (F, f)
A2	$N2$		
AN	Number of observations	R(I)	Relative frequency of R's in category j on noise trials
		RP(I)	Relative frequency of R's in category j on signal + noise trials
AAA	$\partial \ln L/\partial a$		
B	b	SUBNO	Subject number
BBB	$\partial \ln L/\partial b$	SUM(I)	$F(bZ-a)$
CHI	χ^2	SUM1(I)	$f(bZ-a)$
E(I)	$\partial \ln L/\partial X_i$	SUM7(I)	$f(Z)$
F(I)	Absolute frequency of R's in category I on noise trials	SUM10(I)	$F(Z)$
		X(I)	$-Z_k$
FP(I)	Absolute frequency of R's in category I on signal + noise trials		
		XP(J,K)	Element of variance–covariance matrix
H	Correction for a		
HK	Correction for b	XX(J,K)	Element of matrix $\{E\partial^2 \log L/\partial\theta_t\partial\theta_u\}$
		ZDEV	Subroutine to calculate normal deviates from input
HL(I)	Correction for Z_k		

CONVERGENCE CRITERION

Final values are printed out when the sum of the absolute corrections becomes less than 0.001. This constraint is stringent for many applications. If you do not get convergence, reduce constraint to 0.01; if still no convergence, to 0.1. If you are unable to obtain convergence with 0.1, your sample size is probably too small. If such is the case, use the least-squares estimates (the initial values).

To alter the constraint, change statement 0191.

```
0191 IF(TNET.LT.(.001)) SWT = 1
```

OUTPUT NOTES

A	Estimate of $\dfrac{\mu_s - \mu_n}{\sigma_s}$.
B	Estimate of σ_n/σ_s.
Z(K)	Estimate of $\dfrac{X_k - \mu_n}{\sigma_n}$.

MEASURES OF SENSITIVITY

The program also prints common maximum-likelihood estimates of sensitivity and their associated asymptotic variances.

Measure	Equivalent to	Estimate of
A	y-intercept	$(\mu_s - \mu_n)/\sigma_s$
B	s (slope)	σ_n/σ_s
DELTA M	$\Delta m = A/B$	$(\mu_s - \mu_n)/\sigma_n$
D(E)	$d'_e = \dfrac{2A}{B+1}$	$2(\mu_s - \mu_n)/(\sigma_s + \sigma_n)$
A(Z)	area under ROC curve	$F[(\mu_s - \mu_n)/(\sigma_s^2 + \sigma_n^2)^{1/2}]$ F is $N(0,1)$.
D(A)	$2^{1/2}D_{YN} = \dfrac{2^{1/2}A}{(B^2+1)^{1/2}}$ ($2^{1/2}$orthonormal distance)	$\dfrac{2^{1/2}(\mu_s - \mu_n)}{(\sigma_s^2 + \sigma_n^2)^{1/2}}$.

Confidence intervals.   The 95% confidence interval for a measure of sensitivity θ is $\hat{\theta} \pm 1.96$ S.E. $(\hat{\theta})$, where $\hat{\theta}$ is the M.L.E. for θ.

SAMPLE DATA

The data of four subjects are provided to test your implementation of the program.

POOLING OF RESPONSE CATEGORIES

If the computer program stops at IER $= -1$ (statement 0167), then the matrix $\{-E\partial^2 \log L/\partial\theta_t\partial\theta_u\}$ is almost surely singular. In other words, its determinant is zero. This means that the total frequency of usage for some of your response categories is too small for maximum-likelihood theory. To rectify, group or pool infrequently used response categories with adjacent response categories. Use broader and broader response categories until the problem is solved, always remembering that you must have at least three response categories. If this does not solve the problem, use the initial values as your parameter estimates. The initial values are least-squares estimates, and although not optimal, they are acceptable as a first approximation.

BIBLIOGRAPHY

Dorfman, D. D. Standard errors and confidence intervals for measures of sensitivity. Acoustical Society of America Meetings, Miami Beach, Florida, December, 1977.

Dorfman, D. D., and Alf, E., Jr. Maximum-likelihood estimation of parameters of signal-detection theory and determination of confidence intervals—rating-method data. *Journal of Mathematical Psychology*, 1969, **6**, 487–496.

Dorfman, D. D., Beavers, L. L., and Saslow, C. Estimation of signal-detection theory parameters from rating-method data: A comparison of the method of scoring and direct search. *Bulletin of the Psychonomic Society*, 1973, **1**, 207–208.

Green, D. M., and Swets, J. A. *Signal detection theory and psychophysics*. New York: Wiley, 1966.

SAMPLE DATA

The following pages contain the sample data of four subjects, as mentioned in Dorfman's *User's Guide*, which can be used to test your implementation of the program.

```
ENTER (# OF RESP. CAT.-1),SUBJECT #: 5,1

ENTER # OF NOISE-ONLY TRIALS FOLLOWED BY FREQUENCIES.
ENTER 8 NUMBERS/LINE, DELIMITED BY SPACES OR COMMAS.
591,174,172,104,92,41,8

ENTER # OF SIGNAL+NOISE TRIALS FOLLOWED BY FREQUENCIES
ENTER 8 NUMBERS/LINE.
597,46,57,66,101,154,173
```

```
          MAXIMUM LIKELIHOOD ESTIMATES FOR RATING METHOD DATA

                                                    SUBJECT NO.    1
                              INITIAL VALUES

A =     1.0736          B =     0.7179          NO. OF Z(K)"S =  5

-Z(K)=   0.540     -0.215     -0.711     -1.386     -2.211

N1=   591.     N2=   597.

RESPONSE FREQUENCIES

            1       2       3       4       5       6
    N     174.    172.    104.     92.     41.      8.
  S+N      46.     57.     66.    101.    154.    173.

            1       2       3       4       5       6
    N    .2944   .2910   .1760   .1557   .0694   .0135
  S+N    .0771   .0955   .1106   .1692   .2580   .2898

CHI SQUARE=     4.380          LOGL= -1922.405

PROCEDURE CONVERGES --   4 ITERATIONS.

                              FINAL VALUES

A =     1.07210         B =     0.70577

-Z(K)=   0.533     -0.204     -0.710     -1.366     -2.294

CHI SQUARE=     1.497          LOGL= -1920.985

VARIANCE-COVARIANCE MATRIX
  0.0042   0.0014  -0.0015  -0.0014  -0.0013  -0.0011  -0.0002
  0.0014   0.0020  -0.0006  -0.0002   0.0003   0.0012   0.0035
 -0.0015  -0.0006   0.0029   0.0017   0.0012   0.0008   0.0000
 -0.0014  -0.0002   0.0017   0.0025   0.0019   0.0015   0.0012
 -0.0013   0.0003   0.0012   0.0019   0.0028   0.0024   0.0026
 -0.0011   0.0012   0.0008   0.0015   0.0024   0.0045   0.0055
 -0.0002   0.0035   0.0000   0.0012   0.0026   0.0055   0.0129

          A =      1.07209843        VAR(A)=   0.0042
          B =      0.70576882        VAR(B)=   0.0020
   DELTA M=      1.51905043    VAR(DELTA M)=      0.00922597
     D(E)=      1.25702664       VAR(D(E))=      0.00448726
     A(Z)=      0.80946245       VAR(A(Z))=      0.00016406
     D(A)=      1.23873344       VAR(D(A))=      0.00444032
```

ENTER (# OF RESP. CAT.-1),SUBJECT #: 5,2

ENTER # OF NOISE-ONLY TRIALS FOLLOWED BY FREQUENCIES.
ENTER 8 NUMBERS/LINE, DELIMITED BY SPACES OR COMMAS.
591,217,206,97,57,12,2

ENTER # OF SIGNAL+NOISE TRIALS FOLLOWED BY FREQUENCIES
ENTER 8 NUMBERS/LINE.
597,37,54,80,156,165,105

            MAXIMUM LIKELIHOOD ESTIMATES FOR RATING METHOD DATA

                                              SUBJECT NO.   2
                          INITIAL VALUES

A =   1.4008   B =   0.8080   NO. OF Z(K)"S = 5

-Z(K)=   0.339   -0.570   -1.174   -1.983   -2.708

N 1=   591.   N2=   597.

RESPONSE FREQUENCIES

               1   2   3   4   5   6
        N   217.   206.   97.   57.   12.   2.
      S+N   37.   54.   80.   156.   165.   105.

               1   2   3   4   5   6
        N   .3672   .3486   .1641   .0964   .0203   .0034
      S+N   .0620   .0905   .1340   .2613   .2764   .1759

CHI SQUARE=   29.776   LOGL = -1813.267

PROCEDURE CONVERGES --   5 ITERATIONS.

                          FINAL VALUES

A =   1.37889   B =   0.73620

-Z(K)=   0.322   -0.536   -1.147   -2.039   -3.115

CHI SQUARE=   8.308   LOGL = -1802.134

VARIANCE-COVARIANCE MATRIX
  0.0056   0.0022 -0.0016 -0.0016 -0.0013 -0.0001   0.0025
  0.0022   0.0026 -0.0006 -0.0001   0.0008   0.0033   0.0072
 -0.0016 -0.0006   0.0027   0.0015   0.0011   0.0004 -0.0005
 -0.0016 -0.0001   0.0015   0.0027   0.0021   0.0019   0.0018
 -0.0013   0.0008   0.0011   0.0021   0.0037   0.0040   0.0052
 -0.0001   0.0033   0.0004   0.0019   0.0040   0.0099   0.0142
  0.0025   0.0072 -0.0005   0.0018   0.0052   0.0142   0.0301

          A =   1.37888801   VAR(A)=   0.0056
          B =   0.73620337   VAR(B)=   0.0026
    DELTA M=   1.87297162   VAR(DELTA M)=   0.01179265
       D(E)=   1.58839458   VAR(D(E))=   0.00496915
       A(Z)=   0.86659104   VAR(A(Z))=   0.00011540
       D(A)=   1.57037169   VAR(D(A))=   0.00497623

```
ENTER (# OF RESP. CAT.-1),SUBJECT #: 5,3

ENTER # OF NOISE-ONLY TRIALS FOLLOWED BY FREQUENCIES.
ENTER 8 NUMBERS/LINE, DELIMITED BY SPACES OR COMMAS.
591,334,99,26,42,43,47

ENTER # OF SIGNAL+NOISE TRIALS FOLLOWED BY FREQUENCIES
ENTER 8 NUMBERS/LINE.
597,81,44,26,32,66,348
```

```
          MAXIMUM LIKELIHOOD ESTIMATES FOR RATING METHOD DATA

                                                SUBJECT NO.    3
                          INITIAL VALUES

A=      1.2279           B=      0.7165          NO. OF Z(K)"S =  5

-Z(K)=  -0.164     -0.621      -0.761     -1.027     -1.409

N1=   591.     N2=   597.

RESPONSE FREQUENCIES

           1        2        3        4        5        6

    N    334.      99.      26.      42.      43.      47.
  S+N     81.      44.      26.      32.      66.     348.

           1        2        3        4        5        6


    N    .5651   .1675   .0440   .0711   .0728   .0795
  S+N    .1357   .0737   .0436   .0536   .1106   .5829

CHI SQUARE=     5.368            LOGL= -1578.787
PROCEDURE CONVERGES --    3 ITERATIONS.



                          FINAL VALUES

A=    1.22457           B=     0.71560

-Z(K)=  -0.166    -0.606      -0.771     -1.016     -1.417

CHI SQUARE=     2.829            LOGL= -1577.664

VARIANCE-COVARIANCE MATRIX
  0.0064   0.0034  -0.0020  -0.0016  -0.0014  -0.0011  -0.0003
  0.0034   0.0042  -0.0008  -0.0000   0.0004   0.0010   0.0025
 -0.0020  -0.0008   0.0027   0.0020   0.0019   0.0016   0.0012
 -0.0016  -0.0000   0.0020   0.0027   0.0026   0.0024   0.0022
 -0.0014   0.0004   0.0019   0.0026   0.0029   0.0028   0.0027
 -0.0011   0.0010   0.0016   0.0024   0.0028   0.0035   0.0035
 -0.0003   0.0025   0.0012   0.0022   0.0027   0.0035   0.0054

          A=        1.22456822        VAR(A)=    0.0064
          B=        0.71560202        VAR(B)=    0.0042
   DELTA M=        1.71124199    VAR(DELTA M)=      0.01416964
      D(E)=        1.42756677       VAR(D(E))=      0.00504027
      A(Z)=        0.84033895       VAR(A(Z))=      0.00015137
      D(A)=        1.40834709       VAR(D(A))=      0.00512797
```

```
ENTER (# OF RESP. CAT.-1),SUBJECT #: 5,4

ENTER # OF NOISE-ONLY TRIALS FOLLOWED BY FREQUENCIES.
ENTER 8 NUMBERS/LINE, DELIMITED BY SPACES OR COMMAS.
591,513,54,17,4,1,2

ENTER # OF SIGNAL+NOISE TRIALS FOLLOWED BY FREQUENCIES
ENTER 8 NUMBERS/LINE.
597,206,121,107,45,51,67
```

```
         MAXIMUM LIKELIHOOD ESTIMATES FOR RATING METHOD DATA
                                              SUBJECT NO.    4
                            INITIAL VALUES

A =     1.5094            B=     0.9552          NO. OF Z(K)"S =  5

-Z(K)=  -1.117    -1.744    -2.263    -2.571    -2.708

N1=    591.     N2=   597.

RESPONSE FREQUENCIES

           1       2       3       4       5       6
     N   513.    54.     17.     4.      1.      2.
    S+N  206.    121.    107.    45.     51.     67.

           1       2       3       4       5       6


     N   .8680  .0914  .0288  .0068  .0017  .0034
    S+N  .3451  .2027  .1792  .0754  .0854  .1122

CHI SQUARE=     62.507          LOGL= -1306.974

PROCEDURE CONVERGES --   5 ITERATIONS.



                            FINAL VALUES

A =    1.39528         B=    0.88741

-Z(K)=  -1.119    -1.715    -2.256    -2.536    -2.932

CHI SQUARE=     2.077          LOGL= -1285.528

VARIANCE-COVARIANCE MATRIX
 0.0248   0.0142  -0.0052   0.0011   0.0084   0.0125   0.0186
 0.0142   0.0105  -0.0013   0.0038   0.0095   0.0126   0.0173
-0.0052  -0.0013   0.0042   0.0033   0.0026   0.0022   0.0017
 0.0011   0.0038   0.0033   0.0066   0.0083   0.0094   0.0110
 0.0084   0.0095   0.0026   0.0083   0.0152   0.0178   0.0217
 0.0125   0.0126   0.0022   0.0094   0.0178   0.0228   0.0280
 0.0186   0.0173   0.0017   0.0110   0.0217   0.0280   0.0380

         A =      1.39528209        VAR(A)=    0.0248
         B =      0.88741229        VAR(B)=    0.0105
    DELTA M=      1.57230422   VAR(DELTA M)=       0.00762448
       D(E)=      1.47851330     VAR(D(E))=       0.01067576
       A(Z)=      0.85166746     VAR(A(Z))=       0.00030363
       D(A)=      1.47588977     VAR(D(A))=       0.01133853
```

LISTING

The following pages contain the listing of the computer program for determining maximum-likelihood estimates of ROC parameters from rating-scale data.

```
C   PROGRAM DORFALF (RSCORE)
C   RATING METHOD PROGRAM--LATEST MODIFICATIONS
C   BY LYNN BEAVERS NOV. 22, 1972.
C
C   MODIFICATION BY B. FREEMAN MAY,1977 FOR USE ON BBN-TENEX.
C   CHANGES INCLUDE:
C        A.   TELETYPE INPUT OF DATA IN PLACE OF CARD INPUT.
C        B.   USE OF SINGLE-PRECISION COMPUTATIONS INSTEAD OF
C                  DOUBLE-PRECISION.
C        C.   DATA OUTPUT IN DECIMAL FORMAT INSTEAD OF
C                  SCIENTIFIC NOTATION.
C        D.   OUTPUT FORMAT CHANGED FROM WIDE PAPER TO NARROW PAPER.
C        E.   THE LARGE NUMBER IN SUBROUTINE "ZDEV" WAS CHANGED
C                  TO TENEX'S LARGEST REAL NUMBER.
C        F.   ADDITION TO PRINTOUT OF 3 NUMBERS: S, DELTA M,
C                  AND VARIANCE DELTA M.
C   EDIT BY B. FREEMAN  MARCH,1978
C   A THIRD VERSION OF 'RSCORE' WAS SENT THAT INCORPORATED 'F.' ABOVE
C   AND OUTPUT SOME ADDITIONAL PARAMETER ESTIMATES ALSO.
C   THE EDIT  INCLUDES THIS NEW SECTION CALLED 'PARAMETER ESTIMATES'.
C   NOTE:  THE PARTS OF THE ORIGINAL PROGRAM THAT WERE NOT USED
C   WERE LEFT IN AS COMMENTS.
C
C
        INTEGER SUBNO,SWT
        DIMENSION XXDUM(200)
        REAL LOGL,X(16),R(17),RP(17),SUM(18),SUM1(18),SUM7(18),
       1SUM10(18),E(16),HL(16),XX(18,18),XP(18,18),CR(16),F(17),FP(17)
        REAL*8 DSUMM,DSUMN,DSUM(18),DSUM10(18),DF(17),DFP(17)
        CALC(Y)=.5*(1.+.196854*Y+.115195*Y**2+.000344*Y**3+
       1.019527*Y**4)**(-4)

C   ENTER THE (# OF RESPONSE CAT. - 1), SUBJECT NUMBER.
3       TYPE 3012
3012    FORMAT('0ENTER (# OF RESP. CAT.-1),SUBJECT #: ',$)
        READ(5,1,END=2)KK,SUBNO
1       FORMAT(2I)
        KKK=KK+1
C
C   READ IN  FREQUENCIES FOR NOISE AND SIGNAL PLUS NOISE
C   INTO ARRAYS R AND RP, RESPECTIVELY
        TYPE 3014
3014    FORMAT(' ENTER # OF NOISE-ONLY TRIALS FOLLOWED BY FREQUENCIES.'/
       1' ENTER 8 NUMBERS/LINE, DELIMITED BY SPACES OR COMMAS.'/)
        READ(5,70)A1,(R(I),I=1,KKK)
70      FORMAT(8F)
        TYPE 3016
3016    FORMAT(' ENTER # OF SIGNAL+NOISE TRIALS FOLLOWED BY FREQUENCIES
       1'/' ENTER 8 NUMBERS/LINE.'/)
        READ(5,70)A2,(RP(I),I=1,KKK)
C
C   CARD INPUT
C3      READ(5,1,END=2)KK,SUBNO
C1      FORMAT(I2,2X,I5)
C       KK=KK+1
C       READ(5,70)A1,(R(I),I=1,KKK)
C       READ(5,70)A2,(RP(I),I=1,KKK)
C70     FORMAT(8F 10.0)
C
```

```
          DO 71983 I=1,KKK
          DF(I)=0.0D0
          DFP(I)=0.0D0
          DF(I)=R(I)
          DFP(I)=RP(I)
          F(I)=R(I)
          FP(I)=RP(I)
          R(I)=R(I)/A1
          RP(I)=RP(I)/A2
71983     CONTINUE
C
          DO 14 I=2,KK
          X(I)=0.
14        CR(I)=0.
C
C   FIND CUMULATIVE SUMS OF THE PROBABILITIES STARTING AT
C   THE RIGHT AND CUMULATING TO THE LEFT INTO ARRAYS X AND CR
C   FOR NOISE AND SIGNAL PLUS NOISE
C
          CR(KK)=RP(KKK)
          X(KK)=R(KKK)
          DO 12 I=2,KK
          CR(KK-I+1)=CR(KKK-I+1)+RP(KKK-I+1)
12        X(KK-I+1)=X(KKK-I+1)+R(KKK-I+1)
C   TEST FOR 1.'S AND CORRECT BY SUBTRACTING 1-1/2N AND TEST
C   FOR 0'S AND CORRECT BY CHANGING TO 1/2N THEN CALL SUBROUTINE ZDEV
C   TO TRANSFORM THE CUMULATIVE PROBABILITIES IN THE ARRAYS
C   TO STANDARD NORMAL DEVIATES.
C
          Q=0.
          DO 29 I=1,KK
          IF(X(I).EQ.0.)X(I)=1./(2.*A1)
          IF(X(I).GE.1.)X(I)=1.-(1./(2.*A1))
          P=X(I)
          CALL ZDEV(P,Q,D,IER)
          X(I)=Q
          IF(CR(I).EQ.0.)CR(I)=1./(2.*A2)
          IF(CR(I).GE.1.)CR(I)=1.-(1./(2.*A2))
          P=CR(I)
          CALL ZDEV(P,Q,D,IER)
          CR(I)=Q
29        CONTINUE
          IZ=KK-1
C
C   STARTING FROM THE RIGHT, TEST TO SEE IF SDN(I+1) IS EQUAL TO
C   OR LESS THAN SDN(I) AND IF SO MAKE SDN(I+1)=SDN(I)+.1
C
          DO 4 I=1,IZ
          IF(X(IZ-I+1).LE.X(IZ-I+2))X(IZ-I+1)=X(IZ-I+2)+.1
4         IF(CR(IZ-I+1).LE.CR(IZ-I+2))CR(IZ-I+1)=CR(IZ-I+2)+.1
C
C   CALCULATE LEAST SQUARES SOLUTIONS
C
          SUMX=0.
          SUMY=0.
          SUMXY=0.
          SUMX2=0.
          XK=KK
          DO 13 I=1,KK
          SUMX=SUMX+X(I)
          SUMX2=SUMX2+X(I)**2
          SUMY=SUMY+CR(I)
          SUMXY=SUMXY+CR(I)*X(I)
13        CONTINUE
```

```
        XMEAN=SUMX/XK
        YMEAN=SUMY/XK
        B=(XK*SUMXY-SUMX*SUMY)/(XK*SUMX2-SUMX**2)
        AA=YMEAN-B*XMEAN
        PI=3.1415926
        ZA=1./SQRT(2.*PI)
        NN=KK+2
        SWT=0
        LL=0
C   GET INTEGRALS AND DENSITIES
        DO 2000 J=1,NN
        DO 2000 K=1,NN
        XX(J,K)=0.
2000    XP(J,K)=0.
2001    LL=LL+1
        SUM(1)=0.
        SUM(NN)=1.
        SUM7(1)=0.
        SUM7(NN)=0.
        DO 6 I=2,KKK
        Y=-X(I-1)*B-AA
        CALL NDTR(Y,SUM(I),SUM1(I))
6       CONTINUE
        SUM1(1)=0
        SUM1(NN)=0.
        SUM10(1)=0.
        SUM10(NN)=1.
        DO 46 I=2,KKK
        Y=-X(I-1)
        CALL NDTR(Y,SUM10(I),SUM7(I))
46      CONTINUE
19867   FORMAT(10E12.4)
        IF(LL.NE.1)GO TO 601
        WRITE(5,6000)
6000    FORMAT('1',T10,'MAXIMUM LIKELIHOOD ESTIMATES FOR RATING
        1 METHOD DATA')
        WRITE(5,6008)SUBNO
6008    FORMAT('0',T55,'SUBJECT NO. ',I4)
        WRITE(5,6001)AA,B,KK
C6001   FORMAT('0',T30,'INITIAL VALUES',/'0A= ',E15.8,10X,'B= ',E15.8,
6001    FORMAT('0',T30,'INITIAL VALUES',/'0A= ',F10.4,10X,'B= ',F10.4,
        1T50,'NO. OF Z(K)"S = ',I2)

        WRITE(5,6002)(X(I),I=1,KK)
C6002   FORMAT('0-Z(K)= ',12(E15.8,1X))
6002    FORMAT('0-Z(K)= ',12(F7.3,3X))
        WRITE(5,6003)A1,A2
6003    FORMAT('0N1= ',F6.0,5X,'N2= ',F6.0)
        WRITE(5,8000)
8000    FORMAT(/1X,'RESPONSE FREQUENCIES ')
        WRITE(5,6004)(I,I=1,KKK)
        WRITE(5,6543)
6543    FORMAT('0')
        WRITE(5,8009)(F(I),I=1,KKK)
8009    FORMAT('     N ',17(F6.0,1X))
        WRITE(5,8010)(FP(I),I=1,KKK)
8010    FORMAT('  S+N ',17(F6.0,1X))
        WRITE(5,6004)(I,I=1,KKK)
        WRITE(5,6543)
6004    FORMAT(/' ',8X,17(I2,5X))
        WRITE(5,6009)(R(I),I=1,KKK)
6009    FORMAT('     N ',17(F6.4,1X))
        WRITE(5,6010)(RP(I),I=1,KKK)
6010    FORMAT('  S+N ',17(F6.4,1X))
C
C   GET FIRST PARTIALS
C   WITH RESPECT TO A
```

```
601     AAA=0.
        DO 4000 I=2,KKK
4000    AAA=AAA-SUM1(I)*(FP(I-1)/(SUM(I)-SUM(I-1))-FP(I)/(SUM(I+1)
       1-SUM(I)))
C  WITH RESPECT TO B
        BBB=0.
        DO 3001 I=2,KKK
3001    BBB=BBB-SUM1(I)*X(I-1)*(FP(I-1)/(SUM(I)-SUM(I-1))-FP(I)/
       1(SUM(I+1)-SUM(I)))
C  WITH RESPECT TO Z'S
        DO 3002 I=2,KKK
        Q1=-SUM1(I)*B*(FP(I-1)/(SUM(I)-SUM(I-1))-FP(I)/(SUM(I+1)
       1-SUM(I)))
        Q2=-SUM7(I)*(F(I-1)/(SUM10(I)-SUM10(I-1))-F(I)
       1/(SUM10(I+1)-SUM10(I)))
3002    E(I-1)=Q1+Q2
C  GET EXPECTED SECOND AND MIXED PARTIALS
C  WITH RESPECT TO A
        XX(1,1)=0.
        DO 3003 I=2,KKK
3003    XX(1,1)=XX(1,1)-SUM1(I)*((SUM1(I)-SUM1(I-1))
       1/(SUM(I)-SUM(I-1))-(SUM1(I+1)-SUM1(I))/(SUM(I+1)
       2-SUM(I)))
        XX(1,1)=A2*XX(1,1)
C  WITH RESPECT TO B
        XX(2,2)=0.
        DO 3004 I=2,KKK
        D=X(I-1)
        IF(I.EQ.KKK)GO TO 26
        IF(I.EQ.2)GO TO 25
        DD=X(I-2)
        DDD=X(I)
        GO TO 3004
25      DD=0.
        DDD=X(I)
        GO TO 3004
26      DD=X(I-2)
        DDD=0.
3004    XX(2,2)=XX(2,2)-SUM1(I)*X(I-1)*((SUM1(I)*D-SUM1(I-1)
       1*DD)/(SUM(I)-SUM(I-1))-(SUM1(I+1)*DDD-SUM1(I)*D)/
       2(SUM(I+1)-SUM(I)))
        XX(2,2)=A2*XX(2,2)
C  WITH RESPECT TO A AND B
        XX(1,2)=0.
        DO 3005 I=2,KKK
3005    XX(1,2)=XX(1,2)-SUM1(I)*X(I-1)*((SUM1(I)-SUM1(I-1))/
       1(SUM(I)-SUM(I-1))-(SUM1(I+1)-SUM1(I))/(SUM(I+1)-SUM(I)))
        XX(1,2)=A2*XX(1,2)
        XX(2,1)=XX(1,2)
C  WITH RESPECT TO A AND Z'S
        DO 3006 I=2,KKK
        XX(1,I+1)=-(A2*B*SUM1(I)*((SUM1(I)-SUM1(I-1))/(SUM(I)
       1-SUM(I-1))-(SUM1(I+1)-SUM1(I))/(SUM(I+1)-SUM(I))))
3006    XX(I+1,1)=XX(1,I+1)
C  WITH RESPECT TO B AND Z'S
        DO 3007 I=2,KKK
        XIL2=0.0
        IF(I.GT.2)XIL2=X(I-2)
        XX(2,I+1)=-(A2*SUM1(I)*B*((SUM1(I)*X(I-1)-SUM1(I-1)*XIL2)/
       1(SUM(I)-SUM(I-1))-(SUM1(I+1)*X(I)-SUM1(I)*X(I-1))
       1/(SUM(I+1)-SUM(I))))
3007    XX(I+1,2)=XX(2,I+1)
C  WITH RESPECT TO Z'S AND MIXED WITH RESPECT TO Z'S
        DO 3010 I=2,KKK
        IF(I.EQ.KKK)GO TO 3008
        XX(I+1,I+2)=(A2*SUM1(I)*SUM1(I+1)*B**2)/
       1(SUM(I+1)-SUM(I))+(A1*SUM7(I)*SUM7(I+1))/
       2(SUM10(I+1)-SUM10(I))
```

```
           XX(I+2,I+1)=XX(I+1,I+2)
3008       XX(I+1,I+1)=-(A2*(SUM1(I)*B)**2*(1./(SUM(I)-SUM(I-1))
           1+1./(SUM(I+1)-SUM(I)))+A1*SUM7(I)**2*(1./(SUM10(I)
           2-SUM10(I-1))+1./(SUM10(I+1)-SUM10(I))))
3010       CONTINUE
C  INVERT MATRIX
           DO 200 I=1,NN
           DO 200 J=1,NN
200        XX(I,J)=-XX(I,J)
19866      FORMAT(7E15.6)
           CALL MSTR(XX,XXDUM,18,0,1)
           CALL SINV(XXDUM,NN,.001,IER)
           IF(IER.EQ.-1)STOP 1
           IF(IER.GT.0)WRITE(5,201)IER
201        FORMAT(' LOSS OF SIGNIFICANCE.  STEP ',I5,'+1')
           CALL MSTR(XXDUM,XP,18,1,0)
           IF(SWT.EQ.1)GO TO 11
C  FORM SOLUTION VECTOR
           H=AAA*XP(1,1)+BBB*XP(1,2)
           DO 130 I=1,KK
130        H=H+E(I)*XP(1,I+2)
           HK=AAA*XP(2,1)+BBB*XP(2,2)
           DO 131 I=1,KK
131        HK=HK+E(I)*XP(2,I+2)
           DO 2200 I=1,KK
           HL(I)=AAA*XP(I+2,1)+BBB*XP(I+2,2)
           DO 2200 K=3,NN
2200       HL(I)=HL(I)+E(K-2)*XP(I+2,K)
C  ITERATE
           AA=AA+H
           B=B+HK
           DO 140 I=1,KK
140        X(I)=X(I)+HL(I)
           IF(LL.EQ.1)GO TO 11
           IF(LL.GT.200)GO TO 2011
C  CHECK FOR MAXIMIZATION
           TNET=ABS(H)+ABS(HK)
           DO 4500 I=1,KK
4500       TNET=TNET+ABS(HL(I))
           IF(TNET.LT.(.001))SWT=1
           GO TO 2001
C  GET VALUE OF CHI SQUARE
11         SUMM=0.
           SUMN=0.
           DO 5000 I=2,NN
           SUMN=SUMN+A2*(RP(I-1)-(SUM(I)-SUM(I-1)))**2/
           1(SUM(I)-SUM(I-1))
5000       SUMM=SUMM+A1*(R(I-1)-(SUM10(I)-SUM10(I-1)))**2/
           1(SUM10(I)-SUM10(I-1))
           CHI=SUMM+SUMN
C  GET VALUE OF LOG L
C          DSUMN=0.0D0
C          DSUMM=0.0D0
           SUMN=0.
           SUMM=0.
           DO 5001 I=2,NN
C          DSUM(I)=0.0D0
C          DSUM(I-1)=0.0D0
C          DSUM10(I)=0.0D0
C          DSUM10(I-1)=0.0D0
C          DSUM(I)=SUM(I)
C          DSUM(I-1)=SUM(I-1)
C          DSUM10(I)=SUM10(I)
C          DSUM10(I-1)=SUM10(I-1)
C          IF((DSUM(I)-DSUM(I-1)).LE.0.0D0)GO TO 800
           IF((SUM(I)-SUM(I-1)).LE.0)GO TO 800
C          DSUMM=DSUMM+DFP(I-1)*DLOG(DSUM(I)-DSUM(I-1))
           SUMM=SUMM+FP(I-1)*ALOG(SUM(I)-SUM(I-1))
```

```
C 800    IF((DSUM10(I)-DSUM10(I-1)).LE.O.ODO)GO TO 5001
800      IF((SUM10(I)-SUM10(I-1)).LE.O)GO TO 5001
C        DSUMN=DSUMN+DF(I-1)*DLOG(DSUM10(I)-DSUM10(I-1))
         SUMN=SUMN+F(I-1)*ALOG(SUM10(I)-SUM10(I-1))
5001     CONTINUE
C        LOGL=DSUMN+DSUMM
         LOGL=SUMN+SUMM
         IF(LL.EQ.1)GO TO 72
C   WRITE OUT FINAL VALUES, ETC., IF LAST ITERATION.
         WRITE(5,555)LL
555      FORMAT(////'OPROCEDURE CONVERGES -- ',I3,' ITERATIONS.')
556      WRITE(5,6005)AA,B
C6005    FORMAT(//'0',T30,'FINAL VALUES',/'OA= ',E15.8,10X,'B= ',E15.8)
6005     FORMAT(//'0',T30,'FINAL VALUES',/'OA= ',F10.5,10X,'B= ',F10.5)
         WRITE(5,6002)(X(I),I=1,KK)
         WRITE(5,6006)CHI,LOGL
6006     FORMAT('OCHI SQUARE= ',F9.3,10X,'LOGL= 'F9.3)
         WRITE(5,6007)
6007     FORMAT('OVARIANCE-COVARIANCE MATRIX')
         DO 312 I=1,NN
312      WRITE(5,6022)(XP(I,J),J=1,NN)
6022     FORMAT(' ',18(F7.4,1X))
C
C        WRITE(6,6008)SUBNO
C        WRITE(6,7020)
C7020    FORMAT('0',T21,'PARAMETER ESTIMATES')
C   COMPUTING PARAMETER ESTIMATES
C   XP(1,1)=VARIANCE(AA); XP(2,2)=VARIANCE(B)
C   XP(1,2)=COVARIANCE(AA,B)
         DTAM=AA/B
         VAA=XP(1,1)
         VB=XP(2,2)
         VAB=XP(1,2)
         VRDTAM=((1./B**2)*VAA)+((AA**2/B**4)*VB)-2.*(AA/B**3)*VAB
         DE=2*AA/(B+1)
         VRDE=4*((VAA/(B+1)**2)+(AA**2*VB/(B+1)**4)-(2*AA*VAB/(B+1)**3))
         V=AA/SQRT(B**2+1)
         DA=V*SQRT(2.0)
C   CALL SUBROUTINE NDTR FOR PROBABILITY AND DENSITY FUNCTIONS OF V
         CALL NDTR(V,P,D)
         VRPA=D**2*((VAA/(B**2+1))+((AA**2)*(B**2)*VB/((B**2+1)
        1**3))-(2*AA*B*VAB/((B**2+1)**2)))
         VRDA=2*((VAA/(B**2+1))+(AA**2*B**2*VB/(B**2+1)**3)-
        1(2*AA*B*VAB/((B**2+1)**2)))
         WRITE(5,7000)AA,VAA
C7000    FORMAT('0A= ',3E15.8,T40,'VAR(A)= ',F7.4)
7000     FORMAT('0     A= ',F15.8,T30,'     VAR(A)= ',F7.4)
         WRITE(5,7001)B,VB
C7001    FORMAT('0B= ',E15.8,T40,'VAR(B)= ',F7.4)
7001     FORMAT('      B= ',F15.8,T30,'     VAR(B)= ',F7.4)
         WRITE(5,7003)DTAM,VRDTAM
C7003    FORMAT('ODELTA M= ',E15.8,T40,'VAR(DELTA M)= ',E15.8)
7003     FORMAT(' DELTA M= ',F15.8,T30,'VAR(DELTA M)= ',F15.8)
         WRITE(5,7004)DE,VRDE
C7004    FORMAT(' OD(E)= ',E15.8,T40,'VAR(D(E))= ',E15.8)
7004     FORMAT('    D(E)= ',F15.8,T30,'   VAR(D(E))= ',F15.8)
         WRITE(5,7005)P,VRPA
C7005    FORMAT('OP(A)= ',E15.8,T40,'VAR(P(A))= ',E15.8)
7005     FORMAT('    A(Z)= ',F15.8,T30,'   VAR(A(Z))= ',F15.8)
         WRITE(5,7006)DA,VRDA
C7006    FORMAT('OD(A)= ',E15.8,T40,'VAR(D(A))= ',E15.8)
7006     FORMAT('    D(A)= ',F15.8,T30,'   VAR(D(A))= ',F15.8)
         GO TO 3
72       WRITE(5,6006)CHI,LOGL
         GO TO 2001
2011     WRITE(5,6011)
6011     FORMAT('ODOES NOT CONVERGE -- 200 ITERATIONS')
         GO TO 556
```

```
2          CALL EXIT
           END


           SUBROUTINE NDTR(X,P,D)
C
C-----------------------------------------------------------------
C
C          PURPOSE
C
C             COMPUTES Y = P(X) = PROBABILITY THAT THE RANDOM
C             VARIABLE DISTRIBUTED NORMALLY (0,1), IS LESS THAN
C             OR EQUAL TO X.  F(X), THE ORDINATE OF THE NORMAL DENSITY
C             AT X, IS ALSO COMPUTED.
C
C          USAGE
C
C             CALL NDTR(X, P, D)
C
C          DESCRIPTION OF PARAMETERS.
C             X--INPUT SCALAR FOR WHICH P(X)IS COMPUTED.
C             P--OUTPUT PROBABILITY.
C             D--OUTPUT DENSITY
C
C          REMARKS
C
C             MAXIMUM ERROR IS .0000007.
C
C          SUBROUTINE AND SUBPROGRAMS REQUIRED
C
C             NONE.
C
C          METHOD
C
C
C             BASED ON APPROXIMATIONS IN C. HASTINGS, APPROXIMATIONS
C             FOR DIGITAL COMPUTERS, PRINCETON UNIVERSITY PRESS,
C             PRINCETON, N.J., 1955.  SEE EQUATION 26.2.17,
C             HANDBOOK OF MATHEMATICAL FUNCTIONS, ABRAMOWITZ AND
C             STEGUN, DOVER PUBLICATIONS, INC., NEW YORK.
C
C
C-----------------------------------------------------------------
C
           AX=ABS(X)
           T=1.0/(1.0+0.2316419*AX)
           D=0.3989423*EXP(-X*X/2.0)
           P=1.0-D*T*((((1.330274*T-1.821256)*T+1.781478)*T-
          10.3565638)*T+0.3193815)
           IF(X)1,2,2
1          P=1.0-P
2          RETURN
           END


           SUBROUTINE SINV(A,N,EPS,IER)
           DIMENSION A(1)
           DOUBLE PRECISION DIN,WORK
C
C-----------------------------------------------------------------
C          PURPOSE
C             INVERT A GIVEN SYMMETRIC POSITIVE DEFINITE MATRIX
C
C          USAGE
C             CALL SINV(A,N,EPS,IER)
C
```

```
C          DESCRIPTION OF PARAMETERS
C             A     - UPPER TRIANGULAR PART OF THE GIVEN SYMMETRIC
C                     POSITIVE DEFINITE N BY N COEFFICIENT MATRIX.
C                     ON RETURN A CONTAINS THE RESULTANT UPPER
C                     TRIANGULAR MATRIX.
C             N     - THE NUMBER OF ROW (COLUMNS) IN GIVEN MATRIX.
C             EPS   - AN INPUT CONSTANT WHICH IS USED AS RELATIVE
C                     TOLERANCE FOR TEST ON LOSS OF SIGNIFICANCE.
C             IER   - RESULTING ERROR PARAMETER CODED AS FOLLOWS:
C                     IER=0  - NO ERROR
C                     IER=-1 - NO RESULT BECAUSE OF WRONG INPUT PARAME-
C                              TER N OR BECAUSE SOME RADICAND IS NON-
C                              POSITIVE (MATRIX A IS NOT POSITIVE
C                              DEFINITE, POSSIBLY DUE TO LOSS OF SIGNI-
C                              FICANCE)
C                     IER=K  - WARNING WHICH INDICATES LOSS OF SIGNIFI-
C                              CANCE.  THE RADICAND FORMED AT FACTORIZA-
C                              TION STEP K+1 WAS STILL POSITIVE BUT NO
C                              LONGER GREATER THAN ABS(EPS*A(K+1,K+1)).
C          REMARKS
C             THE UPPER TRIANGULAR PART OF GIVEN MATRIX IS ASSUMED TO BE
C             STORED COLUMNWISE IN N*(N+1)/2 SUCCESSIVE STORAGE LOCATIONS.
C             IN THE SAME STORAGE LOCATIONS THE RESULTING UPPER TRIANGU-
C          LAR MATRIX IS STORED COLUMNWISE TOO.
C             THE PROCEDURE GIVES RESULTS IF N IS GREATER THAN 0 AND ALL
C          CALCULATED RADICANDS ARE POSITIVE.
C
C          SUBROUTINES AND FUNCTION SUBPROGRAMS REQUIRED.
C             MFSD
C
C          METHOD
C             SOLUTION IS DONE USING THE FACTORIZATION BY SUBROUTINE MFSD.
C
C-------------------------------------------------------------------------
C
C    FACTORIZE GIVEN MATRIX BY MEANS OF SUBROUTINE MFSD
C          A=TRANSPOSE(T) * T
           CALL MFSD(A,N,EPS,IER)
           IF(IER)9,1,1
C
C          INVERT UPPER TRIANGULAR MATRIX T
C          PREPARE INVERSION-LOOP
    1      IPIV=N*(N+1)/2
           IND=IPIV
C
C          INITIALIZE INVERSION-LOOP
           DO 6 I=1,N
           DIN=1.D0/DBLE(A(IPIV))
           A(IPIV)=DIN
           MIN=N
           KEND=I-1
           LANF=N-KEND
           IF(KEND)5,5,2
    2      J=IND
C
C          INITIALIZE ROW-LOOP
           DO 4 K=1,KEND
           WORK=0.D0
           MIN=MIN-1
           LHOR=IPIV
           LVER=J
C
C          START INNER LOOP
           DO 3 L=LANF,MIN
           LVER=LVER+1
           LHOR=LHOR+L
           WORK=WORK+DBLE(A(LVER)*A(LHOR))
C          END OF INNER LOOP
```

```
          A(J)=-WORK*DIN
4         J=J-MIN
C
C         END OF ROW-LOOP
C
5         IPIV=IPIV-MIN
6         IND=IND-1
C
C         END OF INVERSION LOOP
C
C         CALCULATE INVERSE(A) BY MEANS OF INVERSE(T)
C         INVERSE(A)=INVERSE(T)*TRANSPOSE(INVERSE(T))
C         INITIALIZE MULTIPLICATION LOOP
          DO 8 I=1,N
          IPIV=IPIV+I
          J=IPIV
C
C         INITIALIZE ROW-LOOP
          DO 8 K=I,N
          WORK=0.D0
          LHOR=J
C
C         START INNER LOOP
          DO 7 L=K,N
          LVER=LHOR+K-I
          WORK=WORK+DBLE(A(LHOR)*A(LVER))
7         LHOR=LHOR+L
C
C         END OF INNER LOOP
C
          A(J)=WORK
8         J=J+K
C
C         END OF ROW- AND MULTIPLICATION-LOOP
C
9         RETURN
          END


          SUBROUTINE MFSD(A,N,EPS,IER)
          DIMENSION A(1)
          DOUBLE PRECISION DPIV,DSUM
C
C------------------------------------------------------------------------
C
C         PURPOSE
C           FACTOR A GIVEN SYMMETRIC POSITIVE DEFINITE MATRIX
C
C         DESCRIPTION OF PARAMETERS
C           A      - UPPER TRIANGULAR PART OF THE GIVEN SYMMETRIC
C                    POSITIVE DEFINITE N BY N COEFFICIENT MATRIX.
C                    ON RETURN A CONTAINS THE RESULTANT UPPER
C                    TRIANGULAR MATRIX.
C           N      - THE NUMBER OF ROW (COLUMNS) IN GIVEN MATRIX.
C           EPS    - AN INPUT CONSTANT WHICH IS USED AS RELATIVE
C                    TOLERANCE FOR TEST ON LOSS OF SIGNIFICANCE.
C           IER    - RESULTING ERROR PARAMETER CODED AS FOLLOWS:
C                    IER=0  - NO ERROR
C                    IER=-1 - NO RESULT BECAUSE OF WRONG INPUT PARAME-
C                             TER N OR BECAUSE SOME RADICAND IS NON-
C                             POSITIVE (MATRIX A IS NOT POSITIVE
C                             DEFINITE, POSSIBLY DUE TO LOSS OF SIGNI-
C                             FICANCE)
C                    IER=K  - WARNING WHICH INDICATES LOSS OF SIGNIFI-
C                             CANCE.  THE RADICAND FORMED AT FACTORIZA-
C                             TION STEP K+1 WAS STILL POSITIVE BUT NO
C                             LONGER GREATER THAN ABS(EPS*A(K+1,K+1)).
C         REMARKS
C           THE UPPER TRIANGULAR PART OF GIVEN MATRIX IS ASSUMED TO BE
C           STORED COLUMNWISE IN N*(N+1)/2 SUCCESSIVE STORAGE LOCATIONS.
```

```
C                 IN THE SAME STORAGE LOCATIONS THE RESULTING UPPER TRIANGU-
C              LAR MATRIX IS STORED COLUMNWISE TOO.
C                 THE PROCEDURE GIVES RESULTS IF N IS GREATER THAN 0 AND ALL
C              CALCULATED RADICANDS ARE POSITIVE.
C                 THE PRODUCT OF RETURNED DIAGONAL TERMS IS EQUAL TO THE
C              SQUARE ROOT OF THE DETERMINANT OF THE GIVEN MATRIX.
C
C              SUBROUTINES AND FUNCTION SUBPROGRAMS REQUIRED
C                 NONE
C
C              METHOD
C                 SOLUTION IS DONE USING THE SQUARE-ROOT METHOD OF CHOLESKY.
C              THE GIVEN MATRIX IS REPRESENTED AS PRODUCT OF 2 TRIANGULAR
C              MATRICES, WHERE THE LEFT HAND FACTOR IS THE TRANSPOSE OF
C                 THE RETURNED RIGHT-HAND FACTOR.
C
C----------------------------------------------------------------
C
C              TEST ON WRONG INPUT PARAMETER N
               IF(N-1)12,1,1
    1          IER=0
C
C              INITIALIZE DIAGONAL-LOOP
               KPIV=0
               DO 11 K=1,N
               KPIV=KPIV+K
               IND=KPIV
               LEND=K-1
C
C              CALCULATE TOLERANCE
               TOL=ABS(EPS*A(KPIV))
C
C              START FACTORIZATION-LOOP OVER K-TH ROW
               DO 11 I=K,N
               DSUM=0.D0
               IF(LEND)2,4,2
C
C              START INNER LOOP
    2          DO 3 L=1,LEND
               LANF=KPIV-L
               LIND=IND-L
    3          DSUM=DSUM+DBLE(A(LANF)*A(LIND))
C              END OF INNER LOOP
C
C              TRANSFORM ELEMENT A(IND)
    4          DSUM=DBLE(A(IND))-DSUM
               IF(I-K)10,5,10
C
C              TEST FOR NEGATIVE PIVOT ELEMENT AND FOR LOSS OF SIGNIFICANCE
    5          IF(SNGL(DSUM)-TOL)6,6,9
    6          IF(DSUM)12,12,7
    7          IF(IER)8,8,9
    8          IER=K-1
C
C              COMPUTE PIVOT ELEMENT
    9          DPIV=DSQRT(DSUM)
               A(KPIV)=DPIV
               DPIV=1.D0/DPIV
               GO TO 11
C
C              CALCULATE TERMS IN ROW
   10          A(IND)=DSUM*DPIV
   11          IND=IND+I
C
C              END OF DIAGONAL-LOOP
               RETURN
```

```
12        IER=-1
          RETURN
          END



          SUBROUTINE MSTR(A,R,N,MSA,MSR)
          DIMENSION A(1),R(1)
C
C-----------------------------------------------------------------
C
C         PURPOSE
C           CHANGE STORAGE MODE OF A MATRIX
C
C         DESCRIPTION OF PARAMETERS
C           A - NAME OF INPUT MATRIX
C           R - NAME OF OUTPUT MATRIX
C           N - NUMBER OF ROWS AND COLUMNS IN A AND R
C         MSA - ONE DIGIT NUMBER FOR STORAGE MODE OF MATRIX A
C                   0 - GENERAL
C                   1 - SYMMETRIC
C                   2 - DIAGONAL
C         MSR - SAME AS MSA EXCEPT FOR MATRIX R
C
C         REMARKS
C         MATRIX R CANNOT BE IN THE SAME LOCATION AS MATRIX A
C         MATRIX A MUST BE A SQUARE MATRIX
C
C         SUBROUTINES AND FUNCTION SUBPROGRAMS REQUIRED
C           LOC
C
C         METHOD
C           MATRIX A IS RESTRUCTURED TO FORM MATRIX R
C         MSA MSR
C          0   0   MATRIX A IS MOVED TO MATRIX R
C          0   1   THE UPPER TRIANGLE OF ELEMENTS OF A GENERAL MATRIX
C                  ARE USED TO FORM A SYMMETRIC MATRIX
C          0   2   THE DIAGONAL ELEMENTS OF A GENERAL MATRIX ARE USED
C                  TO FORM A DIAGONAL MATRIX
C          1   0   A SYMMETRIC MATRIX IS EXPANDED TO FORM A GENERAL
C                  MATRIX
C          1   1   MATRIX A IS MOVED TO MATRIX R
C          1   2   THE DIAGONAL ELEMENTS OF A SYMMETRIC MATRIX ARE
C                  USED TO FORM A DIAGONAL MATRIX
C          2   0   A DIAGONAL MATRIX IS EXPANDED BY INSERTING MISSING
C                  ZERO ELEMENTS TO FORM A GENERAL MATRIX
C          2   1   A DIAGONAL MATRIX IS EXPANDED BY INSERTING MISSING
C                  ZERO ELEMENTS TO FORM A SYMMETRIC MATRIX
C          2   2   MATRIX A IS MOVED TO MATRIX R
C
C-----------------------------------------------------------------
C
          DO 20 I=1,N
          DO 20 J=1,N
C
C         IF R IS GENERAL, FORM ELEMENT
C
          IF(MSR)5,10,5
C
C         IF IN LOWER TRIANGLE OF SYMMETRIC OR DIAGONAL R, BYPASS
C
5         IF(I-J)10,10,20
10        CALL LOC(I,J,IR,N,N,MSR)
C
C         IF IN UPPER AND OFF DIAGONAL OF DIAGONAL R, BYPASS
C
          IF(IR)20,20,15
```

```
C
C        OTHERWISE FORM R(I,J)
C
 15      R(IR)=0.0
         CALL LOC(I,J,IA,N,N,MSA)
C
C        IF THERE IS NO A(I,J), LEAVE R(I,J) AT 0
C
         IF(IA)20,20,18
 18      R(IR)=A(IA)
 20      CONTINUE
         RETURN
         END



         SUBROUTINE ZDEV(P,X,D,IE)
C
C-----------------------------------------------------------------------
C
C        PURPOSE
C          COMPUTES X = P**(-1)(Y), THE ARGUMENT X SUCH THAT Y=P(X)=
C          THE PROBABILITY THAT THE RANDOM VARIABLE U, DISTRIBUTED
C          NORMALLY(0,1), IS LESS THAN OR EQUAL TO X.  F(X), THE
C          ORDINATE OF THE NORMAL DENSITY, AT X, IS ALSO COMPUTED.
C
C        DESCRIPTION OF PARAMETERS
C          P    - INPUT PROBABILITY.
C          X    - OUTPUT ARGUMENT SUCH THAT P=Y=THE PROBABILITY THAT
C                 U, THE RANDOM VARIABLE, IS LESS THAN OR EQUAL TO X.
C          D    - OUTPUT DENSITY, F(X).
C          IER  - OUTPUT ERROR CODE
C                 = -1 IF P IS NOT IN THE INTERVAL (0,1), INCLUSIVE.
C                     X=D=.99999E+38 IN THAT CASE
C                 = 0 IF THERE IS NO ERROR.  SEE REMARKS, BELOW.
C
C        REMARKS
C          MAXIMUM ERROR IS 0.00045.
C          IF P=0, X IS SET TO -(10)**38.  D IS SET TO 0.
C          IF P=1, X IS SET TO  (10)**38. D IS SET TO 0.
C  NOTE:   ORIGINAL PROGRAM SET X TO + OR -(10)**74.
C
C        SUBROUTINES AND SUBPROGRAMS REQUIRED.
C        NONE
C
C        METHOD
C          BASED ON APPROXIMATIONS IN C. HASTINGS, APPROXIMATIONS FOR
C          DIGITAL COMPUTERS, PRINCETON UNIV. PRESS, PRINCETON, N.J.,
C          1955.  SEE EQUATION 26.2.23, HANDBOOK OF MATHEMATICAL
C          FUNCTIONS, ABRAMOWITZ AND STEGUN, DOVER PUBLICATIONS,INC.,
C          NEW YORK.
C
C-----------------------------------------------------------------
C
         IE=0
C        X=.99999E+74
         X=.99999E+38
         D=X
         IF(P)1,4,2
 1       IE=-1
         GO TO 12
 2       IF(P-1.0)7,5,1
C4       X=-.99999E+74
 4       X=-.99999E+38
 5       D=0.0
         GO TO 12
C
```

```
7          D=P
           IF(D-0.5)9,9,8
8          D=1.0-D
9          T2=ALOG(1.0/(D*D))
           T=SQRT(T2)
           X=T-(2.515517+0.802853*T+0.010328*T2)/(1.0+1.432788*T+0.189269
          1*T2+0.001308*T*T2)
           IF(P-0.5)10,10,11
10         X=-X
11         D=0.3989423*EXP(-X*X/2.0)
12         RETURN
           END



           SUBROUTINE LOC(I,J,IR,N,M,MS)
C
C-------------------------------------------------------------------
C          PURPOSE
C             COMPUTE A VECTOR SUBSCRIPT FOR AN ELEMENT IN A MATRIX
C    OF SPECIFIED STORAGE MODE.
C
C          DESCRIPTION OF PARAMETERS
C          I     - ROW NUMBER OF ELEMENT
C          J     - COLUMN NUMBER OF ELEMENT
C          IR    - RESULTANT VECTOR SUBSCRIPT
C          N     - NUMBER OF ROWS IN MATRIX
C          M     - NUMBER OF COLUMNS IN MATRIX
C          MS    - ONE DIGIT NUMBER FOR STORAGE MODE OF MATRIX
C                        0 - GENERAL
C                        1 - SYMMETRIC
C                        2 - DIAGONAL
C
C    SUBROUTINES AND FUNCTION SUBPROGRAMS REQUIRED
C          NONE
C
C          METHOD
C          MS=0      SUBSCRIPT IS COMPUTED FOR A MATRIX WITH N*M ELEMENTS
C                    IN STORAGE (GENERAL MATRIX)
C          MS=1      SUBSCRIPT IS COMPUTED FOR A MATRIX WITH N*(N+1)/2 IN
C                    STORAGE (UPPER TRIANGLE OF SYMMETRIC MATRIX).  IF
C                    ELEMENT IS IN LOWER TRIANGULAR PORTION, SUBSCRIPT IS
C                    CORRESPONDING ELEMENT IN UPPER TRIANGLE.
C          MS=2      SUBSCRIPT IS COMPUTED FOR A MATRIX WITH N ELEMENTS
C                    IN STORAGE (DIAGONAL ELEMENTS OF DIAGONAL MATRIX).
C                    IF ELEMENT IS NOT ON DIAGONAL (AND THEREFORE NOT IN
C                    STORAGE, IR IS SET TO ZERO.
C
C-------------------------------------------------------------------
C
           IX=I
           JX=J
           IF(MS-1)10,20,30
10         IRX=N*(JX-1)+IX
           GO TO 36
20         IF(IX-JX)22,24,24
22         IRX=IX+(JX*JX-JX)/2
           GO TO 36
24         IRX=JX+(IX*IX-IX)/2
           GO TO 36
30         IRX=0
           IF(IX-JX)36,32,36
32         IRX=IX
36         IR=IRX
           RETURN
           END
```

APPENDIX *E*

References to ROC Applications

This appendix gives references to applications of the ROC grouped according to the four fields in which a substantial body of such literature exists: medicine, military monitoring, industrial monitoring, and information retrieval. Introductions to the literature in those fields were given by Swets and Green (1978); a more extensive summary of the medical literature was presented by Swets (1979), and of the literatures on military and industrial monitoring by Swets (1977).

To characterize briefly these literatures, the work on medical diagnosis is concentrated on evaluation of various forms of imagery as read by humans, but it attends also to assessment of relative performances of various classes of human readers. Diagnoses made by automatic devices or based on nonimage data have received essentially no study with ROC techniques. The emphasis in military monitoring has been on the fact that human observers usually issue a declining number of true-positive reports over time, and on the extent to which this decline reflects diminishing sensitivity rather than a progressively more conservative detection criterion. The focus to date in industrial monitoring has been on human visual inspection of all products of a manufacturing or processing activity. Applications of ROC techniques remain to be made to evaluation of devices for nondestructive testing, such as those that sense cracks in materials (as in airplane wings) or malfunctioning machinery (as in nuclear power plants). One article in the field of information retrieval describes the field's general level of accomplishment (Swets, 1969). Most of the remainder of the literature is theoretical; ROC theory is used to help in modeling the retrieval process, whether the process is effected by librarians or computers.

MEDICAL DIAGNOSIS

Ackerman, L. V. Computer classification of radiographs and Xerograms of the breast (Ph.D. thesis, University of Michigan, 1971).

Ackerman, L. V., and Gose, E. E. Breast lesion classification by computer and Xeroradiograph. *Cancer,* 1972, **30,** 1025–1035.

Alcorn, F. S., and O'Donnell, E. Mammogram screeners: Modified program learning for nonradiologic personnel. *Radiology,* 1968, **90,** 336–338.

Alcorn, F. S., and O'Donnell, E. The training of nonphysician personnel for use in a mammography program. *Cancer,* 1969, **23,** 879–884.

Alcorn, F. S., O'Donnell, E., and Ackerman, L. V. The protocol and results of training nonradiologists to scan mammograms. *Radiology,* 1971, **99,** 523–529.

Anderson, T. McD., Jr., Mintzer, R. A., Hoffer, P. B., Lusted, L. B., Smith, V. C., and Pokorny, J. Nuclear image transmission by Picturephone evaluation by ROC curve method. *Investigative Radiology,* 1973, **8,** (4), 244–250.

Andrus, W. S., and Bird, K. T. Radiology and the receiver operating characteristic (ROC) curve. *Chest,* 1975, **67,** 378–379.

Andrus, W. S., Dreyfuss, J. R., Jaffer, F., and Bird, K. T. Interpretation of roentgenograms via interactive television. *Radiology,* 1975, **116,** 25–31.

Andrus, W. S., Hunter, C. H., and Bird, K. T. Remote interpretation of chest roentgenograms. *Chest,* 1975, **67,** (4), 463–468.

Bacus, J. W. The observer error in peripheral blood cell classification. *American Journal of Clinical Practice,* 1972, **59,** 223–230.

Blackwell, R. J., Shirley, I., Farman, D. J., and Michael, C. A. Ultra-sonic "B" scanning as a pregnancy test after less than six weeks amenorrhoea. *British Journal on Obstetrics and Gynaecology,* 1975, **82,** 108–114.

Bunch, P. C., Hamilton, J. F., Sanderson, G. K., and Simmons, A. H. A free response approach to the measurement and characterization of radiographic observer performance. *Optical Instrumentation in Medicine, VI,* 1977, **127,** 124–135.

Crassini, B., and Broerse, J. Auditory-visual integration in neonates: A signal detection analysis. *Journal of Experimental Child Psychology,* 1980, **29,** 144–155.

Dowdy, A. H., LaGasse, L. D., Roach, P., and Wilson, D. Lay screeners in mammographic survey programs. *Radiology,* 1970, **94,** 619–621.

Goodenough, D. J. The use of ROC curves in testing the proficiency of individuals in classifying pneumoconiosis. *Radiology,* 1975, **114,** 472–473.

Goodenough, D. J., and Metz, C. E. Effect of listening interval on auditory detection performance. *Journal of the Acoustical Society of America,* 1974, **55,** (1), 11–116.

Goodenough, D. J., Metz, C. E., and Lusted, L. B. Caveat on use of the parameter d' for evaluation of observer performance. *Radiology*, 1973, **106**, 565–566.

Goodenough, D. J., Rossmann, K., and Lusted, L. B. Radiographic applications of signal detection theory. *Radiology*, 1972, **105**, 199–200.

Hessel, S. J., Herman, P. G., and Swensson, R. G. Improving performance by multiple interpretations of chest radiographs: Effectiveness and cost. *Radiology*, 1978, **127**, 589–594.

IAEA Co-ordinated research programme on the intercomparison of computer-assisted scintigraphic techniques. *Medical Radionuclide Imaging*, 1977, **1**, 585–615.

Keeler, E. B. The value of a diagnostic test. The Rand Paper Series, P-5603, 1976, 1–15.

Kundel, H. L. Factors limiting roentgen interpretation—Physical and psychologic. In E. J. Potchen (Ed.), *Current concepts in radiology*. St. Louis: Mosby, 1972, 1–29.

Kundel, H. L. Images, image quality and observer performance. *Radiology*, 1979, **132**, 265–271.

Kundel, H. L., Revesz, C., and Stauffer, H. M. The electro-optical processing of radiographic images. *Radiologic Clinics of North America*, 1969, **3**, 447–460.

Ling, D., Ling, A. H., and Doehring, D. G. Stimulus, response, and observer variables in the auditory screening of newborn infants. *Journal of Speech and Hearing Research*, 1970, **13**, 9–18.

Lusted, L. B. *Introduction to medical decision making*. Springfield, Ill.: Thomas, 1968.

Lusted, L. B. Perception of the roentgen image: Applications of signal detectability theory. *Radiologic Clinics of North America*, 1969, **3**, 435–445.

Lusted, L. B. Decision-making studies in patient management. *New England Journal of Medicine*, 1971, **284**, 416–424.

Lusted, L. B. Signal detectability and medical decision-making. *Science*, 1971, **171**, 1217–1219.

Lusted, L. B. Observer error, signal detectability, and medical decision making. In J. A. Jacquez (Ed.), *Computer diagnosis and diagnostic methods*. Springfield, Ill.: Thomas, 1972, 29–44.

Lusted, L. B. Receiver operating characteristic analysis and its significance in interpretation of radiologic images. In E. J. Potchen (Ed.), *Current concepts in radiology*, Vol. 2. St. Louis: Mosby, 1975, 117–230.

Lusted, L. B. Twenty years of medical decision making studies. Presented at the *Third Annual Symposium for Computer Applications in Medical Care*, Silver Spring, Maryland, October 1979. (To be published in the Conference Proceedings.)

McNeil, B. J., and Adelstein, S. J. Measures of clinical efficacy. The value of case finding in hypertensive renovascular disease. *New England Journal of Medicine*, 1975, **293**, (5), 221–226.

McNeil, B. J., Hessel, S. J., Branch, W. T., Bjork, L., and Adelstein, S. J. Measures of clinical efficacy: III. The value of the lung scan in the evaluation of young patients with pleuritic chest pain. *Journal of Nuclear Medicine*, 1976, **17**, 163–169.

McNeil, B. J., Varady, P. D., Burrows, B. A., and Adelstein, S. J. Cost effectiveness in hypertensive renovascular disease. *New England Journal of Medicine*, 1975, **293**, 216–221.

McNeil, B. J., Weber, E., Harrison, D., and Hellman, S. Use of signal detection theory in examining the results of a contrast examination: A case study using the lymphangiogram. *Radiology*, 1977, **103**, 613–618.

Metz, C. E. Basic principles of ROC analysis. *Seminars in Nuclear Medicine*, 1978, **VIII**, 4, 283–298.

Metz, C. E., and Goodenough, D. J. Quantitative evaluation of human visual detection performance using empirical receiver operating characteristic curves. In C. E. Metz, S. M. Prizer, and G. L. Brownell (Eds.), *Information processing in scintigraphy.* Oak Ridge, Tenn.: USERDA Technical Information Center, 1975, 140–145.

Metz, C. E., and Goodenough, D. J. On failure to improve observer performance with scan smoothing: A rebuttal. *Journal of Nuclear Medicine,* 1973, **14,** (11), 873–876.

Metz, C. E., Goodenough, D. J., and Rossman, K. Evaluation of receiver operating characteristic curve data in terms of information theory, with applications in radiography. *Radiology,* 1973, **109,** 297–303.

Metz, C. E., Starr, S. J., and Lusted, L. B. Observer performance in detecting multiple radiographic signals: Prediction and analysis using a generalized ROC approach. *Radiology,* 1975, **121,** 337–347.

Metz, C. E., Starr, S. J., and Lusted, L. B. Quantitative evaluation of medical imaging. Presented at IAEA Symposium on Medical Radioisotope Imaging, Los Angeles, California, 1976. In *Medical radionuclide imaging,* Vol. 1. Vienna: International Atomic Energy Agency, 1977, 491–504.

Metz, C. E., Starr, S. J., and Lusted, L. B. Quantitative evaluation of visual detection performance in medicine: ROC analysis and determination of diagnostic benefit. In G. A. Hayes (Ed.), *Medical images.* London: Wiley, 1977, 220–241.

Metz, C. E., Starr, S. J., Lusted, L. B., and Rossman, K. Progress in evaluation of human observer visual detection performance using the ROC curve approach. In C. Raynaud and A. E. Todd-Pokropek (Eds.), *Information processing in scintigraphy.* Orsay, France: Commissariat a l'Energie Atomique, Departement de Biologie, Service Hospitalier Frederic Joliot, 1975, 420–439.

Mobley, W. H., and Goldstein, I. L. The effects of payoff on the visual processing of dental radiographs. *Human Factors,* 1978, **20,** (4), 385–390.

Morgan, R. H., Donner, M. W., Gayler, B. W., Margulies, S. I., Rao, P. S., and Wheeler, P. S. Decision processes and observer error in the diagnosis of pneumoconiosis by chest roentgenography. *American Journal of Roentgenology, Radiology Therapy and Nuclear Medicine,* 1973, **117,** 757–764.

Moskowitz, M., Milbrath, J., Gartside, P., Zermeno, A., and Mandel, D. Lack of efficacy of thermography as a screening tool for minimal and stage I breast cancer. *New England Journal of Medicine,* 1976, **295,** 249–252.

Nishiyama, H., Lewis, J. T., Ashare, A. B., and Saenger, E. L. Interpretation of liver images: Do training and experience make a difference? *Journal of Nuclear Medicine,* 1975, **16,** 11–16.

Oster, Z. H., Larson, S. M., Strauss, H. W., and Wagner, H. N. Jr. Analysis of liver scanning in a general hospital. *Journal of Nuclear Medicine,* 1975, **16,** 450–453.

Revesz, G., and Haas, C. Television display of radiographic images with superimposed simulated lesions. *Radiology,* 1972, **102,** 197–199.

Revesz, G., and Kundel, H. L. Effects of non-linearities on the television display of X-ray images. *Investigative Radiology,* 1971, **6,** 315–320.

Revesz, G., and Kundel, H. L. Videodisc storage of radiographs. *Radiology,* 1973, **106,** 91–93.

Ritchings, R. T., Isherwood, I., Pullan, B. R., and Kingsley, D. Receiver operating characteristic curves in the evaluation of hard copies of computed tomography scans. *Journal of Computer Assisted Tomography,* 1979, **3,** (3), 423–425.

Sheft, D. J., Jones, M. D., Brown, R. F., and Ross, S. E. Screening of chest roentgenograms by advanced roentgen technologists. *Radiology,* 1970, **94,** 427–429.

Starr, S. J., Metz, C. E., Lusted, L. B., and Goodenough, D. J. Visual detection and localization of radiographic images. *Radiology,* 1975, **116,** 533–538.

Swensson, R. G. A two-stage detection model applied to skilled visual search by radiologists. *Perception & Psychophysics*, 1980, **27**, (1), 11–16.

Swensson, R. G., Hessel, S. J., and Herman, P. G. Omissions in radiology: Faulty search or stringent reporting criteria? *Radiology*, 1977, **123**, 563–567.

Swets, J. A. Signal detection in medical diagnosis. In J. A. Jazquez (Ed.), *Computer diagnosis and diagnostic methods*. Springfield, Ill., Thomas, 1972, 8–28.

Swets, J. A. ROC analysis applied to the evaluation of medical imaging techniques. *Investigative Radiology*, 1979, **14**, (2), 109–121.

Swets, J. A., Pickett, R. M., Whitehead, S. F., Getty, D. J., Schnur, J. A., Swets, J. B., and Freeman, B. A. Assessment of diagnostic technologies. *Science*, 1979, **205**, 753–759.

Swets, J. A., and Swets, J. B. ROC approach to cost–benefit analysis. *IEEE Proceedings of the Sixth Conference on Computer Applications in Radiology*, 1979, 203–206.

Tolles, W. E., Horvarth, W. J., and Bostrom, R. C. A study of the quantitative characteristics of exfoliated cells from the female genital tract: I. Measurement methods and results. *Cancer*, 1961, **14**, 437–454.

Tolles, W. E., Horvath, W. J., and Bostrom, R. C. A study of the quantitative characteristics of exfoliated cells from the female genital tract: II. Suitability of quantitative cytological measurements for automatic prescreening. *Cancer*, 1961, **14**, 455–468.

Turner, D. A. An intuitive approach to receiver operating characteristic curve analysis. *Journal of Nuclear Medicine*, 1978, **19**, (2), 213–220.

Turner, D. A. Scintillation camera versus rectilinear scanner for liver imaging. *Journal of Nuclear Medicine*, 1975, **17**, (5), 419–421.

Turner, D. A., Fordham, E. W., Pagano, J. V., Ali, A. A., Ramos, M. V., and Ramachandran, P. C. Brain scanning with the Anger multiplane tomographic scanner as a second examination. *Radiology*, 1976, **121**, 115–124.

Turner, D. A., Ramachandran, P. C., Ali, A. A., Fordham, E. W., and Ferry, T. A. Brain scanning with the Anger multiplane tomographic scanner as a primary examination. *Radiology*, 1976, **121**, 125–129.

Uchida, I., Onai, Y., Ohashi, Y., Tomaru, T., and Irifune, T. Quantitative diagnosis of breast thermograms by a computer. *Nippon Acta Radiologica*, 1979, **30**, 401–411.

MILITARY MONITORING

Baddeley, A. D., and Colquhoun, W. P. Signal probability and vigilance: A reappraisal of the "signal-rate" effect. *British Journal of Psychology*, 1969, **60**, (2), 169–178.

Benedetti, L. H., and Loeb, M. A comparison of auditory monitoring performance in blind subjects with that of sighted subjects in light and dark. *Perception & Psychophysics*, 1972, **11**, 10–16.

Coates, G. D., Loeb, M., and Alluisi, E. A. Influence of observing strategies and stimulus variables on watchkeeping performances. *Ergonomics*, 1972, **15**, 379–386.

Colquhoun, W. P. Effects of raised ambient temperature and event rate on vigilance performance. *Aerospace Medicine*, 1969, **40**, (4), 413–417.

Colquhoun, W. P. Training for vigilance: A comparison of different techniques. *Human Factors*, 1966, **8**, 7–12.

Colquhoun, W. P. Sonar target detection as a decision process. *Journal of Applied Psychology*, 1967, **51**, 187–190.

Colquhoun, W. P., and Edwards, R. S. Practice effects on a visual vigilance task with and without search. *Human Factors*, 1970, **12**, (6), 537–545.

Craig, A. Is the vigilance decrement simply a response adjustment towards probability matching? *Human Factors,* 1978, **20,** (4), 441–446.

Craig, A. Discrimination, temperature, and time of day. *Human Factors,* 1979, **21,** (1), 61–68.

Craig, A. Nonparametric measures of sensory efficiency for sustained monitoring tasks. *Human Factors,* 1979, **21,** (1), 69–78.

Craig, A. Broadbent and Gregory revisited: Vigilance and statistical decision. *Human Factors,* 1977, **19,** (1), 25–36.

Craig, A. Vigilance for two kinds of signal with unequal probabilities of occurrence. *Human Factors,* 1979, **21,** (6), 647–653.

Crider, A., and Augenbraun, C. B. Auditory vigilance correlates of electrodermal response habituation speed. *Psychophysiology,* 1975, **12,** (1), 36–40.

Davenport, W. G. Auditory vigilance: The effects of costs and values on signals. *Australian Journal of Psychology,* 1968, **20,** 213–218.

Davenport, W. G. Vibrotactile vigilance: The effects of costs and values on signals. *Perception & Psychophysics,* 1969, **5,** 25–28.

Davies, D. R., Hockey, G. R. J., and Taylor, A. Varied auditory stimulation, temperament differences and vigilance performance. *British Journal of Psychology,* 1969, **60,** (4), 453–457.

Davies, D. R., Lang, L., and Shackleton, V. J. The effects of music and task difficulty on performance at a visual vigilance task. *British Journal of Psychology,* 1973, **64,** (3), 383–389.

Davies, D. R., and Parasuraman, R. Cortical evoked potentials and vigilance: A decision theory analysis. In R. R. Mackie (Ed.), *Vigilance: Relationships among theory, physiological correlates and operational performance.* New York: Plenum, 1977, 285–306.

Deaton, M. A., Tobias, J. S., and Wilkinson, R. T. The effect of sleep deprivation on signal detection parameters. *Quarterly Journal of Experimental Psychology,* 1971, **23,** 449–452.

DeMaio, J., Parkinson, S. R., and Crosby, J. V. A reaction time analysis of instrument scanning. *Human Factors,* 1978, **20,** (4), 467–471.

Guralnick, M. J. Effects of event rate and signal difficulty on observing responses and detection measures in vigilance. *Journal of Experimental Psychology,* 1973, **99,** (2), 261–265.

Guralnick, M. J. Observing responses and decision processes in vigilance. *Journal of Experimental Psychology,* 1972, **93,** (2), 239–244.

Guralnick, M. J., and Harvey, K. C. Response requirements and performance in a visual vigilance task. *Psychonomics Science,* 1970, **20,** (4), 215–217.

Hatfield, J. L., and Loeb, M. Sense mode and coupling in a vigilance task. *Perception & Psychophysics,* 1968, **4,** 29–36.

Hatfield, J. L., and Soderquist, D. R. Coupling effects and performance in vigilance tasks. *Human Factors,* 1970, **12,** 351–359.

Hatfield, J. L., and Soderquist, D. R. Practice effects and signal detection indices in an auditory vigilance task. *Journal of the Acoustical Society of America,* 1969, **46,** (6), 1458–1463.

Jerison, H. J. Signal detection theory in the analysis of human vigilance. *Human Factors,* 1967, **9,** 285–288.

Jerison, H. J., Pickett, R. M., and Stenson, H. H. The elicited observing rate and decision processes in vigilance. *Human Factors,* 1965, **7,** 107–128.

Johnston, W. A., Howell, W. C., and Williges, R. C. The components of complex monitoring. *Organizational Behavior and Human Performance,* 1969, **4,** 112–124.

Levine, J. M. The effects of values and costs on the detection and identification of signals in auditory vigilance. *Human Factors*, 1966, **8**, 525–537.

Loeb, M. On the analysis and interpretation of vigilance: Some remarks on two recent articles by Craig. *Human Factors*, 1978, **20**, (4), 447–451.

Loeb, M., and Alluisi, E. A. Influence of display, task and organismic variables on indices of monitoring behavior. *Acta Psychologica, Attention and Performance III*, 1970, **33**, 343–366.

Loeb, M., and Binford, J. R. Examination of some factors influencing performance on an auditory monitoring task with one signal per session. *Journal of Experimental Psychology*, 1970, **83**, (1), 40–44.

Loeb, M., and Binford, J. R. Variation in performance on auditory and visual monitoring tasks as a function of signal and stimulus frequencies. *Perception & Psychophysics*, 1968, **4**, 361–367.

Loeb, M., and Binford, J. R. Modality, difficulty, and 'coupling' in vigilance behavior. *American Journal of Psychology*, 1971, **84**, (4), 529–541.

Loeb, M., Hawkes, G. R., Evans, W. O., and Alluisi, E. A. The influence of d-amphetamine, benactyzene, and chlorapromazine on performance in an auditory vigilance task. *Psychonomic Science*, 1965, **3**, 29–30.

Lucas, P. Human performance in low-signal-probability tasks. *Journal of the Acoustical Society of America*, 1967, **42**, 158–178.

Mackworth, J. F. Performance decrement in vigilance, threshold, and high-speed perceptual motor tasks. *Canadian Journal of Psychology*, 1964, **18**, 209–223.

Mackworth, J. F. The effect of true and false knowledge of results on the detectability of signals in a vigilance task. *Canadian Journal of Psychology*, 1964, **18**, 106–117.

Mackworth, J. F. Deterioration of signal detectability during a vigilance task as a function of background event rate. *Psychonomic Science*, 1965, **3**, 421–422.

Mackworth, J. F. Effect of amphetamine on the detectability of signals in a vigilance task. *Canadian Journal of Psychology*, 1965, **19**, 104–110.

Mackworth, J. F. Decision interval and signal detectability in a vigilance task. *Canadian Journal of Psychology*, 1965, **19**, 111–117.

Mackworth, J. F. The effect of signal rate on performance in two kinds of vigilance task. *Human Factors*, 1968, **10**, 11–18.

Mackworth, J. F. *Vigilance and attention: A signal detection approach*. Baltimore: Penquin, 1970.

McCann, P. H. Variability of signal detection measures with noise type. *Psychometric Science*, 1969, **15**, (6), 310–311.

Milosevic, S. Changes in detection measures and skin resistance during an auditory vigilance task. *Ergonomics*, 1975, **18**, (1), 1–8.

Milosevic, S. Detection du signal en fonction du critere de response. *Le Travail Humain*, 1969, **32**, (1–2), 81–86.

Milosevic, S. Effect of time and space uncertainty on a vigilance task. *Perception & Psychophysics*, 1974, **15**, (2), 331–334.

Parasuraman, R. Memory load and event rate control sensitivity decrements in sustained attention. *Science*, 1979, **205**, 924–927.

Parasuraman, R., and Davies, D. R. A taxonomic analysis of vigilance performance. In R. R. Mackie (Ed.), *Vigilance: Relationships among theory, physiological correlates and operational performance*. New York: Plenum, 1977, 559–574.

Poulton, E. C., and Edwards, R. S. Interactions and range effects in experiments on pairs of stresses. *Journal of Experimental Psychology*, 1974, **102**, (4), 621–628.

Swets, J. A. Comment: Adaptation-level theory and signal-detection theory and their relation to vigilance experiments. In M. H. Appley (Ed.), *Adaptation-level theory*. New York: Academic Press, 1971, 49–53.

Swets, J. A. Signal detection theory applied to vigilance. In R. R. Mackie (Ed.), *Vigilance: Relationships among theory, physiological correlates and operational performance*. New York: Plenum, 1977, 705–718.

Swets, J. A., and Kristofferson, A. B. Attention. *Annual Review of Psychology*, 1970, **21**, 339–366.

Taub, J. M., and Berger, R. J. Performance and mood following variations in the length and timing of sleep. *Psychophysiology*, 1973, **10**, (6), 559–570.

Taub, J. M., and Berger, R. J. Acute shifts in the sleep–wakefulness cycle: Effects on performance and mood. *Psychosomatic Medicine*, 1974, **36**, (2), 164–173.

Taylor, M. M. The effect of the square root of time in continuing perceptual tasks. *Perception & Psychophysics*, 1966, **1**, 113–119.

Taylor, M. M. Detectability theory and the interpretation of vigilance data. *Acta Psychologica*, 1967, **27**, 390–399.

Teichner, W. H. The detection of a simple visual signal as a function of time of watch. *Human Factors*, 1974, **16**, (4), 339–353.

Thurmond, J. B., Binford, J. R., and Loeb, M. Effects of signal to noise variability over repeated sessions in an auditory task. *Perception & Psychophysics*, 1970, **7**, (2), 100–102.

Tickner, A. H., and Poulton, E. C. Monitoring up to 16 synthetic television pictures showing a great deal of movement. *Ergonomics*, 1973, **16**, (4), 381–401.

Tyler, D. M., Waag, W. L., and Halcomb, C. G. Monitoring performance across sense modes: An individual differences approach. *Human Factors*, 1972, **14**, (6), 539–547.

Watson, C. S., and Nichols, T. L. Detectability of auditory signals presented without defined observation intervals. *Journal of the Acoustical Society of America*, 1976, **59**, 655–668.

Williges, R. C. Manipulating the response criterion in visual monitoring. *Human Factors*, 1973, **15**, (2), 179–185.

Williges, R. C. The role of payoffs and signal ratios in criterion changes during a monitoring task. *Human Factors*, 1971, **13**, (3), 261–267.

Williges, R. C. Within-session criterion changes compared to an ideal observer criterion in a visual monitoring task. *Journal of Experimental Psychology*, 1969, **81**, (1), 61–66.

Williges, R. C., and North, R. A. Knowledge of results and decision making performance in visual monitoring. *Organizational Behavior and Human Performance*, 1972, **8**, 44–57.

INDUSTRIAL MONITORING

Adams, S. K. Decision making in quality control: Some perceptual and behavioral considerations. In C. G. Drury and J. G. Fox (Eds.), *Human reliability in quality control*. New York: Halsted, 1975, 55–69.

Baker, E. M. Signal detection theory analysis of quality control inspection performance. *Journal of Quality Technology*, 1975, **7**, (2), 62–71.

Bloomfield, J. R. Theoretical approaches to visual search. In C. G. Drury and J. G. Fox (Eds.), *Human reliability in quality control*. New York: Halsted, 1975, 19–29.

Buck, J. R. Dynamic visual inspection: Task factors, theory and economics. In C. G. Drury and J. G. Fox (Eds.), *Human reliability in quality control*. New York: Halsted, 1975, 165–187.

Chapman, D. E., and Sinclair, M. A. Ergonomics in inspection tasks in the food industry.

In C. G. Drury and J. G. Fox (Eds.), *Human reliability in quality control*. New York: Halsted, 1975, 231–251.

Craig, A., and Colquhoun, W. P. Vigilance: A review. In C. G. Drury and J. G. Fox (Eds.), *Human reliability in quality control*. New York: Halsted, 1975, 71–87.

Drury, C. G. The effect of speed working on industrial inspection accuracy. *Applied Ergonomics*, 1973, **4**, (1), 2–7.

Drury, C. G. Human decision making in quality control. In C. G. Drury and J. G. Fox (Eds.), *Human reliability in quality control*. New York: Halsted, 1975, 45–53.

Drury, C. G., and Addison, J. L. An industrial study of the effects of feedback and fault density on inspection performance. *Ergonomics*, 1973, **16**, (2), 159–169.

Drury, C. G., and Fox, J. G. The imperfect inspector. In C. G. Drury and J. G. Fox (Eds.), *Human reliability in quality control*. New York: Halsted, 1975, 11–16.

Embrey, D. E. Training the inspector's sensitivity and response strategy. In C. G. Drury and J. G. Fox (Eds.), *Human reliability in quality control*. New York: Halsted, 1975, 189–195.

Fox, J. G., and Haslegrave, C. M. Industrial inspection efficiency and the probability of a defect occurring. *Ergonomics*, 1969, **12**, (5), 721.

Geyer, L. H., Patel, S., and Perry, R. F. Detectability of multiple flaws. *Human Factors*, 1979, **21**, (1), 7–12.

Moray, N. Attention, control, and sampling behavior. In T. B. Sheridan and G. Johannsen (Eds.), *Monitoring behavior and supervisory control*. New York: Plenum, 1976, 221–244.

Morral, J. The analysis of an inspection task in the steel industry. In C. G. Drury and J. G. Fox (Eds.), *Human reliability in quality control*. New York: Halsted, 1975, 217–230.

Murrell, G. A. A reappraisal of artificial signals as an aid to a visual monitoring task. *Ergonomics*, 1975, **18**, (6), 693–700.

Sheehan, J. J., and Drury, C. G. The analysis of industrial inspection. *Applied Ergonomics*, 1971, **2**, (2), 74–78.

Smith, G. L. Jr. Inspector performance on microminiature tasks. In C. G. Drury and J. G. Fox, (Eds.), *Human reliability in quality control*. New York: Halsted, 1975, 149–163.

Smith, L., and Barany, J. W. An elementary model of human performance on paced visual inspection tasks. *Association of International Industrial Engineers*, 1970, **2**, 298–308.

Tsao, Y.-C., Drury, C. G., and Morawski, T. B. Human performance in sampling inspection. *Human Factors*, 1979, **21**, (1), 99–105.

Wallack, P. M., and Adams, S. K. A comparison of inspector performance measures. *Association of International Industrial Engineers Transactions*, 1970, **2**, 97–105.

Wallack, P. M., and Adams, S. K. The utility of signal-detection theory in the analysis of industrial inspector accuracy. *Association of Industrial Engineers Transactions*, 1969, **1**, (1), 33–44.

Weiner, E. L. Individual and group differences in inspection. In C. G. Drury and J. G. Fox (Eds.), *Human reliability in quality control*. New York: Halsted, 1975, 101–122.

Zunzanyika, X. K., and Drury, C. G. Effects of information on industrial inspection performance. In C. G. Drury and J. G. Fox (Eds.), *Human reliability in quality control*. New York: Halsted, 1975, 189–195.

INFORMATION RETRIEVAL

Bookstein, A. The anomalous behavior of precision in the Swets model, and its resolution. *Recall and Precision*, 1974, **25**, 374–380.

Brookes, B. C. The measures of information retrieval effectiveness proposed by Swets. *Journal of Documentation,* 1968, **24,** 41–54.

Carmon, J. L. A discriminant function index for information system evaluation. *Journal of the American Society for Information Sciences,* 1974, **25,** 118–122.

Cooper, W. S. On selecting a measure of retrieval effectiveness. *Journal of the American Society for Information Sciences,* 1974, **25,** 87–100.

Cooper, W. S. On selecting a measure of retrieval effectiveness: Part II. Implementation of the philosophy. *Journal of the American Society for Information Sciences,* 1974, **25,** 413–424.

Farradane, J. The evaluation of information retrieval systems. *Journal of Documentation,* 1974, **30,** (2), 195–209.

Heine, M. H. Design equations for retrieval systems based on the Swets model. *Journal of the American Society for Information Sciences,* 1974, **25,** 183–198.

Heine, M. H. Distance between sets as an objective measure of retrieval effectiveness, *Information Storage Retrieval,* 1973, **9,** 181–198.

Heine, M. H. The inverse relationship of precision and recall in terms of the Swets model. *Journal of Documentation,* 1973, **29,** 81–84.

Heine, M. H. Measures of language effectiveness and Swetsian hypotheses. *Journal of Documentation,* 1975, **31,** (4), 283–287.

King, D. W., and Bryant, E. C. The evaluation of information services and products. In D. W. King and E. C. Bryant (Eds.), *Measures for evaluating identification systems.* Washington, D.C.: Information Resources Press, 1971.

Kraft, D. H. A decision theory view of the information retrieval situation: An operations research approach. *Journal of the American Society for Information Science,* 1973, **24,** 368–376.

Kraft, D. H., and Bookstein, A. Evaluation of information retrieval systems: A decision theory approach. *Journal of the American Society for Information Science,* 1978, **29,** 31–40.

Kraft, D. H., and Hill, T. W. Jr. A journal selection model and its implications for a library system. *Information Storage Retrieval,* 1973, **9,** 1–11.

Robertson, S. E. The parametric description of retrieval tests: I. The basic parameters. *Journal of Documentation,* 1969, **25,** 1–27.

Robertson, S. E. The parametric description of retrieval tests: II. Overall measures. *Journal of Documentation,* 1969, **25,** 93–107.

Robertson, S. E. A statistical analysis of retrieval tests: A Bayesian approach. *Journal of Documentation,* 1974, **30,** (3), 273–282.

Swanson, D. R. On indexing depth and retrieval effectiveness. *Proceedings of the Second Congress on Information Systems Sciences.* Washington, D.C.: Spartan, 1965, 311–319.

Swets, J. A. Information-retrieval systems. *Science,* 1963, **141,** 245–250. Reprinted in M. Kochen (Ed.), *The growth of knowledge.* New York: Wiley, 1967, 174–184; and T. Saracevic (Ed.), *Introduction to information science.* New York: Bowker, 1970, 576–583.

Swets, J. A. Effectiveness of information retrieval methods. *American Documentation,* 1969, **20,** 72–89. Reprinted in B. Griffith (Ed.), *Key papers in information science.* White Plains, N.Y.: Knowledge Industry Publications, 1980, 349–366.

References

Bamber, D. The area above the ordinal dominance graph and the area below the receiver operating characteristic graph. *Journal of Mathematical Psychology*, 1975, **12**, (4), 387–415.

Barnoon, S., and Wolfe, H. *Measuring the effectiveness of medical decisions*, Springfield, Ill.: Thomas, 1972.

Berg, R. L. (Ed.). *Health status indexes*. Chicago: Hospital Research and Educational Trust, 1973.

Berger, H. Nondestructive measurements: How good are they? *Materials Evaluation*, 1976, **34**, 18A–34A.

Brookes, B. C. The measures of information retrieval effectiveness proposed by Swets. *Journal of Documentation*, 1968, **24**, (1), 41–54.

Coombs, C. H., Dawes, R. M., and Tversky, A. *Mathematical psychology*. Englewood Cliffs, N.J.: Prentice-Hall, 1970.

Dorfman, D. D., and Alf, E., Jr. Maximum likelihood estimation of parameters of signal-detection theory and determination of confidence intervals—Rating method data. *Journal of Mathematical Psychology*, 1969, **6**, 487–496.

Dorfman, D. D., Beavers, L. L., and Saslow, C. Estimation of signal detection theory parameters from rating-method data: A comparison of the method of scoring and direct search. *Bulletin of the Psychonomic Society*, 1973, **1**, (3), 207–208.

243

Drury, C. G., and Addison, J. L. An industrial study of the effects of feedback and fault density on inspection performance. *Ergonomics,* 1973, **16,** (2), 159–169.

Drury, C. G., and Fox, J. G. (Eds.). *Human reliability in quality control.* New York: Halstead, 1975.

DuSoir, A. E. Treatments of bias in detection and recognition models: A review. *Perception & Psychophysics,* 1975, **17,** 167–168.

Edwards, W. How to use multiattribute utility measurement for social decision making. *IEEE Transactions on Systems, Man and Cybernetics,* 1977, **SMC-7,** (5), 326–340.

Egan, J. P. *Signal detection theory and ROC analysis.* New York: Academic Press, 1975.

Egan, J. P., and Clarke, F. R. Psychophysics and signal detection. In J. B. Sidowsky (Ed.), *Experimental methods and instrumentation in psychology.* New York: McGraw-Hill, 1966, 211–246.

Enstrom, J. E., and Austin, D. F. Interpreting cancer survival rates. *Science,* 1977, **195,** 847–851.

Fineberg, H. V. On the use of probability estimates to evaluate diagnostic imaging modalities and observer performance. Unpublished paper, 1977.

Fraser, D. A. S. *Statistics: An introduction.* New York: Wiley, 1958.

Garner, W. R. *Uncertainty and structure as psychological concepts.* New York: Wiley, 1962.

Goodenough, D. J., Metz, C. E., and Lusted, L. B. Caveat on use of the parameter d' for evaluation of observer performance. *Radiology,* 1973, **106,** 565–566.

Goodman, L. A. The multivariate analysis of qualitative data: Interactions among multiple classifications. *Journal of the American Statistical Association,* 1970, **65,** 226–266.

Green, D. M., and Swets, J. A. *Signal detection theory and psychophysics.* New York: Wiley, 1966. Reprinted by Krieger, Huntington, N.Y., 1974.

Guiley, L. R. NDE horror stories. In *Proceedings of the Interdisciplinary Workshop for Quantitative Flaw Definition,* Science Center, Rockwell International, Thousand Oaks, Calif., June 17–20, 1974.

Keeney, R. L., and Raiffa, H. *Decision with multiple objectives: Preferences and value tradeoffs.* New York: Wiley, 1976.

Kendall, M. G. *Rank correlation methods.* New York: Hafner, 1962.

Leaper, D. J. Computer-assisted diagnosis of abdominal pain using estimates provided by clinicians and survey data obtained from real life. In R. M. Pickett and T. J. Triggs (Eds.), *Human factors in health care.* Lexington, Mass.: Heath, 1975, 123–138.

Luce, R. D. Detection and recognition. In R. D. Luce, R. R. Bush, and E. Galanter (Eds.), *Handbook of mathematical psychology.* New York: Wiley, 1963.

Lusted, L. B., Bell, R. S., Edwards, W., Roberts, H. V., and Wallace, D. L. Evaluating the efficacy of radiologic procedures by Bayesian methods. In K. Snapper (Ed.), *Models in metrics for decision makers.* Washington, D.C.: Information Resources Press, 1977.

Mason, I. B. Decision–theoretic evaluation of probabilistic forecasts using the relative operating characteristic. Unpublished paper, Australian Bureau of Meteorology, 1980.

McNeil, B. J., and Adelstein, S. J. Determining the value of diagnostic and screening tests. *Journal of Nuclear Medicine,* 1976, **17,** (6), 439–448.

McNeil, B. J., Collins, J. J., and Adelstein, S. J. Rationale for seeking occult metastases in patients with bronchogenic carcinoma. *Surgery, Gynecology, and Obstetrics,* 1977, **44,** 389–393.

McNeil, B. J., Varady, P. D., Burrows, B. A., and Adelstein, S. J. Measures of clinical efficacy: Cost effectiveness calculations in the diagnosis and treatment of hypertensive renovascular disease. *New England Journal of Medicine,* 1975, **293,** (5), 216–221.

McNeil, B. J., Weichselbaum, R., and Pauker, S. G. Fallacy of the five-year survival in lung cancer. *New England Journal of Medicine,* 1978, **299,** 1397–1401.

McNicol, D. *A primer of signal detection theory.* London: Allen & Unwin, 1972.

Metz, C. E. Basic principles of ROC analysis. *Seminars in Nuclear Medicine,* 1978, **VIII,** (4), 283–298.

Metz, C. E., and Goodenough, D. J. On failure to improve observer performance with scan smoothing: A rebuttal. *Journal of Nuclear Medicine,* 1973, **14,** 283.

Metz, C. E., Starr, S. J., and Lusted, L. B. Quantitative evaluation of visual detection performance in medicine: ROC analysis and determination of diagnostic benefit. In G. A. Hay (Ed.), *Medical images.* London: Wiley, 1977, 220–241.

Metz, C. E., Starr, S. J., Lusted, L. B., and Rossmann, K. Progress in evaluation of human observer visual detection performance using the ROC curve approach. In C. Raynaud and A. Todd-Pokropek (Eds.), *Information processing in scintigraphy.* Orsay, France: Commissariat a l'Energie Atomique, Department de Biologie, Service Hospitalier Frederic Joliot, 1975, 420–439.

National Academy of Sciences. *On the theory and practice of voice identification.* Washington, D.C.: National Academy of Sciences, 1979.

Pauker, S. P., and Pauker, S. G. Prenatal diagnosis: A directive approach to genetic counseling using decision analysis. *Yale Journal of Biological Medicine,* 1977, **50,** 275.

Peterson, W. W., Birdsall, T. G., and Fox, W. C. The theory of signal detectability. *Transactions of the IRE Professional Group on Information Theory,* 1954, **PGIT-4,** 171–212.

Pollack, I., and Madans, A. B. On the performance of a combination of detectors. *Human Factors,* 1964, **6,** 523–532.

Raiffa, H. *Decision analysis.* Reading, Mass.: Addison-Wesley, 1968.

Ransohoff, D. F., and Feinstein, A. R. Problems of spectrum and bias in evaluating the efficacy of diagnostic tests. *New England Journal of Medicine,* 1978, **299,** (17), 926–930.

Schoenbaum, S. C., Hyde, J. N., Bartoshesky, L., and Crampton, K. Benefit-cost analysis of rubella vaccination policy. *New England Journal of Medicine,* 1976, **294,** 306–310.

Schoenbaum, S. C., McNeil, B. J., and Kavet, J. The swine-influenza decision. *New England Journal of Medicine,* 1976, **295,** 759–765.

Simpson, A. J., and Fitter, M. J. What is the best index of detectability? *Psychological Bulletin,* 1973, **80,** (6), 481–488.

Snedecor, G. W., and Cochran, W. G. *Statistical methods.* Ames, Iowa: Iowa State Univ. Press, 1967.

Starr, S. J., Metz, C. E., Lusted, L. B., and Goodenough, D. J. Visual detection and localization of radiographic images. *Radiology,* 1975, **116,** 533–538.

Swets, J. A. Effectiveness of information retrieval methods. *American Documentation,* 1969, **20,** 1.

Swets, J. A. The relative operating characteristic in psychology. *Science,* 1973, **182,** 990–1000.

Swets, J. A. Signal detection theory applied to vigilance. In R. R. Mackie (Ed.), *Vigilance: Relationships among theory, physiological correlates and operational performance.* New York, Plenum, 1977, 705–718.

Swets, J. A. ROC analysis applied to the evaluation of medical imaging techniques. *Investigative Radiology,* 1979, **14,** 2, 109–121.

Swets, J. A., and Birdsall, T. G. The human use of information: III. Decision-making in signal detection and recognition situations involving multiple alternatives. *Transactions of the IRE on Information Theory,* 1956, **IT-2,** 138–165.

Swets, J. A., and Birdsall, T. G. Deferred decision in human signal detection: A preliminary experiment. *Perception & Psychophysics,* 1967, **2,** (1), 15–28.

Swets, J. A., and Green, D. M. Applications of signal detection theory. In H. W. Leibowitz, H. A. Pick, J. E. Singer, A. Steinschneider, and H. Stevenson (Eds.), *Applications of basic research in psychology.* New York: Plenum, 1978, 311–331.

Swets, J. A., Pickett, R. M., Whitehead, S. F., Getty, D. J., Schnur, J. A., Swets, J. B., and Freeman, B. A. Assessment of diagnostic technologies. *Science,* 1979, **205,** 753–759.

Swets, J. A., and Swets, J. B. ROC approach to cost-benefit analysis. *IEEE Proceedings of the Sixth Conference on Computer Applications in Radiology,* 1979, 203–206.

Szucko, J. J., and Kleinmuntz, B. Statistical versus clinical lie detection. *American Psychologist,* 1981, **36,** (5), 488–496.

Torgerson, W. S. *Theory and methods of scaling.* New York: Wiley, 1965.

Torrance, G. W. Toward a utility theory foundation for health status index models. *Health Services Research,* 1976, **11,** (4), 349–369.

Turner, D. A., Fordham, E. W., Pagano, J. V., All, A. A., Ramos, M. V., and Ramachandran, P. C. Brain scanning with the Anger multiplane tomographic scanner as a second examination. *Radiology,* 1976, **121,** 115–124.

Wald, A. *Statistical decision functions.* New York: Wiley, 1950.

Weinstein, M. C., and Stason, W. B. *Hypertension: A policy perspective.* Cambridge, Mass.: Harvard Univ. Press, 1976.

Weinstein, M. C., and Stason, W. B. Foundations of cost-effectiveness analysis for health and medical practices. *New England Journal of Medicine,* 1977, **296,** (13), 717–721.

Whalen, A. D. *Detection of signals in noise.* New York and London: Academic, 1971.

Winer, B. J. *Statistical principles in experimental design.* New York: McGraw-Hill, 1962.

Wolfe, J. N. Breast patterns as an index of risk for developing breast cancer. *American Journal of Roentgenology, Radium Therapy and Nuclear Medicine,* 1976, **126,** (6), 1130–1139.

Wulff, H. R. Clinician's use of methods of investigation. In R. M. Pickett and T. J. Triggs (Eds.), *Human Factors in Health Care,* Lexington, Mass.: Heath, 1975, 139–152.

Wulff, H. R. *Rational diagnosis and treatment.* Oxford: Blackwell, 1976.

Index

**ACADEMIC PRESS
SERIES IN COGNITION AND PERCEPTION**

SERIES EDITORS:
**Edward C. Carterette
Morton P. Friedman**
*Department of Psychology
University of California, Los Angeles
Los Angeles, California*

Stephen K. Reed: *Psychological Processes in Pattern Recognition*

Earl B. Hunt: *Artificial Intelligence*

James P. Egan: *Signal Detection Theory and ROC Analysis*

Martin F. Kaplan and Steven Schwartz (Eds.): *Human Judgment and Decision Processes*

Myron L. Braunstein: *Depth Perception Through Motion*

R. Plomp: *Aspects of Tone Sensation*

Martin F. Kaplan and Steven Schwartz (Eds.): *Human Judgment and Decision Processes in Applied Settings*

Bikkar S. Randhawa and William E. Coffman: *Visual Learning, Thinking, and Communication*

Robert B. Welch: *Perceptual Modification: Adapting to Altered Sensory Environments*

Lawrence E. Marks: *The Unity of the Senses: Interrelations among the Modalities*

Michele A. Wittig and Anne C. Petersen (Eds.): *Sex-Related Differences in Cognitive Functioning: Developmental Issues*

Douglas Vickers: *Decision Processes in Visual Perception*

Margaret A. Hagen (Ed.): *The Perception of Pictures, Vol. 1: Alberti's Window: The Projective Model of Pictorial Information, Vol. 2 Dürer's Devices: Beyond the Projective Model of Pictures*

Graham Davies, Hadyn Ellis and John Shepherd (Eds.): *Perceiving and Remembering Faces*

Hubert Dolezal: *Living in a World Transformed: Perceptual and Performatory Adaptation to Visual Distortion*

Gerald H. Jacobs: *Comparative Color Vision*

Diana Deutsch (Ed.): *The Psychology of Music*

John A. Swets and Ronald M. Pickett: *Evaluation of Diagnostic Systems: Methods from Signal Detection Theory*

in preparation

Trygg Engen: *The Perception of Odors*

C. Richard Puff (Ed.): *Handbook of Research Methods in Human Memory and Cognition*